YOUR

GERMAN SHEPHERD PUPPY

MONTH ▶ BY ▶ MONTH

LIZ PALIKA, DEB ELDREDGE, DVM,
and **JOANNE OLIVIER**

A L P H A

A member of Penguin Group (USA) Inc.

ALPHA BOOKS

Published by Penguin Group (USA) Inc.

Penguin Group (USA) Inc., 375 Hudson Street, New York, New York 10014, USA • Penguin Group (Canada), 90 Eglinton Avenue East, Suite 700, Toronto, Ontario M4P 2Y3, Canada (a division of Pearson Penguin Canada Inc.) • Penguin Books Ltd., 80 Strand, London WC2R 0RL, England • Penguin Ireland, 25 St. Stephen's Green, Dublin 2, Ireland (a division of Penguin Books Ltd.) • Penguin Group (Australia), 250 Camberwell Road, Camberwell, Victoria 3124, Australia (a division of Pearson Australia Group Pty. Ltd.) • Penguin Books India Pvt. Ltd., 11 Community Centre, Panchsheel Park, New Delhi—110 017, India • Penguin Group (NZ), 67 Apollo Drive, Rosedale, North Shore, Auckland 1311, New Zealand (a division of Pearson New Zealand Ltd.) • Penguin Books (South Africa) (Pty.) Ltd., 24 Sturdee Avenue, Rosebank, Johannesburg 2196, South Africa • Penguin Books Ltd., Registered Offices: 80 Strand, London WC2R 0RL, England

International Standard Book Number: 978-1-61564-222-9
Library of Congress Catalog Card Number: 2012941807

14   8   7   6   5

Interpretation of the printing code: The rightmost number of the first series of numbers is the year of the book's printing; the rightmost number of the second series of numbers is the number of the book's printing. For example, a printing code of 12-1 shows that the first printing occurred in 2012.

Printed in the United States of America

Note: This publication contains the opinions and ideas of its authors. It is intended to provide helpful and informative material on the subject matter covered. It is sold with the understanding that the authors and publisher are not engaged in rendering professional services in the book. If the reader requires personal assistance or advice, a competent professional should be consulted.

The authors and publisher specifically disclaim any responsibility for any liability, loss, or risk, personal or otherwise, which is incurred as a consequence, directly or indirectly, of the use and application of any of the contents of this book.

Most Alpha books are available at special quantity discounts for bulk purchases for sales promotions, premiums, fund-raising, or educational use. Special books, or book excerpts, can also be created to fit specific needs. For details, write: Special Markets, Alpha Books, 375 Hudson Street, New York, NY 10014.

Publisher: *Mike Sanders*	**Copy Editor:** *Jan Zoya*
Executive Managing Editor: *Billy Fields*	**Cover and Book Designer:** *Kurt Owens*
Development Editors: *Mark Reddin and Christy Wagner*	**Indexer:** *Heather McNeill*
	Layout: *Ayanna Lacey and Brian Massey*
Senior Production Editor: *Janette Lynn*	**Proofreader:** *John Etchison*

This book is dedicated to Watachie, my first German Shepherd Dog. Watachie taught me so much, including how to communicate with dogs and how to teach them. By doing so, he introduced me to my life's work—both teaching dogs and their owners as well as writing about dogs. Thanks, Watachie. I miss you still. —Liz

Contents at a Glance

Appendixes

Contents

Month 4: The Social Shepherd   47

Month 8: Your Teenage Puppy   155

Month 9: In Search of a Leader 177

Month 11: Your Brilliant Puppy   **227**

Month 12 (and Beyond): Approaching Adulthood 259

Appendixes

Introduction

As a dog-crazy child, Liz read all the books about Rin Tin Tin, Strongheart, and the German Shepherd Dogs of *The Guiding Eye*. She thought German Shepherds were a breed apart, above and beyond all other dogs.

So it stands to reason that her first dog as an adult was a German Shepherd. Watachie was a challenging puppy and chewed up her sofa one day while she was at work. She didn't know anything about raising a puppy, so it's not surprising he was destructive. Shortly after the sofa incident, they enrolled in an obedience class. Watachie and Liz graduated first in that class, even though he was the youngest puppy in class and she was the youngest owner. Over the next few years, he earned his American Kennel Club Utility Dog (UD) title with multiple High in Trial awards along the way. He was a certified search and rescue dog, and they participated in numerous sports. If Liz could figure out how to teach him, Watachie would learn it and do it.

With the tips and advice in this book, you, too, can have a German Shepherd like Watachie. In the following chapters, we share with you the journey a German Shepherd puppy takes from birth to 1 year of age. Huge changes take place in just 12 months.

We talk about what happens when your puppy is still at the breeder's home and offer tips on choosing the right puppy for you. We discuss how old the puppy should be when you bring him home and what may happen if he's too young.

Then, month by month, we explain all the various things that happen with your puppy, including physical development, health, nutrition, social skills, behavior, training, and much more. All these can be complicated subjects individually but when your puppy is growing and changing so rapidly, it's easy to get overwhelmed.

The Extras

Throughout this book, you'll find extra tidbits of information. Here's what to look for:

> **DOG TALK**

These are definitions of some terms you might not be familiar with.

> ## HAPPY PUPPY

These sidebars will help make your German Shepherd puppy a happy dog.

> ## TIPS AND TAILS

These hints can help you deal with specific puppy-raising situations.

Trademarks

All terms mentioned in this book that are known to be or are suspected of being trademarks or service marks have been appropriately capitalized. Alpha Books and Penguin Group (USA) Inc. cannot attest to the accuracy of this information. Use of a term in this book should not be regarded as affecting the validity of any trademark or service mark.

The Littermate

Welcome to the first 2 months of your German Shepherd puppy's life! In this chapter, we explain what your pup experiences from birth through the end of her eighth week. Although you won't be a part of her life right now, and you may not even meet her until later, it's important to understand what's going on now because it impacts her life with you after she joins your family.

Most canine experts feel that who a dog is when she's full grown is a result of 40 percent nature and 60 percent nurture. The nature portion consists of the dog's breed, genetics, and her individual inheritance from her parents and ancestors. The nurture part is made of her experiences after birth, including her mother's care, her littermates, her breeder's care, as well as her health, nutrition, and later, veterinary care.

Although it might not seem like what happens during these first few months before your puppy joins your household should be important, it really is. These first 2 months or so set the stage for the rest of your puppy's life with you.

Physical Development

Amazing changes occur during the first 2 months. At birth, puppies tend to weigh about 1 percent of the mother dog's prepregnancy weight if she has a litter of 6 to 8 puppies. If she has fewer puppies, they may be bigger; if she has more, they may be smaller. However, the 1 percent figure is an average, and smaller and larger puppies are also normal.

From Birth Through Day 14

Newborn German Shepherds look like black fur–covered sausages. They're firm and warm, and their skin is tight. Your newborn puppy can lift her head, although she's very shaky and wobbly. Her eyes are closed, she can't hear yet, she doesn't have any teeth, and the only senses she's using now are her smell, her taste, and her ability to feel her mother and littermates' body warmth.

Newborn German Shepherds have tiny ears that are folded over, and their tails are small and lack the longer coat they'll grow later. When picked up, your puppy curves into a comma shape; this is normal.

During this *neonatal period,* your puppy cannot eliminate on her own and needs her mother's help. She licks the puppy's belly and genitalia to stimulate both urination and defecation.

> **HAPPY PUPPY**
>
> The most important thing your puppy needs right now is her mother. Her mother feeds her, cleans her, warms her, and provides security so she stays calm and can sleep and grow as she needs to.

At this age, your German Shepherd puppy needs a warm environment. She can maintain her body temperature only about 10 degrees above that of her surroundings for a very short period of time. So if the mother dog leaves her puppies to eat or relieve herself, and the room where the puppies are is cool—even if it's in the lower 70s—your puppy will quickly get cold.

Your breeder keeps the room where the puppies are, or the *whelping box* area, quite warm. She places a heating pad or a heat lamp in the area to ensure the puppies stay between 85°F and 90°F.

While burrowing under her littermates for warmth or moving to find her mother's nipple to nurse, your puppy uses swimming motions with her legs. Most of her strength right now is in her front legs. By the time she's 5 to 7 days old, she can lift herself up on her front legs. Her back legs are still too weak to support her, though.

During this stage, 90 percent of your puppy's time is spent sleeping. As she's sleeping, she may twitch and kick and appear as if she's dreaming—perhaps chasing tiny rabbits. (It's unknown if puppies are actually dreaming.) This sleep pattern is called *activated sleep.* All that twitching and kicking while she's sleeping helps your puppy strengthen her muscles. When she's developed enough to stand, that sleep exercise helps make her muscles strong enough so she can hold herself up.

The **neonatal period** is the first 2 weeks of a puppy's life. A **whelping box** is a low-sided enclosure for the mother dog and her puppies. It's made to be a secure place for the puppies when they're born and also contain their inquisitiveness when they're old enough to go exploring. **Activated sleep** consists of kicking, twitching, stretching, and other movements during sleep. This is normal for newborns and helps them develop muscle tone.

Between 1½ and 2 weeks old, your puppy's eyes and ears open. Her eyes are blue, and it takes her a couple days to actually focus her eyes and see clearly, although many puppies can track movements almost right away. Loud noises may startle her as she gets used to listening.

Days 15 Through 28

At 2 to 2½ weeks old, your puppy is beginning to eliminate on her own, and when she can take a few wobbly steps, she'll try to walk away from her littermates to eliminate. This is actually the first demonstration of that instinct to keep her sleeping area clean.

TIPS AND TAILS

It's important that the mother dog and puppies have enough room in the whelping box so the puppies can wander away from each other to eliminate. If the puppy doesn't have enough room and learns to eliminate where the puppies are sleeping and playing, housetraining will be difficult later.

Toward the end of this period, your puppy is sleeping less and becoming more active. She's walking better now and although she's still not very coordinated, she isn't falling down nearly as much as she was just days ago.

By about 4 weeks, your puppy has a full set of very sharp, needlelike baby teeth. Often the mother dog begins weaning the puppies at this point because those baby teeth can hurt her as they nurse.

Days 29 Through 42

By day 29, male German Shepherd puppies may weigh about 9 pounds. Female puppies may weigh, on average, 7 pounds.

Your puppy is walking and even trying to run—or at least move faster. She may even attempt some small jumps or pounces. She's also becoming more interested in exploring things around her. Her senses are becoming more important to her, especially as she uses them more. She's moving her head more as she learns to focus her senses.

Newborn puppies cry only when cold, hungry, or distressed, but now your puppy is discovering her voice and may bark a little. She may also whine, cry, or howl.

> **HAPPY PUPPY**
>
> You don't have to respond to your puppy each time she makes noise. After all, right now she's just learning to use her voice. She may make noise for no reason, or she might bark at her littermates. She's experimenting right now.

By 5 weeks, the mother dog begins to distance herself from the puppies a little more. Although she's probably still nursing at least a few times a day, she's not spending all of her time with the puppies as she did when they were younger. She's still watchful and protective of them, though.

Between 5 and 6 weeks, the breeder gradually reduces the temperature in the whelping box area. The puppies are still getting warmth from each other, the mother dog, and any blankets in their area, but as they grow, they're better able to maintain their own body temperature.

Days 43 Through 60

At 48 days, or 7 weeks old, your male German Shepherd puppy may be close to 20 pounds while your female is closer to 16 pounds. Again, these are average weights, so a puppy who is a little smaller or bigger can very well be normal, too.

During this time, your puppy is becoming more active and is actively playing with her littermates. The puppies' coordination is much better, and they aren't tripping over their own paws nearly as much as they have in the past few weeks.

Health

A newborn German Shepherd's body temperature is cooler than an adult's; it's about 94°F to 97°F compared to the adult's average of 101°F to 102°F. The normal heartbeat for a neonatal puppy is about 200 beats per minute—more than twice what an adult's pulse would be when calm.

By about 4 weeks—from days 22 to 28—your pup's heart rate slows to about 170 beats per minute. Her temperature raises to about 100°F, too.

The Mother Dog's Care

German Shepherd *dams* can be a bundle of emotion. Although most allow their owner, the breeder, to be present at the puppies' birth, others want complete privacy. Their attitude depends on the temperament of the individual female dog as well as the relationship the dog and owner have. More than one pregnant German Shepherd has scoffed at the whelping box and given birth in the owner's bedroom or on the owner's bed because she wanted to be as close as possible to her owner.

> **DOG TALK**
>
> **Dam** refers to the mother dog. *Sire* is the father of the litter.

Besides giving birth, nursing the puppies, and helping them eliminate, mother German Shepherds are also very protective of their puppies. Wise breeders don't invite people over to see the newborn puppies because this tends to cause a lot of anxiety for the mother. She's apt to growl, bark, and even lunge at strangers who want to see her puppies. Good breeders allow the mother the privacy she needs to care for her babies.

Breeder Vigilance

Although the mother dog provides most of the puppies' care, she can't do everything by herself. The breeder is an important part of this process, too. She watches the mother and her puppies so that if problems occur, she can deal with them quickly before harm comes to either the puppies or the mother dog.

Some mother dogs, especially first-time mothers, won't lie still long enough so the puppies can nurse until they're full. The dam might get anxious or restless and get up. The breeder watches to be sure the puppies get enough to eat and reassures a restless mother. The breeder also ensures that the mother doesn't lie down on top of a puppy. This doesn't happen often, but if it does, it can be fatal to the puppy if the mother dog doesn't realize it and move.

The breeder also …

- ❧ Ensures the mother dog doesn't lose too much weight as she nurses the puppies.
- ❧ Watches that the mother dog is producing enough milk so the puppies are satisfied after feeding.
- ❧ Keeps an eye on the mother dog's breasts to be sure she doesn't develop *mastitis.*

🐾 Looks for puppies who aren't thriving as well as the others.

🐾 Ensures the largest puppy isn't preventing smaller puppies from eating.

> **DOG TALK**
>
> **Mastitis** is an infection or abscess of one or more of the mother dog's mammary glands. This is usually caused by bacteria from a scratch or wound in the skin of a nipple. Keeping the puppies' nails trimmed and smooth is one way to help prevent mastitis.

Most of the time, solutions are easy. The breeder can feed the mother dog more or add some protein and fat to her diet, and the smaller puppy can have some supplemental feedings. But the fact remains: these solutions are only easy when the breeder is vigilant about spotting and correcting problems as they occur.

Nutrition

Newborn German Shepherd puppies are born with a strong suckling reflex. A healthy puppy's mouth is warm and wet, and if you put a finger in her mouth, she'll immediately begin to suck on it.

At this point in life, nursing provides not only milk, but also energy. A newborn has no subcutaneous fat, and without those fat reserves to provide energy, all her energy must come from her mother's milk.

Young puppies are prone to dehydration, especially if they don't nurse enough. The puppy's immature kidneys excrete large amounts of urine, and nursing often is needed to maintain a pup's fluid levels. If the puppy's skin is gently pinched and released, a well-hydrated puppy's skin immediately returns to shape. If the skin remains pinched in a fold, the puppy is dehydrated.

If the puppy isn't nursing well, or the mother dog isn't producing enough milk, the breeder supplements the puppy's nutrition with supplemental feedings.

Mother's Milk

During the first day and a half after her puppies are born, the mother dog produces *colostrum*. This important first milk helps nourish the puppies as well as provides protection from infectious diseases. It contains maternal antibodies, too, which kickstart the puppies' immune systems. Canine milk is comprised of about 10 percent fat, 9 percent protein, and 4 percent sugar. It contains about 150 calories per gram.

Colostrum, often defined as "the first milk," is the milk the mother produces right after her puppies are born. This nutritious milk contains vitamins, minerals, protein, antibodies, and other immune-boosting substances her new puppies need.

The mother dog needs excellent nutrition herself to produce milk and continue to produce it for a growing litter. As a general rule, she should have three times the calories now that she ate prior to her pregnancy. Her diet needs to be high in protein and fat. The breeder often feeds the mother dog her normal diet but adds extra meals throughout the day. Or she might add calories by including healthy additions to the mother's meals such as cooked pasta, cottage cheese, grated and steamed carrots, cooked chopped chicken hearts, cooked and deboned chicken, or molasses.

German Shepherd puppies nurse from six to eight times every day when first born. The puppies compete for the nipples, with the largest puppy usually taking the nipple he wants. However, a determined smaller puppy can also be successful. The breeder keeps an eye on the smallest puppy in the litter to be sure she gets a chance to nurse, too.

A neonatal German Shepherd puppy gains from 65 to 90 grams per day, depending on the mother's size and the puppy's size at birth. The puppy continues to gain weight steadily each day as she grows. Ideally, the breeder weighs the puppies at birth and then daily as they grow so she knows they're steadily gaining weight.

Supplementation

Most of the time, supplementation isn't needed. German Shepherd mothers produce a lot of milk for their litters, and additional feeding isn't usually necessary. As long as all the puppies are steadily gaining weight and none of them are crying and restless, everything is probably fine.

However, sometimes puppies need help. A small puppy in the litter who cannot compete with larger siblings may need supplemental feeding to catch up. A puppy who loses weight after birth but after 48 hours isn't regaining that lost weight needs supplemental feeding. If the litter is large—10 or more puppies—several or all of the puppies may need some supplemental feeding. If the mother isn't producing enough milk, or if the mother isn't producing *any* milk, supplemental (or replacement) feeding is necessary. At any given time after feeding, if a puppy is restless and crying, she may not have gotten enough to eat and might need supplemental feeding.

If supplemental feeding is needed, the breeder uses a commercial formula made specifically for puppies to supplement or replace the mother dog's milk. These are usually available as liquids (canned) or as powder the breeder mixes prior to feeding.

> ### TIPS AND TAILS
>
> Breeders know to never give straight cow's milk to puppies. It causes diarrhea, which could in turn cause death. Cow's milk is less calorie-dense than dog's milk, and it derives more calories from lactose than from protein or fat. Goat's milk is marginally better than cow's milk, but breeders still opt for other options when possible.

The breeder feeds the puppy using a small bottle with a nipple. She holds the puppy upright (head up) or on her belly as she would be with her mother, not on her back (as with a human infant), which could cause the puppy to choke.

Weaning

Your puppy's baby teeth begin coming in between the third and fourth week, and most are entirely through the gums by 4 weeks. Although the mother dog continues to nurse the litter for another week or so, she's going to start cutting them back— *weaning* them—at about 4 weeks.

> ### DOG TALK
>
> **Weaning** is the process of changing the puppy from nursing on her mother to eating food. Ideally, this shouldn't happen abruptly but instead should be a process spread out over a few days to a week or so.

Many breeders begin offering some formula formulated for nursing puppies close to day 21 in preparation for weaning. Many puppies, however, have no idea this offering is food if it's offered in a saucer or bowl and simply make a mess crawling through it. At some point, however, some of the food ends up in the puppy's mouth, and she discovers it tastes good.

Ideally, puppies should nurse until the mother dog has had enough, or until the puppies are 5 or 6 weeks old. If the litter is a large one or if the mother dog's condition deteriorates—she is thin and her coat is dry and thin—the breeder weans the litter. Some mother dogs give their all to the litter, and her health shouldn't be allowed to suffer.

To help the mother dog wean her puppies, the breeder removes her from her puppies about 2 hours before each scheduled meal. This way, the puppies are hungry at feeding time. The breeder provides either a quality dog food for all life stages or a puppy food specifically for weaning puppies or a home-cooked recipe approved for puppies.

Meat-based foods are preferable and more attractive to the puppies, although some breeders use a dampened dry kibble food. Dry kibbles shouldn't be used at this age because the puppies could choke on a piece of kibble. For this reason, many breeders recommend a gruel the puppies can lap up.

Puppies initially play in the food rather than eat it. But at some point, they all remember they're hungry and discover this new stuff tastes good.

The breeder puts the mother dog back in with her puppies after they've eaten. She probably finishes any leftover food from the saucers, from the floor, and from the puppies.

The breeder allows the puppies to continue to nurse during this introduction to food. This ensures the puppies are well nourished during the transition, and also helps prevent diarrhea due to a rapid introduction to a new food.

> **TIPS AND TAILS**

An 8-week-old German Shepherd puppy—male or female—weighs 20 pounds and needs about 1,300 calories per day. A 16-pound puppy needs 1,100 calories per day.

Gradually, over several days or even a week, the puppies nurse less and less. Eventually, the mother dog stops allowing the puppies to nurse or only allows them to nurse for just a few seconds. At this point, the breeder cuts back the mother dog's feeding to her prepregnancy amounts and schedule.

Grooming

For the first month, the mother dog takes care of almost all the puppies' grooming needs. She washes them after birth—this is a part of the bonding process between the mother dog and her babies. She also washes their faces after nursing and licks their bellies and genitalia to stimulate elimination.

Many breeders trim the tiny puppies' sharp toenails within the first few days so the nails don't scratch and irritate the mother dog's belly as the puppies nurse. Most breeders use a set of small canine nail clippers to do this, followed by a nail file to smooth each nail after trimming.

Once the puppies start the weaning process, the mother dog is less interested in keeping the puppies clean, and the breeder steps in to get this done. She washes their faces after each meal, as well as their feet and anything else that gets covered in food. Sometimes the entire puppy ends up in the food bowl, but that's okay. These grooming sessions introduce the puppy to body care and get her used to being handled.

Social Skills

Although it may seem like there isn't much that can be done as far as social skills during the first 2 months of life, that's not true. Your puppy's mom and littermates provide a great introduction to life with other dogs, as we discuss in the next section. But during this time, wise breeders also begin working on social handling techniques that aid the puppy as she grows up.

> **TIPS AND TAILS**
>
> In their Bio Sensor dog-training programs, the U.S. Army exposes puppies to several exercises early in life. Dogs exposed to these exercises, which cause neurological stimuli, are found to be more able to handle stress, both in daily living and also in new situations later in life. Their physical functions improve as well, including cardiac function, adrenal function, physical tolerance to stress, and immune system strength.

Beginning on the third or fourth day after the puppies are born and continuing through the third week, the breeder puts each puppy through some daily exercises. These include …

- 🐾 Holding the puppy upright, with her head up and tail down, securely in both hands for 3 to 5 seconds.
- 🐾 Holding the puppy securely and reversing the direction, with her head down and her tail up, for 3 to 5 seconds.
- 🐾 Holding the puppy securely on her back with her feet upward for 3 to 5 seconds.
- 🐾 Using a cotton-tip swab, tickling the puppy between the toes of one paw (any paw) for 3 to 5 seconds.
- 🐾 Placing the puppy paws down on a cool, damp towel and allowing her to stand or explore for 3 to 5 seconds.

In addition to these exercises, the breeder also handles the puppies each day. This can include petting, cuddling, and, as the puppies get older, playing with them.

Behavior

Between days 22 and 28, the puppies begin to recognize their own species and alert to other dogs. They watch other dogs in their household, if the mother dog allows those dogs to get close to her puppies, and the puppies begin to interact with the other adult dogs.

Safe, friendly, healthy dogs in the household are often allowed to interact with the puppies if the mother dog okays it. Initially, the older dog might just lie down and let the puppies crawl on her or investigate her. The breeder might even let her lead them on adventures, provided the puppies are safe. She also may wash their faces and bottoms or bring them toys. All these interactions begin the puppies' socialization to other dogs.

At this age, your puppy is also able to bond with people. Wise breeders have various members of her family hold your puppy, pet her gently, and otherwise let her get used to people other than just herself. This helps prepare the puppy for bonding with you and your family later.

At this time, the breeder also supplies some things for the puppy to play with and explore. A cardboard box, a round, empty oatmeal container, a feather, and other safe items that have a different sound, texture, or smell are just what your puppy needs to check out at this age.

> ### HAPPY PUPPY
>
> When a puppy is introduced to a variety of sights, sounds, smells, and surfaces during early puppyhood, she learns to explore the unknown and investigate new things. Most importantly, she learns to cope with change. This will serve her well in adulthood.

The Importance of Mom's Teaching

The importance of the mother dog extends far beyond simply giving birth to the puppies and nursing them. Her attitude also affects the puppies.

A first-time mother dog who is uneasy with her new job can make her babies uneasy, too. They may fuss more than normal, may not gain weight as they should, and may not sleep as deeply as they need. A fearful mother dog can make her babies fearful, as can an overly aggressive mother. Ideally, your breeder uses only female German Shepherds with calm, stable, happy temperaments for breeding.

The breeder can also affect both the mother dog's state of emotions and her litter's emotions in turn. The breeder needs to be calm and relaxed around the mother dog, both during the birth of her litter and afterward. A calm, relaxed, happy breeder is more apt to have a calm, relaxed, happy German Shepherd mother dog.

As the puppies in her litter begin to play and wrestle with each other—and with her—the mother German Shepherd becomes an active teacher. If a puppy pounces on her tail and bites it too hard, she probably gets up, swinging her tail away, and she may even growl at the puppy. As she gets older and bigger, her correction increases until she understands the message that she needs to control the strength of her bite. This lesson, called *bite inhibition,* is very important to her life with people.

> **DOG TALK**
>
> Bite inhibition is a lesson a puppy's mother and littermates teach her that helps her control her bite. She soon learns to bite hard enough to communicate but not so hard as to injure.

Inexperienced breeders often interfere with the mother dog's lessons, feeling she's being mean to her puppies. When such breeders stop these lessons, they're doing the puppies a disservice, as the mother dog is teaching her puppies to accept rules for social behavior. Her body language (her postures and facial expressions), her growl, and her actions all teach her puppies something important.

Littermates Teach, Too

The puppies begin to play with each other and play fight at about $2\frac{1}{2}$ weeks old. They are adorable when they do this. They're clumsy and uncoordinated and fall down constantly, yet they make tiny growls, roll with each other, and try to pounce. While they play, their muscles gain strength as their actions teach each other important lessons.

When the puppies play, they interact with each other, teaching each other how to play and how hard to bite. When one puppy is too rough, her littermates tell her, via cries and other reactions, that she's not playing nicely. If she continues to play too roughly, a puppy may even be temporarily shunned by another littermate. This doesn't last very long, and soon the pups are all romping and rolling together again.

Your Puppy Comes Home

Month 2	Month 3	Month 4
	Socialization at home with new owner and other pets	
	Fear imprint period	
	Begin house and crate training	
	Rapid growth	
	1st DHPP vaccines	

Sometime this month, which covers weeks 9 through 12, your new German Shepherd puppy leaves his mother and littermates and becomes your new family member. This can be exciting, nerve-wracking, worrisome, and wonderful, all at the same time.

Before your puppy comes home, you have a lot of work to do. You need to get your house and yard ready for him, plus do some shopping. We share the essentials you need to stock up on in this chapter. We also give you tips for choosing the right puppy for you, with some help from the breeder if necessary. Know ahead of time that the first days and weeks after your puppy comes home will be stressful for you, your family, and your new puppy, but rest assured: we tell you how you can make it better.

Preparing for Your Puppy

Your puppy is going to need some supplies. Some—like dog food, a leash and collar, a crate, and a few chew toys—are necessities. But don't go overboard buying treats of all kinds and a basketful of toys. He can get by with one type of treat and two or three toys to start.

Food: Find out what the breeder is feeding the puppies, and get a good supply of that food. You don't have to continue feeding this, especially if you have a different food or diet in mind, but it takes time to switch foods correctly so your puppy doesn't get an upset tummy. You want some of the old food on hand as you introduce a new food. (More on this later in the chapter.)

Food and water bowls: Your pup's bowls should be heavy and sturdy enough so he can't pick them up or tip them over. You don't want him to go without water, after all. Liz has two water bowls, one inside and a larger one outside. The food bowl doesn't need to be fancy, but it should be unbreakable. Plastic bowls generally aren't recommended because many dogs develop acne on their chin after long-term use of plastic bowls.

Crate: An appropriate-size crate is a necessity. Get one large enough to house your puppy when he's full grown—the breeder can give you some recommendations depending on how big her adult German Shepherds are. We recommend wire or plastic crates. The soft-sided ones aren't the best for puppies. (See the section on crate training later in this chapter for more information.) Many crates now come with dividers so you can create a smaller area for the puppy and make it larger as he grows.

Collar: A soft nylon, cotton, or leather buckle-type collar is best—not just to hook the leash to, but also as a place for your puppy's identification tag. Opt for an adjustable collar you can make larger as your puppy grows. The collar should be snug enough so it doesn't get in the puppy's way but yet loose enough so it pulls off should it get caught on something. It can be snugged up so it won't pull off when you begin taking your puppy on walks.

Leash: A 4- or 6-foot-long leash with a sturdy snap that hooks to his collar is best to use when walking your puppy. You'll also use the leash to train him. Get a leather or cloth leash, not chain. The chain is tough on your hands and could break your puppy's teeth if he tried to play with it, as puppies so often do. Stay away from adjustable-length leads for now. That'll just teach your puppy to pull, among other problems.

Identification: Before you bring home your puppy, have a tag made with your cell phone number on it. You can have another tag made later that has your puppy's name, once you choose it. But right now, you need some means of being contacted should your new puppy panic and dash away. When you get his collar, hang the ID tag on it immediately so you don't forget.

Chew toys: Choose some sturdy toys for your puppy to play with. They should be made of nontoxic materials and be strong enough he can't chew off small pieces and swallow them. Kong Genius toys are great, as are the Planet Dog Orbee toys.

> **TIPS AND TAILS**

Don't give your puppy old shoes or socks to play with. Not only can these items be dangerous—a swallowed sock can cause a blockage that requires intestinal surgery—but these toys teach your puppy that chewing on socks and shoes is good. That's a bad lesson!

Grooming supplies: You don't need to get a lot of grooming supplies now. Just get the basics, and add more as your puppy gets in his adult coat. Start with a pair of scissor-type dog nail clippers, a pin brush, and some puppy-safe shampoo.

Cleaning supplies: These are also a necessity. Not only will your puppy have an accident or two as he learns housetraining skills, but he'll also track in leaves and mud on occasion. Vinegar is a great nontoxic cleaner, but you may also want an enzymatic cleaner for accidents. Read the labels of any cleaner you're considering buying to be sure it's safe to use with a puppy in the house. As your puppy gets his adult coat, he's going to shed, and for that you need a good, sturdy vacuum.

Pooper-scooper: You'll be picking up dog feces for the next 13 to 14 years, and a pooper-scooper for the backyard makes this chore easier. Choose the kind made of a flat shovel and a rake. Also have a small trash can with a lid handy. Line the trash can with a garbage bag, dump the scooped waste in that, and every other day or so, take the trash bag to the outside trash can.

Plastic bags: As you walk your pup, you'll need a supply of plastic bags to pick up after him. Many commercial brands are available in small rolls, or you can recycle your plastic newspaper or grocery bags.

Baby gates: A gate (or two) isn't a necessity, but it can make housetraining efforts easier by keeping the puppy out of certain areas of the house. A gate can block off the hallway or certain rooms or keep the puppy confined to one room. Get the taller gates, because your German Shepherd is going to be a big puppy very soon.

After your puppy joins your household, you may find that you need some other items—maybe some more cleaning supplies or a couple more baby gates. You can buy those later as needed.

> ### HAPPY PUPPY
>
> Your puppy's name is going to be a part of him for his entire life. Choose a name that will suit him as a large, dignified German Shepherd. At the same time, choose a name that's not negative: Killer, Chomper, and Fang all have negative associations and will cause people to look upon him as potentially dangerous. Choose a name that makes you smile as you say it.

Puppy-Proof Your House

Your German Shepherd puppy may be a little reserved or even timid when you first bring him home. After all, he's away from his mother and littermates, with strange people, and in a different place. This won't last long, and soon he'll be curious, much bolder, and exploring his new world.

Before he comes home, you need to be sure your house is safe for him be in. That means looking at your house from his point of view—not yours. If you lie on your stomach on the floor, lift your head, and look around your house, you'll be seeing it from a German Shepherd puppy's point of view. It's much different, isn't it?

To protect your valuables, and even not-so-valuables, and to keep your puppy safe, you need to puppy-proof your house. For example, in the kitchen, install child-proof latches on the lower cupboards that contain potentially harmful products.

In addition, put the following items away in a safe place:

❧ Floor cleaning and waxing products

❧ Insect and rodent traps, sprays, and other controls

❧ Kitchen and oven cleaners

❧ Candy and chocolate

❧ Grease and spices

❧ Knives and other sharp implements

In the bathroom, safely put away all these products:

❧ Medicines, vitamins, and minerals

❧ Makeup, nail polish, nail polish remover, and lotions

❧ Hair products, including hair coloring, sprays, and gels

❧ Shower, bathroom, toilet, and floor cleaners

❧ Bath products, including bubble bath, shower gels, and soaps

❧ Personal hygiene products

In the living areas, put out of reach or tuck safely away these things:

❧ Cell phones, electronic devices, remote controls, batteries, and chargers

❧ Pens, pencils, felt-tip markers, crayons, craft supplies

❧ Electrical cords

Houseplants are attractive to puppies. The dirt smells good, especially if the plant has been potted using compost, blood meal, or manure. But many houseplants are dangerous to pets. Check out Appendix C for a list of dangerous ones.

If you do a good job puppy-proofing the house, you can not only help keep your puppy safe but also minimize any damage your puppy might do to your stuff. Replacing cell phones, remote controls, wiring, or worse yet, furniture, can get expensive.

Your German Shepherd puppy doesn't have to have free run of the house to be happy. As long as he gets plenty of time with you, his freedom can be restricted and he'll still be a happy puppy. Preventing him from getting into trouble helps keep him healthy and safe.

If your puppy has chewed on something and perhaps swallowed pieces, and you're concerned it might be harmful, call your veterinarian right away. If she's not available, call the emergency veterinary clinic. Your veterinarian's voicemail should give you the emergency number.

Puppy-Proof the Yard

Although your German Shepherd puppy prefers to spend all his time with you, there will be times when he needs to stay outside for a while. It's important that your yard is safe and secure for him to be in.

The fence around your yard needs to be strong and solid. If there are any gaps in the fence itself, broken boards, or spaces under it, your puppy may work at those until he can squeeze through.

Ideally, he shouldn't be able to see through the fence, either. Keep in mind that German Shepherds are watchful and protective, and if he can see through the fence, he'll bark at anything or anyone he can see. That can quickly turn into a problem behavior.

Also in your yard …

🐾 Put away gloves, trowels, and other gardening tools.

🐾 Store all fertilizers, insecticides, and other chemicals out of reach.

🐾 Be careful using any chemicals around your puppy; be sure they're safe to use.

🐾 Put away any kids' toys.

🐾 For the time being, put away lawn chairs, cushions, umbrellas, and decorative garden things.

🐾 Be sure the puppy can't get to the pool or spa cover or the spa's electrical cord.

🐾 Protect any cables, cords, and hoses.

Encourage all family members to get in the habit of putting away anything they use in the backyard when they have finished their chore or activity. If things are put away, the puppy can't chew on them.

Check the plants in the backyard to be sure none are poisonous for your pup. (See Appendix C for a list of potentially poisonous plants.) In addition, think about putting temporary fencing around favorite plants, potted plants, flower gardens, and vegetable gardens. It's going to be a couple years before your puppy understands what he can play with and what he needs to ignore. Your plants don't have to suffer in the meantime.

If you have a pool, either in ground or above, think about how you'll protect your puppy from accidentally getting in the pool. A puppy who falls in and can't get out by himself will become exhausted trying to climb out and may drown. Fencing around the pool, with a locking gate, is the best solution.

If you have a nice backyard and take joy in keeping it looking good, think about building a dog run for your German Shepherd puppy. This would not, and should not be, your puppy's permanent default place where he spends all his time. However, it could be where he could be safe and out of trouble when he needs to be left alone.

Your Pup's Professional Staff

You need a few pet professionals to help you with your German Shepherd, both now as a puppy and throughout his life. Although you can certainly change professionals if you find yourself unhappy with someone, it's nice to have some people lined up before you bring home your puppy. Then, if you need help, you have someone to call.

The first and most important professional in your puppy's professional staff is a veterinarian. You should have your puppy seen by a veterinarian soon after bringing him home to ensure he's healthy and to get him started on vaccinations.

Ideally, the veterinarian should not be afraid of German Shepherds. Unfortunately, if the vet has had a bad experience with the breed, she may be worried about them, and this could cause problems with your new puppy. So feel free to ask veterinarians you're considering if this is a problem.

> **TIPS AND TAILS**
>
> The veterinarian should also be knowledgeable of the common health problems German Shepherds face. Don't hesitate to ask prospective veterinarians if they're familiar with the breed. This is a reasonable question.

Choosing a veterinarian doesn't have to be difficult, but you should do more than simply pick the closest clinic to you. Ask dog-owning neighbors where they take their dogs and whether they're happy with the vet and her staff. Are the prices reasonable? Cost isn't everything—the quality of care is—but you should also be able to afford that care.

Find out whether the veterinarian is available after hours or in case of an emergency. If she's not, what emergency clinic(s) does she work with? What are her payment policies? What pet insurance companies does she accept? What credit cards does she take? Find out all this information; it's important.

You'll also want a trainer. Originally, German Shepherds were bred to be working dogs and not pets. Although they're obviously kept as pets today, the happiest German Shepherds are those whose owners understand that these dogs need both physical and mental challenges. Training is a huge part of this.

As with veterinarians, ask dog-owning friends and neighbors who they recommend. Local veterinarians can also refer you to reputable trainers. If a couple different trainers' names keep coming up, call those trainers and talk to them. What kind of training do they offer? Do they have puppy classes as well as obedience classes? How about private training in case there's a behavioral problem later?

Ask about training methods, too. Every trainer has his or her own style of teaching people and training dogs, but if you aren't comfortable with that style, it won't work for you. Also, go watch the trainer's class to see if you'll be able to work with that trainer.

Next up is a groomer. Many dog owners think of professional groomers as people who work with poodles and only give dogs fancy haircuts. Although that's true, German Shepherd owners should appreciate groomers, too.

German Shepherds shed. They shed all year round, and twice a year, usually the spring and fall, they shed *a lot*. The adult German Shepherd coat is a double coat with coarser outer guard hairs and a thick soft undercoat. That undercoat is the biggest shedding issue; there's a lot of undercoat there.

A professional groomer can take your German Shepherd for the day, brush out his coat, bathe him, and brush him again. When done on a regular basis, this significantly cuts down on the hair floating around your house.

As with other professionals, ask friends and neighbors for referrals. You can also ask your veterinarian who she recommends. When you talk to a local groomer, as with the veterinarian, ask if she is comfortable with German Shepherds. Visit the grooming shop. Is it clean? Do the dogs look comfortable?

You might also want a pet-sitting service or a boarding kennel. Many dog owners enjoy vacations more when they can bring their dog with them. Unfortunately, there will be times you can't bring your German Shepherd with you. In that case, you need someone to come to your house to care for him, or he needs to go to a boarding kennel.

> ### TIPS AND TAILS
>
> Appendix E contains a list of resources, including professional organizations for veterinarians, trainers, pet professionals, and pet sitters, so you can find professionals in your area.

As with other professionals, you can get referrals from other dog owners, but ask your veterinarian for a referral, too. When you find a sitter, ask her to come over and meet your German Shepherd—long before you ever leave on vacation. After all, this breed is protective and often won't let strangers in the house. You want to be sure your German Shepherd thinks of the pet sitter as a friend.

Choosing Your Puppy

Choosing the right German Shepherd puppy for you and your family is at the same time the hardest and yet easiest thing you have to do. The decision is hard because how can you tell what that cute little ball of fluff is going to grow up to be? What's the difference between two puppies in the same litter? Yet at the same time, it's easy because all the puppies are so wonderful.

Yet choosing the right puppy for you is important. This German Shepherd is going to be your companion for his lifetime—the next 13 to 14 years—so choosing wisely is important.

Where to Find a Puppy

The best source of a healthy German Shepherd puppy is from a reputable breeder. A reputable breeder is someone who knows her breed inside and out.

She keeps up on the latest information concerning health, genetics, diseases, testing, and more, and she shows her German Shepherds in dog shows, obedience trials, agility, tracking, or schutzhund competitions. She chooses the best dogs possible to breed and tests those dogs for health concerns prior to breeding.

When you meet her, she'll answer any questions you have about her dogs and also ask you just as many questions to see if you'll be an appropriate owner for one of her puppies. She sells her puppies with a contract and will take back any of her puppies, no matter what their age, if at any time they cannot remain in their home. A reputable breeder also will be available to answer questions for the life of your dog.

> ## TIPS AND TAILS
>
> Before breeding, a good breeder tests her German Shepherds' hips and elbows for dysplasia, and tests them for congenital cardiac disease and autoimmune thyroiditis, as well—all of which can be registered through the Orthopedic Foundation for Animals. She'll also have her dogs tested for Von Willebrand's disease and degenerative myelopathy. (For more information, see Month 12.) Ideally, she'll have her dogs pass a temperament test, too. (See the German Shepherd Dog Club of America website at gsdca.org for more information.)

You can sometimes find German Shepherd puppies at your local shelter or through a German Shepherd rescue group. These can often be wonderful puppies, and by adopting one, you're potentially saving the puppy's life. Just understand that this puppy is an unknown; you don't know the parents, whether they were healthy and had good temperaments, or how the puppies were raised.

Don't buy a German Shepherd from a child with a box of puppies outside the grocery store or from a flea market or pet store. Not only are these puppies unknowns and bred by someone who obviously didn't have the puppies' best interest at heart; but by buying a puppy from these people, you give them incentive to continue irresponsible breeding.

You can find a reputable breeder by going to the German Shepherd Dog Club of America's website or the Canadian counterpart (see Appendix E), or do an internet search for a local German Shepherd club. Talk to your veterinarian; she may have a client who is a reputable breeder. If you see a healthy, well-mannered German Shepherd while out on a walk, ask the owners where they got their dog and whether they would recommend that breeder.

What Is Important to You?

Although most German Shepherds share many characteristics, they are not all alike. Different dogs vary in size, color, coat, and temperament. Deciding what's important to you helps you make a better choice.

When the puppies are born and it's time for you to choose the right puppy for you and your family, you have a lot to think about. As you mull over the following points, feel free to talk to the breeder about them. After all, she knows her dogs better than anyone else.

First, look at temperament. This breed is devoted, affectionate, and loyal—in fact, no other breed in existence has the reputation for loyalty like this one. German Shepherds have, and will, die for their owners.

They can also be one-person dogs. This is great if the relationship is of a police officer and his K9 handler. However, it's not good if the dog will only listen to one person in the family. Therefore, socialization and interaction with other people is important to offset this character trait.

German Shepherds tend to be aloof with strangers, and they take their time getting to know people. This breed is also protective of people, home, yard, and even car.

German Shepherds range in temperament from very bold and outgoing to quiet and more reserved. When choosing a puppy, choose a temperament that will work well, or flatter, your own. If you choose a puppy with a temperament very different from your own, the two of you will clash and the relationship will suffer. For example, if you tend to be quiet and reserved yourself, don't choose the biggest, boldest, most outgoing puppy. Although you may think he would help pull you out of your shell, instead, he might make you uncomfortable.

A better choice might be a puppy who is just a little more outgoing than you. This puppy could help you be a little more extroverted without making you feel threatened. The same applies to you if you're a natural extrovert. Don't get a reserved puppy; you would make him feel uncomfortable all the time.

There's a distinct difference in appearance between male and female German Shepherds. Males are larger, have broader heads, look distinctly masculine, and can be bolder in temperament. Females are smaller, finer boned, and have a more feminine (although definitely not weak) appearance. Females are often more protective of their people.

Male German Shepherds tend to stand between 24 to 26 inches tall at the point of the shoulders and weigh between 85 and 100 pounds. Females are about 20 to 22 inches tall and weigh from 60 to 75 pounds.

The German Shepherd Dog Club of America maintains the breed standard, or written description of the breed (see Month 10). Although some people breed very large German Shepherds, a giant dog is not called for within the standard.

As touched on earlier, German Shepherds have a double coat—a medium to long outer coat and a thick soft under coat. The length of the outer coat can vary to a degree; some dogs have a slightly shorter outer coat while others have a longer one.

Some dogs have what's often referred to as a lush coat, a longer outer coat that may be longer over the entire body, with thick hair behind the ears, around the ruff, and on the tail. This coat is inherited and is fairly common. The genetics that produces this coat also helps create a thick coat in dogs with the more normal medium-length coat. Although this coat isn't desired for conformation show dogs, it's perfectly acceptable for working dogs or pets.

German Shepherds have a range of colors. The most common is called black and tan. The dog has black on his face, ears, and tail, and a black saddle on the back. The "tan" portion can range from a yellowish-cream through brownish-tan to dark, reddish-rust. The range of markings can be minimal with very little tan or with very little black. Other colors include all black, sable (no saddle, and the hair coat looks wolf- or coyote-like), or white.

Various coat colors do not affect temperament or trainability. Although you can take coat color into account when choosing your puppy—after all, people do have personal preferences for color—the puppy's temperament is much more important than color.

Let the Breeder Help You

As you consider all the aspects of the breed, and think about what you want from your dog in the future, talk to the breeder. Let her know your thoughts, concerns, and hopes for your dog. Be honest and realistic about your plans.

If you're hoping to compete in *schutzhund* with this puppy when he grows up, for example, the breeder can steer you toward a puppy with a bold, courageous personality who has a strong *prey drive* toward toys. The breeder can also guide you to a calmer, steady puppy if you're looking for a quiet companion dog. So let the breeder know your thoughts and goals.

Remember, the breeder knows the parents of this litter and has been watching the puppies since they were born. She knows which puppy was the greediest and first to nurse. She knows which puppy was the first to walk, bark, and play. She knows, too, the puppy who likes to cuddle and the one who likes to give kisses. All this knowledge helps her match the right puppy to the correct family.

Many breeders also do puppy testing, which can also help pinpoint personality traits. These are usually done between 6 and 7 weeks of age, so if your breeder does them, it will probably happen before you ever see the litter. But you can ask the breeder if she did it and what the results were.

One of the most important aspects concerning choosing the right puppy for you is how you feel about that individual puppy. Asking questions, letting the breeder help you, and doing research are all important, but you still have to feel a connection to the puppy you bring home. So as you choose a puppy, let your heart lead you, too.

What Age Is Best?

Do not bring a puppy home before he's at least 8 weeks old. Even though he's weaned by 6 weeks or thereabouts, he needs a couple more weeks with his mother and littermates.

Remember, during those 8 weeks his mom teaches him to accept discipline and that the world is not revolving around him. His littermates teach him how to be a puppy and interact with other puppies. He learns how to play and how hard (or easy) to bite while playing with other puppies. These are important lessons that carry through to his relationships with people, and if he leaves for his new home too early, he misses out on them. Dog trainers and behaviorists routinely try to help puppies who have not had these lessons, and it's impossible to re-create those lessons later.

The traditional age to bring a puppy home has been 8 weeks. Although this age is better than 6 or 7 weeks, 8 weeks can also pose a challenge as many puppies hit a *fear period* at about this age. Anything that frightens the puppy during this time—such as a car ride or a trip to the veterinarian's clinic—can become an ongoing, lifetime fear.

Fear periods are stages in the puppy's life when he becomes worried or afraid for no apparent reason other than his age.

Most German Shepherd experts and behaviorists believe the ideal time to bring home a new German Shepherd puppy is between 9 and 10 weeks. At this age, he's had plenty of time with his mom and littermates, he's weaned and eating well, and he's past that first crucial fear period. He's happy, healthy, bold, and ready for a new life.

Physical Development

This month (weeks 9 through 12) is a time of change. Your German Shepherd is growing rapidly, with male puppies weighing 25 to 30 pounds by the end of the month and females weighing about 20 to 26 pounds on average.

He's still sleeping a lot, so don't be worried when he does. Most of his growing happens while he's sleeping.

Your puppy's motor skills are getting better, too. He's still clumsy, but not as much as he was. He's running, learning how to clamber over small obstacles in his path, and maybe even climbing.

His senses are also better now. He's able to track movements visually, and he's swiveling his ears to follow sounds. His ears may not be standing up right now, but they will stand up soon. His nose is also becoming more important to him, and he's learning to sort through scents. He'll even attempt to follow some scents.

The trademarks of German Shepherds at this age are needle-sharp puppy teeth, that wonderful milky puppy breath, and great big ears. Protect yourself from those teeth by handing your puppy a toy whenever he wants to chew on you. Enjoy the puppy breath now because that disappears far too quickly. And have a laugh at those big ears. He'll grow into them soon enough.

As soon as you choose your puppy at the breeder's home, put a buckle collar on the puppy with an engraved tag with your cell phone number. Don't wait until you get home or until you choose the puppy's name. Put it on right away just in case of an accident.

Health

The vast majority of German Shepherd puppies at this age are healthy, roly-poly balls of fluff with big, dark eyes. They're absolutely adorable.

But you need to look past all that adorableness, stop hugging your puppy for a few seconds, and get started on ensuring he is and will remain healthy.

The Breeder's Health Records

When you sign the contract with the breeder to buy your German Shepherd puppy, she should also give you a copy of your puppy's health record. If you can't find this among the paperwork the breeder gave you, call her and ask for a copy of it. This information is important to have because your veterinarian needs to see what's already been done for your puppy. This prevents duplication or lets him know what needs to be done next.

Breeders normally worm the puppies for roundworms, which are common in puppies, at least once. Your puppy probably also got at least one distemper vaccination, usually at 7 or 8 weeks. Anything given earlier is usually ineffective because the puppy probably has maternal antibodies until he's at least 6 weeks old.

But don't guess as to what the breeder might have done. Get copies of your puppy's records to avoid mistakes later on.

The First Visit to the Vet

Your new puppy should go see the veterinarian very soon after coming home. Many breeders require this within 48 hours, and most include it in their sales contract. There are several reasons why this is important and why your breeder may require it.

This first visit with your veterinarian can establish that your puppy is healthy. Your veterinarian examines your puppy to look for signs of disease or *congenital health defects*. If it turns out your puppy is not healthy, you have the right (if you so desire) to return the puppy to the breeder. If you do this within the first day or so, it won't be so heartbreaking. If you decide to keep the puppy, the breeder should either refund your purchase price, give you a partial refund, or work with you to pay the veterinary costs.

> ### DOG TALK
>
> A **congenital health defect** is one that exists at birth. It can be genetic or can be acquired before or during birth.

Bring a small sample of your puppy's feces to the first visit. The vet will check it for signs of internal parasites.

During the first visit, your veterinarian will give your puppy a thorough exam. She'll check that your pup's eyes are clear and clean. She'll check the eye lids to ensure the lashes aren't turned inward and rubbing against your pup's eyes. Other problems with the eyes can sometimes indicate the presence of diseases elsewhere in the body.

She'll also check your puppy's ears. They should be clean, dry, and pink. Redness, discharge, and matter caked to the inside of the ear are symptoms of a problem. She'll also check for any foreign matter in the ears.

Your veterinarian will take a look at your puppy's teeth to be sure they look good, none are missing, and no problems are visible. She'll also look at the gums, tongue, inside of the mouth, and throat. A normal, healthy puppy will have a pink tongue, gums, and inside of the mouth (black spots are fine), but other colors can point toward health problems.

She'll listen to your puppy's heart for any congenital heart defects and listen to the lungs to be sure your puppy is breathing well and his lungs are clear. The vet will also check the lymph glands on your puppy's neck and at various other locations on the body. An enlarged gland may indicate an infection in the body.

By gently feeling your puppy's abdomen, the vet can verify everything feels as it should. While doing this, she'll watch your puppy to see if he flinches when anything is touched. The flinching could be a sign that something hurts.

The veterinarian will watch your puppy walk, looking for a normal gait and noting any limping or soreness. She'll check over your entire puppy, including the paws and toenails, skin and coat, and under the tail. She'll point out any problems, or potential problems, but hopefully will give your German Shepherd a clean bill of health.

Vaccinations and Vaccination Schedule

When a dog is exposed to or gets sick because of an infectious disease, his immune system creates *antibodies* against the disease. This is called an active immunity and prevents the dog from getting sick from this particular disease again in the future. The dog's immune system continues to make these antibodies long after the source of the infection is gone, and if he's exposed to this same disease again later, his body will produce even more antibodies. This protection generally lasts for the dog's lifetime.

Vaccinations allow for a controlled exposure to an infectious disease so your puppy's body can produce those antibodies. Modified live virus (MLV) vaccines contain live viruses that live in your pup. However, they have been modified so your puppy shouldn't get sick from the virus. The immune system tends to react quickly to these vaccines and produce antibodies right away.

Killed virus vaccinations contain killed viruses so they cannot make the puppy sick. However, although the body does make antibodies in response to killed vaccines, it does so at a slower rate than to a modified live vaccine.

A variety of vaccinations are given to puppies (and adult dogs) on a regular basis. Some of these are considered essential—these are the *core vaccines*—while others are needed by some dogs depending on the dog's geographical location, whether the dog travels or not, and other aspects of the individual situation—these are the *noncore vaccines*. A third category of vaccines are available for specific circumstances.

The diseases and vaccinations normally considered core, or essential, include *distemper, hepatitis, parvovirus,* and *rabies.* Most veterinarians recommend all puppies and dogs be vaccinated with these core vaccines. These diseases are serious, potentially fatal, and difficult to treat.

Canine distemper is a virus similar to the human measles virus. It can affect many of the dog's organs, including the skin, eyes, and intestinal and respiratory tracts. The virus can be transmitted through urine, feces, and saliva, and the first symptoms are usually a nasal and eye discharge. This is a potentially fatal disease, and those dogs who do survive have lasting neurological damage.

Canine hepatitis is a virus found worldwide. It's spread through nasal discharge as well as urine, usually through direct contact. The virus begins with a sore throat— your dog won't want to swallow, drink, or eat. It spreads rapidly to other organs and develops quickly; dogs can die within hours of the first symptoms.

Parvovirus, often referred to simply as parvo, has killed thousands of dogs, usually puppies, and because the virus continues to mutate and change, it's still a deadly threat. This virus is considered the most deadly, dangerous, and fatal disease known to dogs. Vomiting, diarrhea, dehydration, and death are common. Sudden death may also occur from heart damage caused by this disease.

Rabies is almost always fatal once the disease has been contracted. Transmitted through contact with an infected animal, usually a bat, raccoon, or skunk, the first symptom is usually drooling because of problems swallowing, followed by staggering, seizures, and changes from normal behavior. Rabies vaccinations are required by law.

The diseases and vaccines considered noncore—or not essential—include *leptospirosis, parainfluenza, bordetella bronchiseptica,* and *Lyme disease.* Discuss these vaccinations with your veterinarian. She may recommend one or more of them, depending on your pup's location and activities.

Leptospirosis is a bacteria rather than a virus. It affects the kidneys and is passed from the kidneys to the urine and transmitted to other dogs when they sniff the contaminated urine. This disease also attacks the liver. Lepto, as it's called, can be spread to other animals, including people. Symptoms include a fever, nausea, and dehydration, and it can be fatal. Reactions to this vaccine are not uncommon.

> ## TIPS AND TAILS
>
> Wait in your veterinarian's office for half an hour after your puppy receives a vaccination. If he's going to have a reaction, it usually begins in that time period.

Parainfluenza is one of several viruses called canine cough or kennel cough. It's easily spread by coughing, which also happens to be one of the first and primary symptoms. It may turn into pneumonia, but it's generally just a cough that goes away in a week or two.

Bordetella is a bacteria that causes coughing and other respiratory problems. This, too, is one of the diseases classified under the canine cough or kennel cough umbrella. It's very contagious and easily spread from one dog to another through coughing. It's rarely dangerous to healthy dogs, but puppies can get quite sick.

Lyme disease is caused by a bacteria spread by infected ticks. Originally identified in Connecticut, it's now found in all 48 contiguous states. A fever is the first symptom, followed by muscle soreness, weakness, and joint pain. Severe, permanent joint and kidney damage are possible.

New vaccines are continually being developed and introduced. Most have some specific applications. These include *rattlesnake venom* and *porphyromonas.* Talk to your veterinarian about them.

If you live in an area where rattlesnakes are common and your dog likes to chase reptiles, this vaccine could gain your dog some time after a snake bite.

Porphyromonas is a vaccination against the bacteria that causes periodontitis (gum disease).

Vaccinations for dogs are important—they save lives. In fact, many of the diseases that killed thousands of lives—such as canine distemper—are extremely uncommon now because of vaccinations. However, vaccines are not innocuous and can cause problems. They should be given wisely and with caution.

Most veterinarians recommend puppies get their first vaccinations between 6 and 8 weeks of age. If the mother's antibodies are still effective in the puppy's body, that first vaccination may not be effective. That's why most puppies get a series of vaccines early in life. The shots are usually given 3 or 4 weeks apart, and you and your veterinarian can talk about the best vaccination schedule for your puppy.

Internal Parasites

The thought that parasites can be living inside your German Shepherd puppy is absolutely disgusting. Unfortunately, parasites are common, and that's why your veterinarian asked you to bring a stool sample from your puppy to his first exam.

It's fairly common for puppies to have roundworms. In fact, most breeders treat the whole litter as a matter of course. Adult dogs—as well as people—can become infested with them, although this happens far less frequently than in puppies. Roundworms live in the intestinal tract but can migrate to the lungs, trachea, and even the eyes. The eggs are passed out of the puppy (or other animal's) body via the feces. Keeping the yard clean and disposing of feces promptly is the best way to prevent an infestation.

Hookworms can infest both dogs and people. This worm, which also lives in the intestinal tract, grabs on to the intestinal tract tissues and bites, causing the puppy to lose some blood. Unfortunately, the worm does this several times a day, causing a blood loss each time. A puppy with a severe infestation can quickly become anemic. As with roundworms, cleanliness is the key to preventing infestations.

Whipworms—hardy, long-lived worms—reside in the lower part of the intestinal tract, where they can survive for years, causing diarrhea, nausea, and intestinal cramping. The eggs are passed out via the feces and can live in the environment for as long as 5 years. These worms are also more than willing to live in human hosts as well as canine ones. Picking up and properly disposing of feces regularly is important to avoid an outbreak.

Puppies pick up tapeworms through an intermediate host, the flea. When the flea bites the puppy, the puppy chews at that spot and ingests the flea. If the flea is carrying tapeworm eggs, they then hatch in the puppy's intestinal tract. Dogs can also get these parasites by eating rodents such as mice or voles. Tapeworms can cause diarrhea and soft stools. Controlling fleas is the key to preventing tapeworm infestations.

A German Shepherd puppy with a heavy parasite infestation may have a poor coat and unhealthy skin, in addition to soft stools. He'll likely have a full, round belly, too. A puppy with a few parasites may not yet be showing signs, so the easiest way to test for internal intestinal parasites is to take a small piece of fresh stool in to your veterinarian's clinic and have it checked under a microscope. Then if any signs of parasites are present, such as a piece of a worm or parasite eggs, they can be identified and a course of treatment can be prescribed.

Nutrition

Your German Shepherd is an eating machine at this age. He's growing rapidly and needs food to maintain that growth. A 25-pound puppy needs about 1,600 calories a day, while a 30-pound puppy needs about 2,000 calories. These amounts are approximates, however, and vary for each puppy.

To make things even more complicated, as soon as you figure out how much food your puppy needs, he'll need more! Most puppies need more calories just before a growth spurt and slightly less after a growth spurt. It's hard to tell when the growth spurts are beginning; sometimes the only sign is that the puppy always seems hungry. But because many rapidly growing German Shepherd puppies are always hungry anyway, that's not always a definitive sign.

The best thing you can do is simply pay attention to your puppy. If he's so hungry he's trying to eat anything and everything, offer him a little more food throughout the day. If he starts to feel thin, offer him more food then, too. However, if he's getting chubby (or fat), slightly cut back on his food.

If your puppy has diarrhea, slightly cut back on the amount you're feeding. This is a common side effect when puppies get too much food.

Food from the Breeder

Your breeder will give you some of the food he's been feeding your puppy, so continue to offer your pup this familiar food. His first few days home are stressful enough; he doesn't need to change foods now, too.

If you plan on continuing to feed your puppy that food, that's fine, and you can buy more in the next few days. However, if you'd like to change foods, don't do that immediately. Feed your puppy the food he's accustomed to for a couple weeks and then begin adding small amounts of the new food to a slightly decreased amount of the old food. Over a couple weeks, slowly increase the amount of new food while you decrease the old food.

If at any time your puppy has diarrhea, stop adding the new food for a few more days. When his stools are firm again, you can add the new food again, but do so *slowly*. Many German Shepherds have a sensitive digestive system and don't tolerate change well, so make changes slowly.

Feeding Practices

Feeding your German Shepherd puppy involves more than filling a bowl with dry kibble and placing it on the floor so he can nibble all day long. Although *free feeding* your puppy is easy, it's not the best way to feed him.

> **DOG TALK**

Free feeding is the practice of allowing your puppy to eat at his leisure all day long.

Your German Shepherd puppy needs scheduled meals. This helps the housetraining process immensely because he has to relieve himself after eating. If he nibbles all day long, it's much more difficult to tell when he needs to go outside. Plus, if your puppy doesn't feel well, one of the first questions your veterinarian will ask is, "How is his appetite?" If he's free feeding, you won't be able to answer that question.

At this age, your puppy needs three meals a day. Many puppies have a preference for one time or another as their bigger meal. For example, your German Shepherd may want to eat more in the morning, less at lunch, and a medium-size meal in the evening. This is fine as long as all the meals together equal the calories he should be getting.

Feed your puppy in a quiet corner where no one will bother him. He shouldn't have to worry about being stepped on while eating, so be sure he's away from foot traffic.

Don't mess with his food while he's eating. Contrary to what's often suggested, playing with his food won't stop him from guarding it. Instead, it can lead to anxiety over his food. When first introducing him to his food bowl, you can offer him a couple handfuls of food from his bowl by hand but then place his bowl on the floor and leave him alone.

If you have several dogs, give each his or her own bowl, and don't let the older dogs steal the puppy's food. Feeding time should be stress free.

Water

Your puppy's body is about 75 percent water, and losing as little as 15 percent can result in dehydration and even death. Your puppy needs a ready source of clean, fresh water.

The best bowls for German Shepherd puppies are those that are made to be unspillable, such as the bowls with weighted or wider bases. If your puppy spends any time outside, he'll need a second water bowl outside as well as the one inside.

During hot weather, a larger water bowl may be advisable. During cold weather, be sure the outside water bowl isn't frozen.

Keep the water fresh and clean the bowl daily because bacteria can build up from bits of food and saliva dropped into the water.

If you're worried your puppy isn't drinking enough, especially in hot weather, offer him some ice cubes. You can also make some ice cubes out of diluted, low-sodium chicken broth. Just give him these outside so they don't stain your carpet.

Grooming

Grooming is going to be a life-long process for your German Shepherd, so it's important to teach him now that this can be a pleasurable experience. You also want him to know that even if it's not so much fun—such as cleaning his ears or trimming his toenails—he needs to trust you.

The easiest way to do this is by touching him kindly and gently all over his body right from the start. You want him to learn that your hands are never rough or hurtful. The easiest way to do this is by giving him a gentle massage.

Start by sitting on the floor and encouraging your puppy to join you. Bring him up on your lap or between your legs and have him lie down. Don't pin him down, though; this isn't a wrestling match.

When he's comfortable, begin gently rubbing your hands over him. Do this slowly so you relax him. Let your fingers get to know the feel of his body so if he has a lump, cut, imbedded tick, or any other problem, your fingers will find it even if you can't see it through his coat.

Touch him all over, from his nose to the tip of his tail. Feel between each toe and touch each toenail. Run your hands up each leg. Check out his private parts. Even feel down the length of his tail.

After a few days of this, when your pup is used to your touch, introduce a soft bristle brush or a pin brush. After giving your puppy a massage, gently brush him. Move the brush in the direction his hair grows. Don't be concerned so much about getting through his coat to his skin right now. Instead, show your puppy that brushing is simply an extension of that wonderful feeling he gets when you massage him.

Take your time introducing the massage and brushing. After all, you want him to relax and enjoy this. If he does, grooming chores in the future will be much easier.

Social Skills

Your German Shepherd puppy is going to be living in a world with more people than dogs, and he needs to know how to behave in this world. He learned canine social skills from his mother and littermates, and although those are important, he now needs to learn more about living with people.

Socialization Basics

People were a part of your puppy's life from the very beginning because his breeder began handling him, stroking him, and cuddling him even before his eyes were open. Before your puppy left the breeder's place to come home with you, the breeder most likely continued this *socialization* by bringing in a few other people so your puppy met more than just the breeder and her family.

> **DOG TALK**
>
> **Socialization** is the process of introducing your puppy to the world around him, including sights, sounds, smells, and surfaces as well as other people and animals.

The breeder also accustomed the puppies to the sounds and smells of living with people. Your puppy heard the sounds of the vacuum cleaner and garbage disposal as well as the clanging of pots and pans. He smelled dinner cooking and the flowers in a vase on the table. But the socialization that began with the breeder now needs to continue in your house.

Month 3 is the best age for socialization, and you can't procrastinate this. If your veterinarian says your puppy hasn't had all his vaccinations yet and shouldn't meet other dogs right now, that's fine. You can still socialize your puppy to the world around him without risking his health. Simply avoid other dogs and don't allow your puppy to sniff where other dogs have relieved themselves. Take your puppy to outdoor shopping centers, to the local elementary school when the kids are on their way to school, and to the local garden center. There are lots of places where your puppy can see, hear, and smell new things and people and not be at risk for a contagious disease.

The idea of socialization is to teach your German Shepherd that the world is a great place. It's not scary, it's not threatening, and it's not something to worry about. To convey this message, make all introductions fun, happy, and accompanied by verbal praise in a happy tone of voice as well as a few tasty treats.

For example, show your German Shepherd puppy a closed umbrella. Move it around, and encourage him to step up to it and sniff it by saying, "What is it?" Pop a treat in his mouth when he does. Then open the umbrella. If your puppy jumps back, simply ask again, "What is it?" Turn the umbrella upside down on the ground and drop a few treats on it. Point at them and encourage your puppy to come up to the umbrella and get the treats. Praise him.

Use this jolly routine for anything new, especially anything your puppy is worried about. You can even ask your neighbor on the motorcycle or the garbage-truck driver to stop, talk nicely to your puppy, and offer him a treat. The mail carrier and delivery truck driver can also help with socialization.

Your Puppy and Children

Kids and puppies seem to be made for each other. They both love to run, play, and make noise. However, your German Shepherd puppy is going to grow up more quickly than the children in his life, and he'll soon be larger and stronger than they are. It's important that both your puppy and the children in his life know how to interact with each other so no one gets hurt.

As much as realistically possible, keep interactions between your puppy and kids calm and gentle. No wrestling, no tug of war, and no play fighting. Instead, have the kids give your puppy a massage or tummy rub. They can even play hide and seek—let the kids hide and have the puppy find them. Or have the kids throw the ball for the puppy to fetch.

Keep the puppy on a leash when he's interacting with the kids. That way, if he gets overexcited—or the kids get too wound up—you can restrain the puppy until he (or they) settles down.

Don't let the kids run with the puppy. If they run, he's going to chase. When he chases, he's going to want to catch them, and he'll do that with his teeth. Remember, right now your puppy has a mouthful of needle-sharp teeth. In a couple months, he'll lose those and grow some big strong teeth. It's important that he understand he's not allowed to use his teeth when playing with people but most importantly with kids.

To prevent your puppy from biting on the kids or grabbing their clothes, have the kids hand the puppy a dog toy when he starts to get nippy. Teach the puppy, "Get a toy! Good to have a toy!" If he has a toy in his mouth, he can't use his mouth inappropriately.

> **TIPS AND TAILS**
>
> Never leave your German Shepherd alone with children. Puppies and kids can be great friends, but it has to happen with adult supervision. Plus, puppyhood is a great time to teach good habits, and you can only do that if you're there with him.

Kids and dogs—especially a puppy—are the cutest things on the planet. But dogs can hurt children terribly, and dog bites from the family dog happen far too often. Establish some rules for interactions between the puppy and the kids in his life, and enforce those rules to avoid problems.

Behavior

Right now, your puppy's mind is developing just as much as his body is. He's learning all the time, and this is important for you to remember because everything you do with him is teaching him something.

If he cries and you coming running, he's going to remember that. He may begin crying just to get your attention, and that could be a very bad habit. He may also learn that when he sits nicely in front of you and looks at you with those big dark brown eyes, you talk nicely to him and give him a treat. Now that's a good habit to get started!

Keep in mind that he's constantly learning. Think about what the two of you are doing together and what you want him to continue doing as he grows up.

Sleeping Routines

Although your puppy isn't sleeping as much now as he did just a few weeks ago, he is still sleeping a lot. He will sleep, relieve himself, eat, relieve himself, play, and sleep some more.

Your puppy should sleep in his crate. In the "Training" section later in this chapter, we talk about crate training, including why this is so important and how to introduce your puppy to his crate. For now, remember that when your puppy is ready for a nap or when he's going to bed for the night, he needs to be in his crate.

> **HAPPY PUPPY**
>
> Puppies, like young children, can become overexcited and overstimulated, and turn grumpy. When you see your puppy reaching this point, put him in his crate for a nap. He'll be much happier when he wakes up.

How much your puppy will sleep is hard to determine. If he's going through a growth stage, he may sleep more than he does between those growth spurts. Let him sleep as much as he needs to right now.

Your puppy will probably wake up at least once per night, maybe even twice, and need to go outside to relieve himself. When you take him outside, don't interact with him, and certainly don't play with him. Just take him outside, let him relieve himself, quietly praise him, and bring him back to his crate. If you keep things calm and quiet, he should go back to sleep fairly quickly.

Curiosity

Now in his new home, your German Shepherd has an unlimited curiosity about everything around him. Things like the furniture, the kids' toys, your books, the plants out in the yard, and even the lizards in the pile of rocks are all new and exciting to him.

Unfortunately, this curiosity can get him into trouble. Your puppy doesn't know what's safe to play with and what isn't. Nor does he understand that something he chews up may be expensive to replace. This is why puppy-proofing your house and yard is so important.

Your supervision is also important. When your puppy wants to pick up the TV remote control, you can interrupt him with a sharp, "No, that's not yours." Then lead him to one of his toys, and praise him with a happy tone of voice, saying "Here, get your toy! Good to have a toy!" Turn his curiosity into a teaching moment.

He's Biting!

Your German Shepherd puppy doesn't have hands, so he manipulates the world with his mouth. Unfortunately, that means he may chew up things and he may grab people with his mouth (which is why you need to supervise him when he plays with children).

One technique to distract him from biting is to teach your puppy to grab a toy instead. When he has a toy in his mouth, he can't bite or grab clothes. So when you see your puppy getting excited, with you or with the kids, hand him a dog toy and tell him, "Get a toy. Good to have a toy! Yeah!" and make a big fuss over him when he holds that toy in his mouth.

When you see him pick up a toy on his own, praise him even more. "Good to have a toy! Look at you! What a special puppy you are!" Your praise should make him prance and dance.

If your puppy doesn't have a toy and does grab clothes or skin with his teeth, first yell, "Ouch!" in a high-pitched voice, as if you were one of his littermates who was hurt by his teeth. Make direct eye contact with him as his mother would have done when he misbehaved. If his biting stops at that moment, walk him to his toys. If he continues to bite and appears overexcited, take him to his crate for a timeout until he calms down.

Training

If you thought only puppies need training, you're wrong. Training your German Shepherd is an ongoing process for his lifetime.

German Shepherds are working dogs, and a bored German Shepherd of any age is going to get into trouble. Training, no matter whether it's obedience, trick training, or performance sports, keeps your dog's mind challenged and busy, which makes him less likely to get in trouble.

Training Techniques

There are as many different training techniques, methods, and styles as there are dogs, owners, and dog trainers. Although the proponents of each technique tend to think theirs is the best, or easiest, or kindest, as long as the technique is easy to use and humane for the dog, there's really no one technique that's better than another.

The training technique used in this book is a lure-and-reward technique. It's easy for dog owners to understand and use, and it's just as easy for the dogs to learn. It's also kind and humane for the dog.

Here are the basic training steps of this technique:

🐾 Show the dog what you want him to do.

🐾 Praise and reward him for doing it.

🐾 Should he do something you don't want him to do, interrupt him. Then show him what you want him to do, and praise and reward him.

It sounds easy, right? It is.

Say, for example, your German Shepherd puppy is jumping up on your legs, scratching you with his sharp toenails. Plus, you're concerned that when he gets bigger, if he jumps he'll knock the kids down. Here's how to curb this behavior:

🐾 Have your puppy on leash, and hold the leash in your left hand. Have a pocketful of treats and one treat in your right hand.

🐾 Let your puppy sniff the treat, and tell him, "Sweetie, sit," and move the treat over his head toward his tail just slightly. As his head goes up and back, his hips will go down.

🐾 When his hips touch the ground, tell him, "Good boy to sit! Yeah!" and give him the treat.

🐾 Now, use the hand holding the leash to also hold his collar. Use your right hand to pet your puppy while he's sitting. As you pet him, praise him, "Good boy, yes, you are."

🐾 When he's calm, tell him, "Sweetie, okay!" and release his collar so he can get up and move around.

Your puppy jumps on you for attention; if he gets attention while he's sitting, he no longer needs to jump up. So be sure he gets all his petting while sitting!

If he jumps up before you can have him sit, tell him, "No jump," as you take his collar and help him sit using the treat-over-the-nose technique. Then praise him for sitting.

Rather than just telling your puppy what *not* to do, you're teaching him what *to* do instead. This makes training much easier, not to mention a whole lot more fun for you and your puppy.

Crate Training Your Puppy

The crate is your German Shepherd puppy's bedroom. It confines him at night when everyone is sleeping, but it also keeps him safe for short periods of time during the day.

The crate is not a cupboard to store your puppy in all the time; that's abusing the crate. Instead, by using the crate, your puppy learns to control his bladder and bowels, as puppies have an instinct to keep their bed clean.

You want the crate to be a good thing. Ideally, when you say, "Sweetie, go to bed!" your puppy should run to his crate and dash in with his tail wagging wildly. If your puppy hates his crate and you have to push him inside, there's a problem.

> ### TIPS AND TAILS
>
> Crates work well for puppy training because puppies like dark, confined places to hide and sleep. The crate becomes your puppy's safe and secure den.

Crates come in several different types. The hard plastic crate that comes apart so the top can be inverted and stored in the bottom half is the most common type. This one is bulky, but it's easy to clean and easy for dogs to get used to. A wire crate that looks more like a cage is also easy to use. It's often heavy, although it is collapsible and stores flat. The soft-sided nylon crates that look more like carry bags are great for small dogs but are not suitable for German Shepherds. Most will destroy it in minutes.

Whether you choose a plastic crate or a metal one is up to you. Take a look at the variety of crates at your local pet supply store, and think about your ability to move it, store it, and use it. Choose a crate that will give an adult German Shepherd room to stand up, turn around, and lie down. You aren't going to provide this much room for your puppy now, when he's so small, but he's going to need that room as he grows.

When you bring home the crate, section off a part of it. Your puppy needs room to lie down comfortably, but if you give him the whole adult-size crate, he can relieve himself in one corner of the crate and have plenty of room to get away from it. Some crates come with sections you can slide into place just for this purpose, but if your crate doesn't, you can use a heavy cardboard box to make a back portion of the crate inaccessible.

Set up the crate in a room where people in the house hang out. Lots of foot traffic is good. This isn't going to be a permanent location for the crate; it's just here now for introductions.

Prop open the crate door so it won't close accidentally. Grab a good handful of treats, and let your puppy smell the treats. Toss one toward but not into the crate. Let your puppy go eat it and praise him, "Good boy!" Do that a couple more times, and then toss a treat into the crate. When he steps into the crate for the treat, praise him with the command you're going to use, "Good to go to bed! Yeah!" Repeat this a few more times and then stop. Do this each time you walk by the crate throughout the day.

When mealtime comes around, put your puppy's food bowl inside the crate, pushing it to the back. Let him go in the crate, and close the door. Let him eat in peace, and don't open the door immediately after he's finished. Let him figure out the door is closed. Then, if he's calm and quiet, open the door and praise him. If he's barking, pawing at the door, and throwing a temper tantrum, don't let him out. In fact, walk away and go to another room. When he calms down, come back and let him out.

Begin putting him in the crate and closing the door for 2 or 3 minutes every now and then throughout the day. Always give him a treat when he's inside, and never let him out when he's throwing a fit.

Some German Shepherd puppies can learn this lesson all in one day. If your breeder introduced him to the crate when she still had him, your pup will switch over to the crate at your house with no problem.

Once your puppy is used to the crate, put it in the place where you'd like it to remain. In your bedroom is a great place because your puppy can sleep in your room, hearing you and smelling you and being close to you even though you're asleep. If you're short of room, move your bedside table out and put the crate there.

Don't isolate your puppy. If you put him in the laundry room or garage, he'll be very unhappy and behavioral problems such as barking and howling can result. Your German Shepherd puppy needs to be near you.

> **HAPPY PUPPY**

When your puppy is comfortable with the crate, it will become his bed at night and his refuge when he's tired or stressed. Leave the door to the crate open during the day, and let him run in and out as he wishes. You may find him curled up in it sound asleep with the door wide open, and that's wonderful.

One of the biggest benefits of using the crate, besides teaching housetraining skills, is preventing bad behavior from occurring, so don't stop using the crate until your dog is mentally grown up and well trained. For a German Shepherd, this can be

3 to 4 years old. Even then, many owners leave the crate out as the dog's bed and just take the door off so the dog can come and go as he pleases.

Prioritize Housetraining

Housetraining is a basic skill necessary for every dog who lives inside—after all, mistakes can ruin carpet and make life miserable. Plus, a German Shepherd is much too big of a dog to be making messes inside.

Housetraining consists of teaching the puppy where he needs to relieve himself. You may have a certain section of the backyard where you want him to go as well as on a part of your sidewalk where it would be convenient and easy to clean up.

The second part of housetraining is teaching your pup to try to relieve himself when you ask him to. This is just as important as teaching him where to go. For example, if you teach your dog to relieve himself in one corner of the backyard and on the vacant lot in your neighborhood, you also need to be able to ask him to go on command in other places. If you're traveling, he will need to go during the trip.

First of all, decide where you want him to relieve himself. There doesn't have to be anything special about this spot. It just needs to be a place where your puppy has easy access and where you're willing to clean up after him.

To teach him to use this spot, walk him out to that place. That means when your puppy needs to go, such as when he wakes up first thing in the morning, put a leash on him and walk him to the door as you ask him, "Do you have to go?" Then have him go outside with you to the spot. When he relieves himself, praise him enthusiastically, "Good boy to go!"

Don't send your puppy outside all by himself. If you do, you can't teach him where to go, and you can't praise him for doing it. In addition, you really won't know if he's gone or not. He may show up at the door asking to come in and have an accident on the carpet inside the door because he was too busy exploring instead of going.

By taking him out, you can teach him where to go, along with a command that means "Try to go now," and you can reward him for doing it. All of this helps create a reliably housetrained dog.

Housetraining Accidents

Accidents do happen, even when you're vigilant. A puppy can be playing one second and squatting the next. However, accidents usually occur when you get distracted and get busy with something other than the puppy. It happens to all of us.

When an accident happens, how you react is important. After all, the puppy does have to urinate and defecate. If you convey to the puppy that urinating and/or defecating is wrong, he'll try to hide it. He may no longer relieve himself in front of you, even outside. You may find puddles or piles behind the drapes or the sofa.

If you catch your puppy in the act, use your voice to interrupt him, loudly saying "No, not here!" Take him outside, and tell him to go now using your normal, soft voice. Praise him if he has anything left or tries to comply. Then leave him outside while you go back inside to clean up.

If you find an accident after the fact—after the puppy has finished and moved away—do not punish him at all. Don't drag him to it and yell at him, and don't stick his nose in it. He has to go; it's a natural biological action. Bringing him back after the fact won't teach him anything. Instead, take him outside and leave him there while you clean up.

Do not yell at your puppy for accidents. Instead, promise yourself you'll do better next time, either by making sure to take him outside more quickly, by sticking to his schedule, or by supervising him better. You're both learning!

You and Your Puppy

Your new German Shepherd puppy is so small, yet when he first joins your household, he'll be a major disruption. Plus, most new puppy owners try so hard to do everything right that the stress levels in the home can rise significantly.

But you know what? Everything is going to be fine. You have all the help you need right here. So relax and enjoy your puppy.

What to Expect

If at all possible, bring home your new puppy on a Friday if you have Saturday and Sunday off from work. This way, he can get to know you and the household for a few days before he's left all alone when you return to work on Monday.

When you first bring your puppy home, take him from the car to the place where you want him to relieve himself. Let him wander around, sniff, and decide where he wants to go. Have family members leave him alone right now; after all, if he doesn't relieve himself here, he will when he gets inside the house. So let him have some quiet time now, and praise him when he relieves himself.

Inside, the best way for him to meet the family is to have everyone sit on the floor and let the puppy go from person to person. No one should hold or restrain him; just let him get to know everyone. Limit this to people who live in the house, though.

Neighbors and other family members can meet him in a few days. (We talk more about socialization later in this chapter.)

These first interactions with your new German Shepherd puppy need to be calm and quiet. No wrestling with the puppy or play fighting. Instead, show him this new home is safe and in no way threatening to him.

After the first introductions, have everyone in the family go back to a normal routine as much as possible. This helps your puppy learn the routine and how life proceeds in this home. He also needs to spend some time alone now and then throughout the day. Crate training your puppy is a good way for him to spend some time alone. When you can't supervise your puppy, put him in his crate with a chew toy.

Over the next few days, don't be surprised if your puppy cries. This is an entirely new situation for him, with people he doesn't know, and in a strange place. He may be lonely for his littermates, he might not know where to find food or water, and he might even be a little frightened. Just because you understand that your puppy may cry doesn't necessarily mean you should run to him each and every time he cries. If he needs to go outside, take him outside. But if he's been outside and still cries, perhaps because he's alone, offer him a toy or something to chew on and then leave him alone again. When he's quiet, then go give him some attention.

The first few days will be tough for you and your puppy. He'll probably wake you up a few times during the night, he might have some housetraining accidents, he might cry and whine, and he might play fight with those sharp puppy teeth. Just react calmly to all these occurrences. Your confidence will help him be calm, too.

Be a Parent

Your new German Shepherd is a baby, so it's important that you establish yourself as your puppy's adoptive parent. Although this German Shepherd may well become your best friend later, right now he needs a parent's leadership and guidance.

To do this, you'll need to establish some ground rules for your relationship. The most important right now is to be sure he's not treating you like one of his littermates. Don't let him jump on you, climb on top of you, or chew on your pant legs, feet, or hands. If he did any of those things to his mother, she would have growled at him.

Play with your puppy, but if he gets too excited, stop the play time. Just get up and walk away. If he chases you and tries to continue jumping and biting, take him to his crate and give him a time-out for a few minutes or until he calms down.

If you just try to think of yourself as a parent rather than a playmate, you'll be fine. Just don't get frustrated when your puppy doesn't understand right away. After all, you don't look anything like his mother!

The Benefits of Organization

Puppies thrive on a schedule, so organization is going to be your friend right now. If you normally aren't an organized person or don't live with any kind of a schedule, try to change that for at least a few months.

Housetraining is much easier when the puppy has a schedule for eating, napping, and going outside to relieve himself. He's also going to need to go outside after play sessions, and in these early months it'll be about every 2 hours when he's awake.

With some organization, or at least a plan, you can also be sure things are done when they need to be done and you're not procrastinating. Socialization, for example, needs to start very soon. If you don't do it in these early weeks, you can miss that window of time when socialization is so important.

How you organize is of course up to you. Some puppy owners post notes on the refrigerator as reminders, while others use the calendar on their smartphone. You can also use a bulletin or white board. What's most important is that you create a plan. Here's what to make time for:

🐾 Your puppy needs three meals a day right now, although in a couple months, he'll only need two. When are you going to feed him?

🐾 He needs to go outside to relieve himself after waking up, after eating, after playing, and about every 2 hours when awake.

🐾 He needs at least a couple play sessions with you each day as well as time to begin his training.

🐾 Set aside time to begin introducing him to brushing, nail clipping, and other grooming chores.

🐾 Make time for socialization.

You'll to add to this list as time goes on. For example, he'll also need to make a couple trips to the veterinarian over the next several weeks. So create a plan and check it often—for both your sakes.

Month 3 > Month 4 > Month 5

Month 4
Socialization at home with new owner and other pets
Teething begins—heavy chewing period
Enroll in puppy class
Rapid growth ‖ Switch to adult food
2nd DHPP vaccines ‖ 3rd DHPP and rabies vaccines

Month 4 (weeks 13 through 16) brings a lot of changes in your German Shepherd puppy. She's growing fast, and you'll see differences in her almost on a daily basis. Mentally, she's ready to learn, so getting her started on a training routine now is important. You're also going to want to get her used to the grooming chores that will be a part of her life.

This month is one of the most important as far as socialization goes. Your puppy needs to meet a variety of people, other puppies, and dogs, and see, smell, hear, and feel new things. Don't procrastinate; socialization now is vitally important.

Physical Development

By the end of this month, your puppy probably weighs between 35 and 40 pounds, with male puppies weighing a little more than female puppies. She's losing that puppy roundness and beginning to look more like a German Shepherd. She's leggier, and her body is longer, as are her nose and her tail.

She's losing some of her puppy coat, too. You'll start seeing the coat change on her face first as the smooth adult coat appears on her forehead. Then her fluffy puppy coat will be replaced by the smoother adult coat down her back, over her spine, down to her tail, and then gradually down her sides. It really is quite interesting because the adult coat doesn't appear all at once equally all over the body; it comes in gradually.

Your puppy's motor skills are getting better, and she's a little less clumsy all the time. Although after a big growth spurt, expect her to trip over her own paws for a while again until she gets used to the changes.

Teething Begins

At some point during this month your puppy will begin to lose her puppy teeth. When varies by puppy, although for most it's around 15 or 16 weeks. But as with most things concerning development, some puppies start losing teeth sooner or later, so don't worry if it happens that way.

Many times owners discover their puppy is teething when they step on a discarded tooth. Other times, you may see a few drops of blood in your puppy's mouth or blood on a chew toy. If you never find a tooth, your puppy probably swallowed it. Don't worry about this, though, because it will digest in her intestinal tract.

An adult German Shepherd has 42 adult teeth. The incisors are the small teeth at the front of the top and bottom jaws, the canines are the big fangs, the premolars are the next teeth following the canines, and the molars are the last two teeth on either side of the top and bottom jaw. The adult teeth usually come in right under the puppy teeth so while she's teething, your puppy's gums are often swollen and hot.

> ### HAPPY PUPPY
>
> To help alleviate the pain of teething, offer your puppy ice cubes to chew on. If she's not interested in plain ice cubes, make some with diluted low-sodium chicken broth. Just be sure you give her these outside so they don't stain your carpet.

Your German Shepherd puppy's adult teeth don't all come in at the same time. The small incisors are usually the first to be lost and the first to come in during this month. The big canines are next and come in any time during the last half of this month on into the next. The premolars, found in the top and bottom jaw after the canines as you look toward the back of the mouth, generally come in late this month or next month. The molars are last and may not come through the gums until month 7.

If an adult tooth comes in next to a puppy tooth, check to see if the puppy tooth is loose. If it is, it'll probably fall out on its own and you don't have to do anything with it. However, if the puppy tooth is still well anchored and solid, on your next trip to the veterinarian ask him to take a look at it. The puppy tooth might need to be pulled. If allowed to remain, it could cause problems with the adult tooth.

Those Floppy Ears

Your puppy's ears are probably kind of floppy right now, and one day they're up and the next day they're down. They may tilt toward the center of her head, leaning on each other, or they may fall toward the outside of her head, looking like wings.

A German Shepherd's ears usually stand up on their own anytime between 8 weeks and 5 months of age. Until they completely stand up, they can do the floppy ear dance, up and down, especially when the puppy begins losing her puppy teeth and growing in her adult ones. (What do her teeth have to do with her ears? The theory is that so much calcium is going to her teeth that her ears fall down.)

You can help your puppy use her ears and strengthen her ear muscles by encouraging her to move them. Whistle, and when she perks up her ears and looks at you, she'll use the muscles that support her ears. Make other funny noises at different times throughout the day so she perks up her ears, swivels them, and works out those muscles.

At the same time, don't squash her ears. If you mash her ears, fold them back against her head, or otherwise flatten them while petting or playing with your puppy, you could potentially weaken her developing ear muscles. If you really want to pet her on the head, scratch or rub at the base of her ears.

If your puppy's ears haven't stood up at all by this time, you might want to give them a helping hand by taping them up. Not all German Shepherd puppies need their ears taped, but it's not unusual that you'd have to do this.

> **TIPS AND TAILS**

If a German Shepherd puppy's ears aren't standing tall by 7 or 8 months of age, they probably won't stand up. So don't wait too long to decide whether or not to tape her ears.

To tape up your German Shepherd puppy's ears, you need two foam curlers or perm rollers. (Find these in the hair-care department at your local drug or department store.) Take the hard plastic clip out of the roller; you only need the foam part. You also need first-aid adhesive tape $1\frac{1}{2}$ to 2 inches wide.

With the sticky side out, wrap the foam roller in adhesive tape. Place the tape-covered roller in your puppy's ears so the bottom part of the roller doesn't block her ear canal but is below the level of the top of her skull. If the roller is too high in the ear, the ear will simply fall over with the roller in it. If the roller is too low, it will block the ear canal.

Form the ear flap around the roller so it's a pyramid that's wider at the base and narrower at the top. Using more of the adhesive tape, tape the ear into this position.

Now distract your puppy so she gets used to the feel of these things in her ears. Play with her, throw a ball or toy, or brush her. If she begins shaking her head or scratching at her ears, distract her. When she does get the rollers out of her ears or scratches some of the tape off, just repeat the process. You'll probably have to do this many times.

Once you begin taping, continue to do so until your puppy's adult teeth are well grown in and her ears seem to be standing well when untaped. However, if you take the tape and rollers off and the ears fall back down within a day or so, tape them up again.

Although floppy ears certainly won't hurt your dog, German Shepherds are known for their expressive upright ears. It's certainly worth your time and energy to try to help them stand.

Health

Thankfully, most German Shepherd puppies of this age are healthy. However, it's important for you to watch your puppy and learn what's normal for her and what isn't. Then, should you see a change, talk to your veterinarian, your partner in your puppy's health care. When there is a problem, the more you can tell your vet about the changes you've seen, the better able your vet will be able to help your puppy.

Recognizing Signs of Health Problems

Your puppy can't speak to you to tell you when she doesn't feel well, so you have to pay attention to how she behaves and moves to determine when something doesn't look right. Those differences could mean a change in your puppy's health and signal potential problems.

Eating habits: Make a note of any changes in your puppy's eating habits. Although her appetite will often vary depending on how fast she's growing on any given day or week, if your puppy refuses to eat for more than two meals, call your veterinarian.

Vomiting: Vomiting once is not necessarily a problem. Your puppy might have eaten too quickly or perhaps she drank too much water too quickly. But if she vomits repeatedly and can't keep any food down, call your veterinarian.

If you spot anything unusual in the vomit, such as pieces of foreign objects— things that might have been chewed and eaten—save those and call your veterinarian. If you see blood in the vomit, call your veterinarian immediately.

Urine and feces: Watch your German Shepherd puppy's urinary and bowel habits. Long-time dog owners like to joke that no one in the world pays as much attention to feces as dog owners do. There's a good reason for that, because many health problems show up first as changes in the digestive system. If your puppy is straining to urinate or defecate, that's a problem. Diarrhea is also a problem; it can be a symptom of disease, of a dog-food issue, or that your puppy ate something she shouldn't have. Report any blood you see in her urine or feces to your vet right away.

Activity level: Pay attention, too, to changes in your pup's activity, and note any lack of desire to play. German Shepherd puppies like to stay close to their owners as a matter of course, but if your puppy seems clingier than normal, that might be a sign something hurts or she doesn't feel well.

Limping or lameness: Your puppy might trip over her own feet or fall while playing and just be a little sore. However, if she won't put any weight on a limb or limps for more than a few hours, call your veterinarian.

Temperature: By this age, your puppy's normal temperature is the same as an adult German Shepherd's: about 101.5°F to 102°F. If your puppy isn't acting normal, take her temperature. If it's either low or high, call your vet.

Don't hesitate to call your veterinarian if something concerns you. Your vet won't laugh at you if it turns out to be nothing important. In fact, most veterinarians are happiest when their clients do pay attention to their dogs.

When you do call, however, be able to explain exactly what concerns you. Tell your vet what your puppy's appetite is like, how her stools are different from normal; or what her temperature is. Even if you just have a feeling something's wrong, think of how to explain that. Even a description such as, "My German Shepherd puppy doesn't seem to be eager to eat and isn't playing like she normally does. Her temperature is 101.5 and her stools are normal. But her expression looks sad." Your veterinarian will have more questions or will ask you to bring in your puppy for an examination.

Dealing with Fleas

Fleas are tiny insects that live by biting their host—in this case, your German Shepherd puppy. Each time a flea bites, it takes one drop of blood. One flea isn't going to do a great deal of harm, but where there's one flea, there are apt to be hundreds more, and your puppy can potentially lose a drop of blood for each one of these pests.

The bites can also be a problem if your pup is allergic to the flea's saliva, as many German Shepherds are. For many pets, this can cause severe itching and they'll scratch, chew, and even lose hair in the bite area.

If you see what looks like salt and pepper on your puppy's bed, that's an indication your German Shepherd puppy has fleas. The dark bits are excreted blood, and the white specks are flea eggs.

To prevent a flea infestation on your puppy, you have to control the fleas on your puppy as well as in your home and yard. In years past, that meant using pesticides and insecticides everywhere. However, such preventatives are very toxic, and their use has fallen out of favor with most pet owners and veterinarians.

Instead, it's better to begin controlling fleas before they become a problem. Today's topical flea-prevention products usually work well. Not all products are safe for puppies, however, so choose wisely or get a recommendation from your veterinarian.

A good vacuum cleaner is an indispensible tool in your fight against fleas. Vacuum the house daily during flea season. That means getting the floor, the carpet, your pup's bedding, and the furniture. Don't forget to do your car, too. Throw out the sweeper bag or empty the vacuum container afterward.

Diatomaceous earth and boric acid are also often recommended for use in the house. Sprinkle liberally, leave down for a little while (according to package directions), and then vacuum. Sentry makes a spray called Natural Defense Household Spray that can be used in the house, in crates, on bedding, in cabinets, and more, and is considered safe for use around puppies. It uses peppermint, cinnamon, lemongrass, and thyme oils.

Although garlic and brewer's yeast have been recommended for discouraging fleas from biting, these have fallen out of favor with many pet experts. Garlic has been found to be not as healthy for dogs and cats as once thought, and brewer's yeast alone is not very effective.

Pennyroyal oil is often recommended as a natural means of flea control. However, more cases of toxicity have been recognized with its use recently, leading experts to recommend it not be used on your puppy or her bedding.

If your German Shepherd is having a reaction to the flea bites and is scratching, chewing, and acting miserable, call your vet. Your puppy might need some veterinary care to overcome the flea bite reaction or dermatitis.

Taking Care of Ticks

The two most common types of ticks found on dogs are deer ticks and dog ticks—both blood-sucking insects. Ticks can be the cause of several serious diseases, including Lyme disease, Rocky Mountain spotted fever, ehrlichiosis, canine babesiosis, and canine hepatozoonosis. Tick paralysis is also a potential problem with tick bites.

Ticks are usually found on tall grasses or bushes, and when your puppy (or you!) walks past, the tick grabs on. The tick then works its way through your dog's coat to her skin, inserts its head into your dog's skin, and begins to engorge on blood.

The most effective way to find ticks is to examine your German Shepherd puppy often, especially in the spring and fall when ticks are more numerous and active. As you feel all over your puppy, you'll notice ticks as bumps on your puppy's skin. When you find a bump, part the hair and look at the skin. An engorged tick that's full of blood will be about the size of a pencil eraser or slightly larger.

Use a pair of tweezers to remove a tick. Grasp the tick down near the head, close to your puppy's skin, and gently pull the tick straight out. (Commercial tools made specifically for removing ticks are also available.) Don't yank or twist the tick, or the head could break off and remain lodged in your puppy's skin, which could cause an abscess. If you see some redness at the site where the tick was later and it doesn't clear up in a couple days, call your veterinarian.

> **TIPS AND TAILS**
>
> If you find a tick, don't squeeze it with your fingers. Many of the diseases ticks carry can also be transmitted to people.

Nutrition

Most German Shepherd puppies have a huge growth spurt during this month. To fuel that growth, they need good-quality nutrition—and a lot of it!

The food you feed your German Shepherd puppy provides nutrients for everything that happens inside her body, from growth to cell reproduction to energy for activities. So be sure you're feeding her a food that'll do her body good.

Appetite and Growth Spurts

Your German Shepherd puppy's appetite will probably increase just before she begins a big growth spurt, so if your puppy acts famished this month, don't be surprised. Increase her food slightly, and spread the increase across her meals. If you're feeding three times a day, divide that increase in food among all three meals. If you give your puppy the extra food at just one meal, it might be too much and she might not eat it. If she does eat it all, she might have soft stools because of the big increase in food.

Even though your puppy needs more food during a growth spurt, you may find that she's not interested in one of her meals—often the midday meal. If she seems to eat better with just two meals a day, that's fine. Just divide her food into two meals so she continues to get the same total amount of food.

There's no way to predict how much food your German Shepherd puppy will need. Not only is each puppy an individual with unique nutritional needs who grows at her own rate, but each food or diet is different. Begin feeding using the instructions given on the food label, and vary the amount depending on how your German Shepherd does on the food. Look at her weight—heavy or thin—as well as the condition of her skin and coat, the brightness of her eyes, and her energy for play.

After a big growth spurt, your puppy's appetite may decrease a little. This is normal. If she leaves food in her bowl or isn't quite as hungry as she was, just cut back on the amount you're feeding her. A slight decrease is okay. Just be ready to increase the food again when the next growth spurt happens.

The Basics of Nutrition

Dogs are carnivores. They are naturally designed to eat meat and thrive on animal protein. Even though few dogs today actually have to catch prey animals to survive as their wild cousins need to do, their nutritional needs remain the same.

Good nutrition, however, is much more than just feeding your pet meat. There are many components of nutrition, all of which need to be met if your puppy is to thrive. Some German Shepherds do have food sensitivities, especially as adults. Others may have digestive issues, while a few have slower (or faster) metabolisms. Good nutrition must take into account all of your German Shepherd's individual needs.

Your German Shepherd puppy needs the right balance of good-quality proteins, amino acids, enzymes, carbohydrates, fats and fatty acids, vitamins, and minerals.

Proteins, amino acids, and enzymes: Proteins are necessary for muscle building, hormone production, disease fighting, growth, reproduction, and many other bodily processes. Proteins can be found in animal products such as meats and eggs as well as in some plants. Proteins found in meats and eggs are called complete proteins because they contain a balanced and complete assortment of amino acids necessary for good health. Many plants, including cereal grains and legumes, contain proteins, but these plant-based proteins don't contain all the amino acids your dog needs. They're incomplete proteins.

Your pup needs 22 amino acids, 12 of which she can synthesize within her body. These amino acids are called nonessential amino acids because they don't need to be present in the food she eats. The remaining amino acids must be provided by your puppy's food, and because of this, they're called essential amino acids. The essentials include arginine, histidine, isoleucine, leucine, lysine, methionine-cystine, phenylalnine-tyrosine, theonine, tryptophan, and valine.

Enzymes are also proteins. These are catalysts involved in many functions within the body. Enzymes are needed for healing, cell functions, brain functions, and digestion.

Most pet-nutrition experts agree that the best sources of proteins for dogs come from animal sources. Muscle meats, organs, cheeses, yogurt, and eggs are all sources of excellent digestible proteins for your puppy.

Carbohydrates: Carbohydrates are derived from plants and found in two forms: simple and complex. Simple carbs are made of simple sugar molecules, while complex carbohydrates are comprised of several sugar molecules joined together in a chain. Your puppy's body breaks down carbohydrates into glucose, which she uses as energy for a variety of her bodily functions.

Complex carbohydrates are also dietary fiber. Your puppy needs fiber in her intestinal tract to move foods through and to form stools. Without fiber, your German Shepherd puppy could easily become constipated.

Your puppy can easily eat and metabolize carbs such as tubers (carrots, potatoes, sweet potatoes, and yams) as well as greens (green beans, spinach, broccoli, collard greens) as long as they're chopped into smaller pieces and cooked or steamed. Dogs can also eat some fruits, especially apples, bananas, blueberries, and strawberries.

Fats and fatty acids: Fats are vital for the absorption of fat-soluble vitamins. Fats are also needed for hormone processes, for healthy skin and coat, and for energy. There are three essential fatty acids: omega-3, omega-6, and arachidonic acid. These fatty acids are needed for cell structure, development, and function. They also support the immune system and help with the movement of oxygen in the bloodstream. They must be in the correct balance to be of use to your puppy.

Adequate amounts of fats are often provided in your puppy's dog food, and especially from sources such as meat, fish, poultry fat, avocados, and nuts. Commercial kibble-type foods often add fat to the food—in the recipe or sprayed on after cooking—to enhance the flavor of the food.

Vitamins: Vitamins are organic compounds found in foods that perform essential functions in your German Shepherd's body. These can range from helping maintain healthy vision to keeping the coat shiny. There are two types of vitamins: fat soluble (which requires fats in the diet for metabolism of the vitamin) and water soluble (using water in the body for vitamin metabolism).

Fat-soluble vitamins include A, D, E, and K. If your puppy consumes excess fat-soluble vitamins, they are stored in her fat cells until she needs them. If she eats too many, these vitamins can create a toxic situation in her body, cause blood thinning and bleeding, or lead to a variety of other undesirable side effects.

The water-soluble vitamins include the B vitamins and vitamin C. Excess water-soluble vitamins are excreted in the urine and don't cause any problems for your pup.

Minerals: Minerals are originally from the earth, but a good source for your German Shepherd is from the meats she eats as well as raw or slightly steamed vegetables.

Calcium is one of the most abundant minerals in the body. Most of it is found in the bones, but calcium is also necessary for nerve functions and as a co-enzyme for many body functions. Calcium is found in bones, cheese, seeds, nuts, and dark green leafy vegetables. Too much calcium can cause your pup constipation.

Calcium and phosphorus really should be listed as one mineral conjoined—calcium-phosphorus—because one wouldn't be effective without the other. Together, they are vital for strong bones, DNA and RNA structure, and energy. Phosphorus is found in meats and eggs.

> ## TIPS AND TAILS

A ratio of 1.0 or 2.0 parts calcium to 1.0 part phosphorus is needed to ensure both minerals are properly utilized in the body. If the amount of phosphorus far exceeds the amount of dietary calcium, bone abnormalities may occur. Too much calcium with too little phosphorus causes large bone growth but the bones will be less dense.

Another important mineral is zinc, which is a co-enzyme for more than 25 different processes during digestion. It also supports the immune system, is important for healthy skin and coat, and aids in healing. It can be found in meats and eggs.

A good-quality dog food should contain all these elements in the proper amounts. Read the label carefully and/or ask your vet for a recommendation so you can ensure your German Shepherd pup gets the best nutrition possible.

Eating Disorders

German Shepherds have been known to develop two different eating disorders: anorexia and pica. Although these don't always develop during month 4, they can. We address them here so you'll recognize them should one of them develop in your puppy.

Anorexia in people is usually related to a psychological condition regarding weight and appearance. Your German Shepherd has no concept of weight or appearance, but anorexia in dogs can still either have a psychological trigger or a medical cause.

German Shepherds can be quite sensitive to what happens around them, and disruptions can cause your puppy to stop eating or to eat significantly less than normal. For example, school beginning after summer vacation and the kids no longer being home with her all day can disrupt your puppy's life enough that she may lose her appetite.

However, if there haven't been any changes in your puppy's life and she still isn't interested in eating, look for some signs of a health problem, as outlined earlier in this chapter.

If the anorexia has a psychological cause, adding something smelly and tasty to her normal food—such as grated cheese or shredded cooked meat—can usually tempt your puppy to eat. However, if there's a medical reason for the anorexia—such as liver, kidney, or pancreatic disease—even good food probably won't tempt her. If you're concerned about your German Shepherd's eating changes, call your veterinarian.

Pica is an eating disorder that, unfortunately, can be quite common in German Shepherd puppies at this age, especially when they're teething. Many puppies begin chewing on (and swallowing) anything they can get hold of when they're teething because their gums and jaws hurt. If the pica is actually caused by teething, it will go away when her adult teeth come in.

> **DOG TALK**
>
> **Anorexia** is the lack of an appetite or inability to eat. **Pica** is the act of eating nonfood items.

Pica can also have a nutritional cause. Some puppies, especially those who eat a less-than-optimal diet or who aren't metabolizing their food well, will have a craving to satisfy that nutritional need. Malnourished puppies will eat dirt, rocks, compost, wood, and other obviously nonfood items. When changed to a better diet or when the food is supplemented with something to aid the puppy's digestion, this disorder often goes away.

Puppies who develop pica because of teething or a nutritional disorder need to be distracted from eating those strange things. If the puppy swallowed these items, the objects could tear or puncture the dog's intestinal tract, cause a blockage, or otherwise be toxic. A verbal interruption can often stop a puppy from grabbing something, but this means you need to closely watch your puppy. Keeping your house and yard puppy-proofed is important, but because puppies eat strange things that often can't be predicted, supervision is still important.

Unfortunately, some German Shepherds develop a compulsive need to eat strange things and never outgrow it. These dogs won't stop hunting for things when distracted or when their diet is changed. The need to eat different objects becomes an all-encompassing need, and they'll devour socks, plastic bags, wooden sticks, rocks, or other things commonly found around the house or yard. A German Shepherd with an obsessive compulsive disorder needs help from both a veterinarian and a behaviorist. A combination of medications, behavior modification exercises, and close owner supervision can often help.

Grooming

Your German Shepherd puppy doesn't have extensive grooming needs, especially when compared to a breed like Poodles or Bichon Frise. However, that doesn't make grooming any less important for your puppy.

Grooming helps keep your German Shepherd healthy. Cleaning her ears and teeth, wiping the sleep out of her eyes, brushing her regularly, and trimming her toenails are all a part of the process. Plus, by feeling every part of your puppy's body on a regular basis, you can catch minor changes—lumps, cuts or scratches, or ticks—before they turn into major problems.

Keeping your German Shepherd clean is also important. Not only does this help keep the dirt in your house to a manageable level, but a clean puppy is also a healthier one.

Grooming Your German Shepherd Puppy

Although your German Shepherd puppy isn't going to have her full adult coat for a few more months, and she won't be shedding as much now as she will later, you still need to introduce her to several aspects of grooming.

Brushing: You began brushing your puppy last month, just touching and stroking her gently with the brush to get her used to the idea. That gentle introduction should continue until you can brush all over her entire body. Use soft strokes, and be sure you don't scratch her skin through her coat. Next month, you'll learn more about her coat, coat care, and shedding. Right now just focus on teaching her to enjoy her daily brushing and time spent with you.

Trimming toenails: Although your puppy's nails aren't long right now, they will get thicker and stronger as she grows, so getting her used to getting her nails done sooner will save you both time and frustration later. The scissors-type nail clippers usually work best for German Shepherds because they cut larger nails more easily than the guillotine clippers do.

When you give your puppy a massage, or after you brush her, be sure you also handle her paws. Gently massage each toe and pad, and gently handle each nail. When your puppy is comfortable having her paws massaged, then you can clip her nails.

To determine where to trim, look at one nail from the side. Do you see underneath where the end of the nail curves up and then flattens under the base of the nail? You can usually safely trim that curved part. If you hit the quick by accident, dip the nail in some *styptic powder* or scrape the nail over a bar of soap to stop the bleeding until a clot forms. After you trim each nail, praise your puppy and tell her how wonderful she is. Then trim another one.

> **DOG TALK**

Styptic powder contains several ingredients, including ferrous sulfate, and is used to stop minor bleeding.

Paws: While you're working on her feet, take a look at her paws. German Shepherds have shorter hairs on their paws so their feet fur generally doesn't have to be trimmed as many other breeds do. However, if your German Shepherd puppy has a lush coat, or just has longer hair on the underside of her paws, you may want to trim the bottom of her feet. This can help keep her paws cleaner—less dirt tracked into the house—plus it will help her not slip on tile or slippery floors.

When trimming her paw fur, hold the scissors parallel to the paw and don't stick the point of the scissors toward the inside of the paw or between her paw pads. Simply trim the hairs that stick down past the bottom of the pads, the hairs that would fold under the pads when your puppy is walking.

Private parts: Most puppies—males as well as females—keep their private parts clean by licking. However, sometimes they need some help. When that's the case, wet a hand towel or clean rag in warm water, and add just a drop of a gentle soap, like baby shampoo, or a dog shampoo made for puppies. Wash the end of the male's sheath or the female's vulva, rinse well, and dry the area.

You may find feces stuck to your German Shepherd puppy's coat around her anus after she relieves herself. The feces can be washed off, but many owners prefer to avoid this problem by trimming the coat under the tail. To trim safely, hold the scissors parallel to the skin rather than pointing in toward the skin. Don't trim the hair close to the skin, either. Just trim it enough so nothing will stick to it.

Ears: Handle your puppy's ears gently, especially if you're taping them upright. Next month, you'll learn how to clean your pup's ears.

Teeth: To check your puppy's teeth, gently lift her lips on one side of her mouth until you can see her teeth. Move her head and do the same thing on the other side of her mouth. Open her mouth and look inside. You'll begin cleaning her teeth in a few months (month 7), so between now and then, teach her to accept this handling.

It's important to introduce your German Shepherd puppy to grooming now even though some of these chores are pretty basic. Right now, her teeth are brand new and really don't need cleaning, but if you introduce these skills now—even something as simple as handling her mouth—she'll get used to them gradually and will be less apt to argue with you when she needs these things done.

Establishing a Grooming Schedule

Your German Shepherd doesn't necessarily need to be groomed every day, but it's a good idea to do it daily, anyway. Not only will grooming help keep her clean, but giving her a massage and brushing her is a wonderful way to bond with your dog. When your schedule is busy and life is hectic, what better way to spend time with your dog than sitting on the floor with her while giving her a massage?

Think about when the best time would be to do these grooming chores. You might like to watch the news in the evening; that could be a good time to sit on the floor in front of the television and groom your puppy. But no matter when you decide to do it, make it a part of your schedule so you do it every day.

Social Skills

German Shepherds are naturally protective—that's one of the traits people love about the breed. However, without good socialization early in life, your pup can become fearful. With fear, that naturally protective dog can then easily become aggressive, taking the protective instinct too far. An unsocialized, fearful, aggressive German Shepherd is a disaster waiting to happen.

Socialization began early in your puppy's life, but now you really need to concentrate on ensuring your puppy is familiar with and comfortable in her world. You cannot put this off until later. Once this age is past, you can't make up for it later.

Introducing Other Puppies and Dogs

When your puppy's vaccinations are up to date and your veterinarian says she's safe to meet other puppies and dogs, get started on this. Although your puppy spent time with her mom and littermates, they were family. Now your puppy needs to meet other canines.

Talk to friends and neighbors and find out who has a healthy, well-vaccinated dog who is good with puppies. Let your puppy and the adult dog meet in a neutral place, perhaps while on a walk or at the local park. They will sniff each other, and your puppy may roll over and bare her belly. This is normal behavior.

If your puppy is excited and bouncing all over—maybe even jumping on the adult dog—don't be surprised if the adult dog growls at your puppy. This, too, is normal, so let it happen. The adult is teaching your puppy that's she's getting too rowdy and needs to calm down.

> **TIPS AND TAILS**
>
> Don't let your puppy dash up to other dogs or pull hard on the leash to greet them. That's considered just as rude in dogs as it would be for you to rush up to another person and stop 2 inches from her nose. That person would be offended, too. So help your puppy walk calmly up to other dogs, and if she can't be calm, turn and walk the other direction until she calms down.

Introduce your puppy to other puppies, too, and not just other German Shepherds. Let her meet puppies of other breeds, sizes, shapes, and colors. Enrolling in a puppy kindergarten class (see the training section later in this chapter) is a great way for your puppy to meet new puppies.

When your German Shepherd puppy is interacting with other dogs or puppies, let things progress as they will. Don't push the two toward each other, and don't try to force them to play. If they want to sniff the grass side by side, that's fine. In fact, it's good social behavior because it shows each other they're both relaxed and nonthreatening.

Playing with other dogs and puppies is important, but your puppy doesn't have to play with every dog she meets. In fact, socialization also means knowing how to behave in a particular situation. Sometimes your puppy needs to see other dogs and puppies and yet behave herself without playing, jumping and leaping, or barking. Help her sit by holding her collar. Praise her when she's sitting quietly.

Meeting All Kinds of People

Your German Shepherd puppy must meet a variety of people. That means people of different ages, sizes, shapes, and ethnic backgrounds. Puppies who never meet toddlers, for example, may forever be worried about them. After all, toddlers make funny noises, wear diapers, and walk unsteadily. To a puppy unfamiliar with them, toddlers are strange.

Some socialization suggests include …

- ❧ Children of all ages, from infants to teenagers.
- ❧ Babies and toddlers in strollers, walkers, and a parent's backpack.
- ❧ Short people, tall people, skinny people, heavy people, people in casual clothes, people in uniforms, and people all dressed up.
- ❧ People wearing flip-flops, women in heels, guys in heavy boots, and people wearing hats.
- ❧ People in wheelchairs, using walkers, or canes.
- ❧ People of a variety of ethnic backgrounds, especially those different from your own.

It's easy to introduce your puppy to most people because, after all, people love puppies. Just say you're socializing your puppy and ask if they would like to pet her. Have a few dog treats in your pocket, and let them give her a treat.

If she wants to jump on them, just keep a hand on her collar and help her sit. Praise her when she sits nicely for petting.

Maintain control of all introductions. If someone gets too rough with your puppy, move your puppy away. After all, you want these to be positive experiences and if someone gets too rough and scares your puppy, that will be counterproductive to the goal.

Introducing One New Thing Every Day

Last month, you began introducing your puppy to the world around her, and you should continue these lessons this month. Include things that stimulate her senses— sights, sounds, smells, and things for her to touch.

She should see flapping sheets, open trash bags, and billowing skirts. Be sure to show her different things like picnic tables, umbrellas, cardboard boxes, balloons, and upside-down lawn chairs. Also introduce her to household tools being used, like brooms, mops, shovels, and rakes.

Let her hear kitchen noises, like the garbage disposal, dishwasher, microwave, blender, toaster, and pan lids on pans. Run electronics like the vacuum cleaner, washing machine, dryer, and a power screwdriver while she's around. See if you can get her within earshot of a motorcycle going past and the garbage truck on trash day. Loud kids going past on skateboards are something she should hear, too.

Smells are important, too. Walk by a restaurant or two, and let her sniff the air. Amble past a full dumpster on a hot day. (You might not want to inhale as much here!) Go for a walk near the ocean or a lake and let your puppy smell the different odors. Walk by a pasture of horses or goats, too, if possible.

Walking your German Shepherd on different surfaces is also a part of socialization. Walk on concrete, asphalt, sand, dirt, paving stones, bricks, carpet, and tile.

Set a goal of introducing your puppy to something new each and every day this month. It could be something at home, in the backyard, in your neighborhood, or away from home. That something new could be a new broom or dust rag, some new shoes you just bought, or your neighbor's noisy new ATV. Look for new adventures for your puppy.

Just remember to keep all these introductions happy and fun. Bring treats with you, and use a happy tone of voice. Don't drag your puppy up to something that's scary. Instead, talk to her in a happy tone of voice, let her look at (or smell) the scary thing at a safe distance, and when she's ready, let her walk up to it on her own. Praise her when she does approach it.

Behavior

At this age, your German Shepherd puppy's behavior may fluctuate wildly from bravado to fearfulness. To make things even crazier, she may be brave one moment and then do a 180 and be fearful the next.

This doesn't mean anything's wrong with her or that she has a "bad" temperament. She's perfectly normal for a puppy this age.

You and Your Shadow

The happiest German Shepherd in the world is one who can be with her owner 24/7. This breed *loves* to be close to their owners.

German Shepherds need to be in the house around their people. You'll probably notice this month that as you walk around the house, your puppy follows you. She'll trail you from the bedroom to the kitchen, and the kitchen to the living room, and if you let her, she'll even follow you out front when you go outside to get the newspaper. Many German Shepherd owners laughingly complain that it's even hard to go to the bathroom by themselves. When the door is closed, a black nose is always sniffing under the door.

This need to be close means German Shepherds are not good backyard dogs. If left outside along for hours, they'll bark until your neighbors complain, dig up the backyard, and destructively chew anything they can get their jaws around. These dogs aren't bad as far as they're concerned; they're simply unhappy to be away from you.

> ### ▶ HAPPY PUPPY
>
> If you have to leave your puppy during the day, leave her inside the house in her crate. Give her something to chew on or a food-dispensing toy. (See Month 5 for more on food dispensing toys.) If you can't come home during the day, hire a neighbor to come walk your puppy a few times a day. Maybe a local teenager would like to earn some extra money.

Get used to having a shadow. Don't try to make the puppy stay in one room while you walk around. Not only is that too hard for a puppy this age, but it's natural for her to want to follow you. So rather than get angry at her for doing it, just laugh and get used to it.

Bravado and Fear

Your puppy has been in your home for a few weeks now and is probably very comfortable there. She's bonded with you, knows everyone in the immediate family, and has forged a truce with the family cat. That's all wonderful.

What happens now, though, with this comfort level and at this age, is a silly stage of behavior where your German Shepherd puppy begins acting like a miniature guard dog. She may begin barking at people, other dogs, or the trash truck. Her natural—albeit babyish—protective instincts are combining with her comfort level and confidence in you.

But some of this bravado is also the result of a little fearfulness. Remember those fear periods we discussed last month? It's not unusual for puppies to have a small fear period when they're teething. After all, your puppy may not feel too well right now; her gums are swollen and her jaws hurt.

When your puppy begins acting brave, with her back paws firmly planted on your feet (so you can back her up), just step away from her, turn her away from whatever she's barking at, and distract her. When she looks at you, praise her for her attention.

Don't yell at her. This isn't logical behavior on her part, and she's not doing it on purpose. Instead, it's emotional puppy behavior.

> ### TIPS AND TAILS
>
> Distracting your puppy from bravado isn't going to inhibit her natural protective abilities as an adult. Instead, by distracting her now, you can prevent these puppy behaviors from turning into bad habits.

Vocal Discovery

Your puppy has probably been making noises since you brought her home. She cries when she needs to go outside and barks when she wants to come back in. She barks when she plays and whines when the cat scares her.

At some point during this month, your German Shepherd puppy will discover she has a voice … and she'll begin to use it. She may bark when she's feeling brave, and she'll bark when a neighbor is out in his own backyard doing yard work. Your puppy may bark when a dog and owner walk down the street or when she's in the car with you and sees something strange. You may be amazed at how big a bark your puppy has! German Shepherds can, unfortunately, easily become problem barkers. They take their watchful nature to heart and use their voice to tell the world they're on duty.

Neighbors are rarely thrilled about an incessantly barking German Shepherd, so it's important to tell your puppy that all this barking is not needed.

When your puppy begins barking, distract her or get her attention by making a noise, dropping a book, or waving your hands. You want her to stop what she's doing and look at you. If she's on leash, turn her away from what she's barking at and walk the other way as you tell her, "Sweetie, that's enough."

When she stops barking and looks at you, tell her, "Thank you! Good to be quiet!"

Don't yell at her for barking; she'll just think you're barking, too! Don't put an electronic bark collar on a puppy; those are too severe. Instead, interrupt her and praise her for focusing on you.

Training

Your German Shepherd puppy's brain is well developed now and she's ready to learn. Just keep in mind that although she's able to learn, she does have a short attention span. Don't ask her to concentrate on any one thing for very long, and if she's antsy and making mistakes, stop and play with her for a few minutes. Then go back to your training.

Keep your training fun. Having a good time while training doesn't mean it's any less important, but if you and your puppy both enjoy the training you do together, you're both apt to work harder at it.

Collar Touch

Far too many puppies learn to play keep-away when someone tries to touch their collar. Perhaps they learn that a person grabbing the collar means they're going to their crate or punishment will follow. That's a bad habit, though, and one that's potentially dangerous. After all, you need to be able to hold your puppy's collar in many different situations. So it's important to teach your puppy that touching her collar is good.

Here's how to teach her:

- Have the leash attached to your puppy's collar so she doesn't dash away. Have some good treats in one hand, too.

- Let your puppy sniff the treats, say her name in a happy tone of voice, and touch her collar. Jiggle it, and as you do, pop a treat in her mouth.

- Repeat this several times, take a break and play with your puppy, and repeat the exercise a few more times.

Do this collar touch exercise often. You can do it during every training session, during walks, or even when you're playing with your puppy. Let her know that when you touch her collar, good things happen.

Puppy Classes

The beginning of month 4 is a great time to enroll your puppy in a puppy-training class. Most trainers require puppies to have two distemper/parvo combination vaccinations prior to starting the class, and by 13 or 14 weeks of age, most puppies have had those shots.

Often, puppy classes combine training, socialization to other people, and socialization to other puppies in their curriculum. The class is also good for you because you can talk to other puppy owners. It can be a relief to find out your puppy isn't the only one trying to chew up everything in the house or having some housetraining problems. It's good group therapy.

Most puppy classes include the following:

☙ Introductions to the basic obedience skills: sit, down, stay, come, and walk on a leash without pulling.

☙ Problem-prevention tips for common puppy issues, including jumping on people and biting with those needle-sharp puppy teeth.

☙ A chance for puppies to meet and have other people pet your puppy, including the trainers in the class and other puppy owners.

☙ A play session so the puppies can run, chase, and interact with other puppies in the class.

If you've already selected a trainer to work with, contact him and ask when a puppy class is starting. If you don't yet have a trainer, call your veterinarian for a recommendation.

Housetraining Problems

The first goal of housetraining your German Shepherd puppy is to teach her not to relieve herself inside the house. Some dog owners prefer their dog relieve herself in one specific area in the backyard, such as a back corner, rather than all over the place. This is especially nice if there are kids in the family who play in the backyard.

It's also nice if your puppy will try to relieve herself when you ask her to, such as before you bring her inside or when you're traveling and you stop for gas. You could then take her for a walk and ask her to go.

Keep these goals in mind as you train your German Shepherd puppy. It will help as you work through any problems.

Accidents in the crate: If your puppy has accidents in her crate, be sure she isn't spending too much time in there. She can spend the night in the crate and several hours here and there throughout the day, but don't keep her in there all day and all night. She needs to get out, move around, exercise, play, and spend time with you.

If your German Shepherd puppy doesn't like to go in the crate, teach her that something positive happens each time you put her in it. Give her a food-dispensing toy such as a Kong with treats inside it.

Never use the crate to punish your puppy. Don't put her in the crate and then stand there and yell at her. The crate should be her refuge, not her jail cell.

> **TIPS AND TAILS**

If your puppy is overstimulated, you can put her in her crate as a time-out so she can calm down. But don't yell at her or otherwise punish her as you do so. Just be calm and quiet and put her in her crate.

Not going on command: If your puppy doesn't understand your command for her to relieve herself, don't worry. She'll catch on. Just continue taking her outside, and when she begins to go, quietly say the command. When she's done, tell her what a good girl she is, "Good to go potty!" Using whatever word or phrase you decide to use.

Accidents in the house: Preventing accidents from happening is a huge part of housetraining your puppy. After all, every time she relieves herself inside the house, she learns she can. Yelling and screaming at her after she's already done it isn't going to change future behavior. So limit your puppy's freedom. Keep her very close to you so you can see when she needs to get outside. Then maintain a schedule of feeding, play, and naps so you can get her out regularly.

Housetraining takes patience. Your puppy will get it eventually, but all puppies develop at their own pace. Just stick to your routine and schedule, teach your puppy what you want her to do, and praise her when she does.

Using the Leash Outside

Your German Shepherd puppy has become your shadow, following you all over the house from room to room, and she doesn't like to be left behind. So does that mean she'll do the same thing outside? Maybe. But then again, maybe not.

Many German Shepherd puppy owners develop a false sense of security when they find that they have a small German Shepherd shadow. They think their puppy will follow them anywhere, anytime, no matter what, so they let their puppy run free, off leash, even when outside a fenced-in yard.

The puppy might follow the owner, but far too many times something distracting or exciting pops up and the puppy is off like a flash to investigate. She may dash across a busy street or chase a smaller dog. She could be off after a cat or a squirrel and ignore you when you call her to come.

As with so many aspects of puppy training, every time your puppy ignores you, she learns she can. So if your German Shepherd puppy dashes away and ignores your repeated calls to come, she learns that she doesn't have to respond. This will make teaching the "Come" much more difficult.

Instead, keep your German Shepherd puppy on the leash whenever you're outside a fenced-in yard. She can still investigate a squirrel or a gopher hole; you'll just have the other end of the leash.

Most German Shepherds are not mentally grown up until 3 or 4 years old and should be on leash until then. Plus, your puppy should be well trained and be able to demonstrate that she will come when you call her, every time you call, no matter what the distractions.

Teaching the "Sit"

The "*Sit*" is the first obedience exercise you'll teach your German Shepherd puppy because it helps her learn self-control. After all, if she's sitting while being petted, she's not jumping on people. If she's sitting while you fix her food, she's not jumping up to knock the bowl out of your hands. Self-control is a good skill for all German Shepherd puppies to learn.

Here's how to teach the "Sit":

- 😺 Put your puppy on her leash so she can't run away from the lesson.
- 😺 With your left hand, hold the leash close to her collar.
- 😺 Have a treat in your right hand and let her smell the treat.
- 😺 Move your treat hand up from her nose and slightly back over her head. As her head comes up, her hips will move downward. Tell her, "Sweetie, sit."
- 😺 As her hips touch the ground, tell her, "Sweetie, good to sit!" Then give her the treat.

As she eats the treat, pet her and help her remain in the sitting position. After a few seconds, tell her, "Sweetie, *release*," and walk her forward a few steps.

For your puppy, "**Sit**" means lower your hips, keep your front elevated with your front legs straight, and hold still until I release you. "**Release**" is the command that means this is the end of the exercise for the moment.

After you've practiced the sit several times a day for a few days, begin saying "Sit" as you begin to move the treat from her nose rather than waiting until her hips hit the ground. After a lot of practice, you'll be able to say, "Sweetie, sit" and you won't need a treat. But that's months from now.

Teaching the "Stay"

Right now, you can teach your German Shepherd puppy to stay while in the sit position, but eventually she can do the stay while sitting, in a down, or even while in a standing position.

The "**Stay**" command means hold still, in this position, until you go back to release her.

🐾 Put the leash on your puppy so you can help her hold still.

🐾 Ask your puppy to sit, and praise her.

🐾 Hold the leash close to her collar with your left hand and then move your right hand, palm toward your puppy's nose, up and down a few inches as if building an invisible wall. At the same time tell your puppy, "Sweetie, stay."

🐾 If your puppy pops up or lies down, tell her, "No. Sit. Stay." Help her do it.

🐾 After just a few seconds, praise and pet her, then release her.

Over the next few weeks and months, gradually increase the time you ask her to sit and stay. Begin by asking her to hold still for just 5 seconds, then 10 seconds, and then 20. If your puppy begins making a lot of mistakes, you may be pushing her too hard.

Also, over time, you can begin taking a step or two or three away from her. But just as with the first time, if she makes mistakes, you're probably moving too far away too quickly. Take your time. You have lots of time to teach her this.

Teaching "Watch Me"

At this age, your puppy will be distracted by just about everything in her world. Birds, butterflies, and even ants are fascinating to her, never mind kids on skateboards or other dogs. You can't teach her if she isn't paying attention to you, so you need to help her pay attention.

Teaching her to look at you when you tell her, "Sweetie, *watch me,*" teaches her to focus. Plus, because you're going to be sure she likes the rewards for this exercise, paying attention to you will be fun.

> **DOG TALK**
>
> **"Watch me"** means ignore distractions and look at my face, preferably making eye contact.

Find a few really good treats that have a strong smell, like Swiss cheese, your German Shepherd puppy really likes and normally doesn't get. The treats have to be special.

Here's how to teach "Watch me":

- With your puppy on leash, ask her to sit facing you.
- Hold the leash in your left hand, and have the treat in your right hand.
- Let your puppy smell the treat in your hand and then move the treat toward your chin as you tell her, "Sweetie, watch me."
- If she jumps up to get the treat, have her sit again, and this time, use your left hand to hold her collar. Then repeat the verbal command and hand motion.
- As soon as her eyes move to your face, praise her, "Good to watch me! Yeah!" and pop the treat in her mouth.

Repeat this three or four times and then play with your puppy for a few minutes. Then repeat the exercise a few more times.

As your puppy gets better at this, challenge her a little. Take a step to the left and then to the right while asking her to watch you. Then back up a few steps, encouraging her to follow you while watching you. Praise her as she watches you.

The First "Come" Technique

The "*Come*" is one of the most important obedience exercises your German Shepherd puppy can learn. A reliable response to the come will help make life easier. For example, if your German Shepherd is outside in the rain and you want to call her inside before she turns into a muddy mess, having her come when you call her can certainly help.

> ## DOG TALK
>
> "**Come**" means your puppy should look for you and proceed directly to you quickly, without stopping, no matter what the distractions might be.

The come also has the potential of saving her life. If she's heading into danger—toward a street where cars are, for example, or any other danger—being able to call her back to you is vital.

Because come is so important, there are many ways to teach it. In this section, we give you the first technique. It's easy for puppies to learn and understand. In the next section, we share a second technique.

This first technique uses a sound stimulus to make the come exciting. Many trainers use a clicker. When paired with treats, the clicker marks or identifies the behavior you want your puppy to repeat in the future. Other trainers use whistles for teaching the come because the whistle can be heard for a longer distance.

We suggest using a small shaker with dry dog-food kibble inside to mark good behavior. This makes it a little easier for your pup because she probably already knows the sound is equated with food. So make up a small shaker by putting some dry dog-food kibble or dry treats in a small plastic container with a lid.

Here's how to teach your German Shepherd puppy the "Come":

🐾 Have your puppy on leash and have some really good treats (not the dry kibble—you use that for the sound of the food shaking in the container) in your other hand.

🐾 Make a noise with the shaker, and immediately give your puppy a treat. Don't say anything at this point. You want her to associate the sound with a really good treat.

🐾 Do this three or four times, take a break and play with your puppy, and repeat the exercise.

After 2 or 3 days, add the word "Come." Again with your puppy on leash and close to you, shake the noisemaker, say, "Sweetie, come," in a happy tone of voice, and pop a treat in her mouth.

After several days of practicing at this, you can move on to the next step. Keep your puppy on leash, but let her get distracted. Then shake the noisemaker, tell your puppy, "Sweetie, come!" and then back away from her for several steps so she has to follow you. If she dashes after you, praise her enthusiastically and give her a treat.

If the distraction keeps her attention, tug on the leash a little to move her toward you. Then back up several steps and praise her for following you.

As your puppy learns this exercise, keep her on leash and vary the distractions. Practice with the family cat in the same room or while the kids are playing. Keep the exercise fun and rewarding for your puppy. And don't be in a hurry to stop using the noisemaker. Remember, you want these obedience exercises to become new habits, and that takes time. So over the next few months, keep repeating this exercise. Just vary the treats and the distractions.

The Second "Come" Technique

When your German Shepherd puppy understands the first come technique, after a week or so of training, you can add this second technique. For this technique, you need the noisemaker, some good treats, and a longer leash—20 feet is great, but 30 feet is even better.

This technique teaches your German Shepherd puppy that even when she's bold and wants to investigate things at a distance from you, she still needs to come when she's called.

Here's how to teach this second version of the "Come":

 Attach the long leash to your puppy's collar. Have the shaker and a few treats in your other hand.

 Walk around your yard, and let your puppy get distracted. Hold on to the leash, but don't say anything to her or even pay attention to her.

❧ When she's distracted, back away from her, shake the noisemaker, and call her to come. Praise her and pop a treat in her mouth when she comes right away.

If she doesn't come immediately, don't stand there and repeat the command. You want your puppy to respond right away instead of taking her time, so back away from her and tug on the long leash a little to be sure she comes directly to you. Then praise her for coming.

Never scold your puppy for not coming to you. She could easily misunderstand and think that coming to you is bad. So let the leash enforce your command, and keep your voice, your facial expression (smile!), and posture happy.

Teaching "No Pull"

Puppies like to pull. They're always in a hurry to see and smell new things, and people just walk too slowly!

Unfortunately, though, when puppies pull, they can hurt themselves—their neck, shoulders, or joints—and they can hurt you—your arm, shoulder, or back. Using different collars, harnesses, and no-pull equipment isn't the answer because as soon as your puppy isn't wearing that equipment, she'll go back to pulling.

Instead, your puppy needs to learn to walk nicely on the leash without pulling. Luckily, this isn't hard to teach. Here's how to teach "No pull":

❧ Put the leash on your puppy and have some treats in your pocket.

❧ Without saying a word to your puppy, begin walking forward.

❧ If she dashes ahead and begins pulling, simply turn around and go the other direction, taking the leash with you.

❧ When she catches up with you, praise her, "Hey, look at you!" and give her a treat.

Each and every time she pulls, repeat the exercise. When she decides to walk with you, praise her enthusiastically and give her a treat.

The key to this exercise is consistency. If you practice this exercise sometimes but let her pull at other times, her behavior won't be consistent, either. German Shepherds are smart dogs with a strong work ethic. She can learn to walk without pulling, so teach her.

You and Your Puppy

With all the emphasis on housetraining, starting obedience training, teaching your puppy not to bite, and everything else concerned with raising a puppy, it's easy to lose sight of the fact that you should be enjoying your puppy. Be sure you take the time to play with your puppy and enjoy her.

When you play with your German Shepherd puppy, you're also strengthening the bond between the two of you; you're building that relationship. Most play also requires some activity, and that exercise is as good for you as it is for your puppy.

It really doesn't matter what you do to play with your puppy as long as you're not teaching her to fight you. Don't wrestle with her; that's fighting. However, you can play hide and seek. You go hide and call your puppy to come find you. Or throw balls or toys for her to fetch.

> **HAPPY PUPPY**
>
> If your German Shepherd puppy comes up to you and lowers her front end while keeping her hips in the air with her tail wagging, she's inviting you to play. This is called a play bow.

If your puppy begins to play too roughly, bites, or jumps, stop the game. Walk away, pick up the toys, or put your puppy in her crate. Teach her that roughness from her means the end of the game.

If your children are playing with the puppy and she gets too rough, step in and stop the game for your kids. Again, you put her in her crate or leash her so you can stop her from continuing the game.

You can use play to make your training sessions better. By alternating training exercises with some play time, you'll make the training fun for your pup as well as help keep her interest during the training sessions.

Month 4	Month 5	Month 6
	Socialization in public	
	Teething begins—heavy chewing period	
	Ready for basic commands	
	Switch to adult food	
	3rd DHPP and rabies vaccines	

Month 5, which includes weeks 17 through 20, is a time of change for your German Shepherd puppy, and yet much also remains the same.

Your puppy is growing physically, his adult coat is growing in, and it's time to think about spaying or neutering. his mind is developing, too, and his attention span is a little better than it has been so he's ripe for learning. But socialization needs to continue, and he's still teething. Overall, this is a fascinating month.

Physical Development

Your puppy is growing rapidly this month. Every time he wakes up from a nap, he'll seem to have grown, and that could very well be true. By the end of this month, male puppies could weigh about 50 pounds while female puppies could be about 45 pounds.

He's still going to look a little out of proportion, though. His nose is long, his ears are huge, and his tail may even touch the ground. His body looks very long, and his legs are lanky. He's growing so quickly, he'll still be tripping over his own paws at times.

Teething Continues

He's still teething this month. Although most of his puppy teeth will be gone by the end of the month, his adult teeth are still growing in.

He'll still need some ice and toys to chew on because his gums and jaws will bother him. Toys should be interesting enough to keep his attention so he chews on them rather than your shoes or the legs of the table. A Kong or other food-dispensing toy stuffed with tiny slices of apples and carrots, along with some chunks of cheese, and topped off with peanut butter, will keep him busy for a long time. You can even freeze the filled Kong—the cold will help his gums, too. (We talk about food-dispensing toys in more detail later in this chapter.)

> ### HAPPY PUPPY
>
> To make a fun frozen treat for your teething puppy, fill a child's plastic beach pail with water. Put it in the freezer, and when the water is slushy and just beginning to freeze, stir in slices of apples, bits of carrots, shredded chicken, cubed beef, or other good foods. Then finish freezing. When it's frozen solid, pop it out of the pail and give it to your German Shepherd—outside, because it will be messy.

Now, About That Tail ...

An adult German Shepherd's tail is magnificent. It descends from his hips in a saber-like curve with the last tail vertebrae reaching his hocks. The tail's coat is thick and bushy, with the colors from the dog's body blending in. The movement and posture of his tail accentuates every emotion your puppy has.

Right now, however, that tail is overly long, and the tip of it may touch the ground. It appears to be thick with bone and muscle, but there isn't much coat yet. The tail probably still has some puppy coat and coloring, although signs of the adult coat started to appear last month.

Adult dogs tend to carry their tail low, sweeping it from side to side during daily activities. When he's excited, however, his tail is lifted.

At this stage of development, your puppy sometimes may act like he doesn't even have a tail and not express much emotion with it, or he may wag it so wildly he clears everything off your coffee table! In fact, many German Shepherd puppy owners have said the coffee table went away after their puppy cleared it one time too many.

One day this month, you might find that your puppy just realizes he has a tail. He may turn around to look at it, try to chase it, and fall down. Even though this is hysterically funny to you, interrupt your puppy when he does it and distract him with a toy. If he thinks you like this behavior, he may begin doing it for attention, and it can turn into a compulsive behavior. So laugh if you want the first time and then put a stop to it.

Watch his tail for injuries, too. Sometimes puppies wag their tail so hard they hit it up against the edge of the coffee table or even a door frame and injure it. His tail is so long at this point it can also get slammed in a car door—a painful injury for your pup. If your puppy plays with another puppy, that puppy could try to catch your puppy by biting his tail. So keep an eye on his tail, and if it appears sore or painful, check for wounds. Call your veterinarian if you're in doubt.

Health

Although it's still too early to spay or neuter your German Shepherd puppy, it's definitely time to begin thinking about it. If you make a decision ahead of time, you can talk to your veterinarian, find out at what age she prefers to do the surgery, and budget for it.

Your puppy is also old enough now to begin heartworm preventatives, if these pests are a problem in your region. Unfortunately, the territory where these pests are found has spread considerably in recent years. If you don't know whether they're a problem or not, call your veterinarian.

Deciding to Spay or Neuter

Not every German Shepherd needs to be bred. Only the best of the best—those German Shepherds with breed championships and/or multiple working titles, and those who are healthy and sound both physically and mentally—should be bred. Obviously, any dog with physical, structural, or health problems should not be bred. Dogs with any temperament flaws also should not pass along their genetics.

As you're thinking about this decision, keep in mind that breeding dogs is tough. Not only does it require a thorough knowledge of the breed, researching and reading pedigrees, and knowing the breed genetics, but there's the actual breeding, whelping, raising the puppies, and finding the best homes possible for them. Breeding dogs— and doing it correctly, as it should be done—is not for the faint of heart. There's a *lot* more to it than playing with adorable puppies.

If you're curious as to whether your puppy has the possibility to be bred in the future, talk to your breeder, and have her take a look at your puppy. She may be able to tell you that your puppy needs to be spayed or neutered, and she can explain why. Or if you're seriously planning on competing with your puppy in the future, both in *conformation dog shows* as well as obedience and schutzhund, she may well tell you to hold off a little while to see how your puppy grows up.

Conformation dog shows are competitions in which dogs are compared to their breed's description of a perfect dog as well as against the other dogs competing on that day. The Westminster Kennel Club dog show, televised every February, is a conformation dog show.

Spaying a female dog consists of surgical removal of her ovaries and her uterus through a small incision in the abdomen. This is usually done at about 6 months of age. By getting your female German Shepherd puppy spayed, she won't come into season and won't be able to reproduce. Recuperation is usually very easy. She'll probably have to wear a cone to keep her from licking at her stitches and potentially pulling them out. Your veterinarian will recommend she be kept quiet for a week to 10 days. You can do this by keeping her on leash and close to you. When you can't supervise her, put her in her crate.

With males, the surgery consists of castration. The testicles are removed through a small incision forward of the scrotum. As with the females, your veterinarian will tell you to keep your dog quiet for a week to 10 days. He, too, will probably need to wear a cone to keep him from bothering the incision. Again, recuperation is usually very fast.

Spaying a female dog tends to decrease the incidences of breast or mammary-gland cancers. The female dog is also protected against cancers of the reproductive system because it's no longer there. Obviously, a spayed female will no longer come into season twice a year.

There are several benefits to neutering a male dog. He'll have fewer sexually related behaviors, including fighting with other male dogs, trying to escape from the yard, roaming, etc. Leg lifting, marking, and urinating on upright surfaces tend to be decreased as well. Testicular cancer is no longer an issue, considering the testicles have been removed.

Spaying or neutering your dog does have some risks and potential side effects, however. Surgery and anesthesia always come with some risks. Your puppy might bleed during surgery, stop breathing, or even die. There can be complications from the anesthesia (although there are options as to different types of anesthesia that may lower the risks). There might be complications from the surgery, too (although these are rare). Discuss the risks with your veterinarian prior to scheduling the surgery.

Although spaying or neutering your German Shepherd does stop the chance of unexpected reproduction, this should be a well-researched decision rather than an automatic one. Some of the potential problems seen in spayed or neutered dogs can be serious. For example, both spayed females and neutered males have two times the risk of developing osteosarcoma and hemangiosarcoma as intact dogs. Spayed females are more likely to develop urinary incontinence later in life, and males are more prone to urinary tract cancers and prostate cancer. Research is continuing on several other possible issues, including the increased risk of knee injuries.

For most dogs not used for breeding, spaying the female or neutering the male is a real option with noted benefits. However, make an educated decision to do—or not do—this consciously. If you have any questions or concerns, talk to your veterinarian.

If you do decide to spay or neuter your German Shepherd, find out at what age your vet prefers to do the surgery. Some like to wait until the dog's growth plates close (when the bones have finished most of their growth), which for German Shepherds is usually between 9 and 12 months.

Heartworm and Preventatives

Heartworms are a totally unique kind of internal parasite. Rather than living in your dog's intestinal tract like roundworms, hookworms, and other intestinal parasites do, heartworms live, as the name suggests, in your dog's heart. Because of this, your vet's testing of a stool sample won't give a diagnosis of heartworms. Your dog needs a blood test instead.

Heartworms, like tapeworms, have an insect intermediary host. This time it's a mosquito. When a mosquito draws blood from a dog already infested with heartworms, it draws into itself the heartworm larvae that are circulating in the dog's bloodstream. When it bites another dog, the larvae are transferred to the second dog, infecting that one.

As the worms grow inside the dog, the bloodstream carries them to the heart. It takes about 6 months for the larvae to mature in the dog, and when they do, they reproduce. The offspring are called microfilaria.

> **TIPS AND TAILS**
>
> Heartworms have been found in all 50 states, although they're most common along the Eastern seaboard from New Jersey south to Florida, along the Gulf of Mexico to Texas, and up the Mississippi River.

Thankfully, preventatives can ward off an infestation, but a blood test must first be done to be sure your German Shepherd doesn't have heartworms to begin with. The preventatives must be given throughout mosquito season; your veterinarian can provide some guidance as to what that should be.

If your veterinarian determines your German Shepherd has heartworms, he will establish a treatment program. The options vary depending on how many heartworms are present, their location, and your puppy's overall health.

Nutrition

Your puppy is growing tremendously this month, and his appetite will continue to increase before and during growth spurts and level off afterward. Just keep an eye on his weight, and be sure to increase his food a little if he gets too thin.

You shouldn't have to make any other changes in his food or feeding routine this month as long as you're feeding a good-quality food. If you're still feeding the food the breeder provided and you wish to change, or if you're concerned with the quality of your puppy's food, you can make some gradual food changes this month.

Deciding what's a good-quality food for your German Shepherd puppy can be difficult. Remember, his growth and development right now depend upon the food he's eating.

The Dog-Food Industry

In 2010, the pet-food industry sold more than $8 billion in pet foods. This is a gigantic industry designed to provide mass-produced and, for the most part, relatively inexpensive foods to adequately nourish as many pets as possible.

The primary benefit of commercial dog foods is convenience. Dog owners can buy dog food at the grocery store while shopping for the family or at the local pet store. Then while cooking for the family, they can feed the dog, too, quickly and easily giving him a cup of dry kibble food or canned food.

As a general rule, dog-food manufacturers spend a considerable amount of time and money in research. As a result, they are able to produce puppy foods, weight-loss foods, foods for giant-breed dogs, and foods for older dogs, to name a few. They have created foods with unique proteins like duck and rabbit, and unique carbohydrates like sweet potato and barley, so dogs with allergies can eat without problems.

> **HAPPY PUPPY**
>
> Although commercial dog foods (and dog-food companies) do have some problems, many German Shepherds can eat good-quality commercial dog foods with no negative side effects. They'll eat their food eagerly and have bright eyes and a shiny coat as a result.

The dog-food industry is not perfect, and the recalls of 2007 showed us that. Headlines in magazines and newspapers and on websites and blogs screamed that thousands of dogs and cats were becoming ill, some very seriously, and many died, because of tainted food. Although cats seemed to be struck harder and more cats died, both dogs and cats were affected.

After an investigation, Menu Foods, which was manufacturing foods sold under hundreds of labels, appeared to be the primary culprit. In March 2007, the federal Food and Drug Administration (FDA) belatedly issued a recall of 60 million packages of dog and cat foods made by Menu Foods. These foods contained wheat gluten imported from China that had been contaminated with *melamine*.

> ## DOG TALK
>
> **Melamine** is a compound used to make many different items, including dinnerware, shelving, floor tiles, and fireproof fabrics. It's added to cereal-grain glutens because it increases the foods' protein levels in laboratory testing. It also helps processed meats keep their shape.

In the weeks and months that followed, this initial recall turned out to be just the tip of the iceberg. Corn glutens were found to be contaminated, as well as rice gluten. As testing continued, other contaminants were found in assorted dog foods.

At one point, more than 6,000 dogs were known to have fallen ill and at least 3,000 died. These figures are the ones known but are nowhere near accurate, as some dogs fell ill prior to the official recall and many veterinarians were so busy treating sick dogs they never reported any numbers.

If anything good could came out of this horrible time, it's that many dog owners learned that complacency isn't a good thing. A number of websites and blogs post dog-food recalls when they're issued. One is expertrecall.com. We suggest you bookmark and check this site often.

A Quick Look at Commercial Foods

Trying to determine what's the best food for your German Shepherd can be confusing. Everyone has an opinion, and many of those opinions are wildly different. So what do you do?

First, read the labels and ingredient lists on the dog-food packages and learn to decipher what they say. For example, know that if a label says "Beef, wheat germ, wheat middlings, and wheat flour," the food is really a wheat-based one rather than a beef food even though beef is listed first. (Ingredients in the food are listed by weight, not volume.) By breaking the wheat ingredient into three different forms, the manufacturer can list wheat three times, each of which is less in weight than the beef. But when they're combined, they're most likely much more than the beef.

Also, it helps to know what the ingredients are and what they are not. At its website, the Association of American Feed Control Officials (AAFCO) maintains a list of what ingredients are allowed in dog foods and exactly what those ingredients include. For example, the AAFCO states that chicken by-product meal consists of the ground, rendered parts of the carcass of slaughtered chickens and includes necks, feet, undeveloped eggs, and intestines. There are no guidelines as to how many feet may be included in each batch, for example, so each batch is variable and may differ in nutritional value from other batches.

Don't pay too much attention to the guaranteed analysis that lists the percentages of protein, fat, fiber, and moisture in the food. Although many people might tell you your German Shepherd should eat a food that has a certain percentage of protein, the protein percentage on the package isn't necessarily a good guide. For example, melamine was added to foods to boost the protein in the food as determined by laboratory analysis. However, it was not digestible protein and was toxic. But legally, dog food companies cannot put on the packaging how digestible the ingredients are. The guaranteed analysis can be, and often is, misleading.

The best thing to do is look for a good-quality meat as the primary ingredient, followed by either a second-quality meat or good-quality carbohydrates such as sweet potatoes, yams, green vegetables, apples, bananas, papayas, mangos, or other digestible and good foods.

You'll find a variety of different types of commercial foods available, each with advantages and disadvantages:

Dry foods: These foods generally have a moisture content of between 6 and 10 percent, hence the description "dry." These foods are easy to store and use, and depending on the recipe and formulation, may have a moderate shelf life—perhaps 6 months. Dry foods may consist of a variety of ingredients, including meats, carbohydrate sources, and added vitamins and minerals.

> **TIPS AND TAILS**
>
> Cheaper commercial dry dog foods usually contain a high percentage of cereal grains, usually rice, corn, and wheat. These are known to cause allergy problems in many German Shepherds.

Canned foods: These are generally meat-based foods with a moisture content of 80 to 85 percent. They may or may not have vitamins or minerals added. They have a long shelf life—sometimes even a couple of years.

Dehydrated foods: Dehydrated dog treats, especially those made from liver, have been available for many years. Dehydrated foods, however, only became available in the past decade. These foods can be dehydrated raw or lightly cooked foods. The primary advantage to dehydration is that the slow processing doesn't destroy the nutrition in the ingredients as the high temperatures in other processing can. When kept in cool, dry conditions, these foods have a moderate shelf life—usually up to a year.

Frozen foods: These are available in raw food form or cooked. As with any frozen foods, handling is very important. If the food is allowed to thaw at any point, it may become contaminated with bacteria. Buy a reputable brand name, and feel free to ask the company and the store where you buy the food questions about distribution and handling procedures. These foods usually have a fairly short shelf life, although it varies by food and manufacturer.

Although these are the most popular types of commercial foods, there are others. Some foods are now packaged in long tubes, like bologna or sausage, and you can cut off a slice or chunk for feeding. You might also find refrigerated fresh foods or cooked foods. As dog owners demand better-quality foods, manufacturers are responding.

Homemade Foods

Many German Shepherd owners feed their puppy homemade food. Some owners fix their own dog foods because their dogs have allergies or other health problems, while others are concerned about the quality of commercial dog foods.

Raw food diets have become very popular in the last 20 years. They're usually based on raw meats and bones, with vegetables, fruits, and other foods mixed in. Although proponents state that these diets are more natural than commercial foods—and they are—raw diets are not without risk. Raw meats are commonly contaminated with bacteria that can make both dogs and people very ill—sometimes fatally so.

> **TIPS AND TAILS**
>
> Use safe handling techniques with raw meat, including cleaning up all tools, dishes, and the counters with bleach afterward. Wash your hands well, too. Store all meats in the refrigerator or freezer.

If you want to feed your German Shepherd puppy a raw diet, here are some guidelines:

🐾 Use a recipe designed and tested by a canine nutritionist and adhere to that recipe.

🐾 Use bones cautiously, if at all. German Shepherds, even puppies of this age, have strong jaws and can shatter bones. When swallowed, those sharp pieces can perforate the digestive tract. Ground bones can cause an obstruction in the intestinal tract.

🐾 Find a local source of clean, unadulterated meat.

🐾 Find a farmers' market or other source of clean, pesticide-free vegetables and fruit.

🐾 Supplement with a good-quality vitamin and mineral supplement that contains calcium. Feed according to directions for a growing puppy. Don't oversupplement, because more is not better. Too much of a supplement can affect your puppy's growth, especially his bones, as well as his overall health.

Home-cooked meals are somewhat safer because the ingredients are cooked and the bacteria are destroyed. However, if you decide to feed a home-cooked diet, be sure to follow a recipe that's been formulated and tested by a canine nutritionist.

If you decide you want to avoid commercial dog foods, talk to your veterinarian first and get her opinion. If you're both of the same mind that this would be advantageous for your German Shepherd puppy, ask for a referral to a canine nutritionist. These foods can be fed safely, but you need to take care while doing it. Also keep in mind that your German Shepherd puppy depends on these foods for his energy, mental well-being, physical health, and growth. That's a lot of responsibility to put on his food—and on you, if you decide to make it.

Grooming

Last month you saw your puppy's coat begin to change. The adult coat that started to come in was very different from his soft, fluffy puppy coat and began to appear on his tail and up the middle of his back. That coat change continues this month, and gradually more and more of your German Shepherd's puppy coat will be replaced by his adult coat.

All About the Coat

The German Shepherd *breed standard* describes the coat of these dogs in fairly specific terms. The outer coat is dense and of medium length. It's straight but sometimes has a slight wave, and it's almost coarse. The face, head, legs, and paws all have a shorter coat, while the back of the legs has slightly longer hair called feathers and the neck has longer hair that creates a ruff.

> ### DOG TALK
>
> A **breed standard** is a written description of the perfect German Shepherd. The German Shepherd Dog breed standard was created by the German Shepherd Dog Club of America and was patterned after the German breed standard. The breed was recognized in 1908, the present breed standard was approved in 1978, and it was reformatted in 1994.

Dogs with a lush coat have a slightly longer coat and have more length in the feathers, ruff, and tail. Even the lush coat is a medium-length coat as compared to many other breeds. It's just longer and fluffier than the normal German Shepherd coat.

The German Shepherd undercoat is soft and dense and is a great insulator. Although both the outer and under coats are shed, the undercoat is what's shed so profusely toward the end of winter and on into spring.

Brushing Your German Shepherd Puppy

When your dog's adult coat has fully come in, it requires a thorough brushing at least once a week, and twice a week is better. Right now, though, as your puppy's coat is being shed and he's still getting used to grooming, a daily brushing is best.

When you went shopping for supplies before you brought home your puppy, hopefully you bought a pin brush. A pin brush gets its name from its long metal or plastic bristles topped with a bead of plastic or rubber so you don't scratch or scrape your puppy's skin. You can use the pin brush all over your puppy.

As the adult coat grows in, you'll also need a rake. This is a brush with a row of straight, rigid metal teeth. Try to find one that's Teflon coated because these move through the coat more easily. Use the rake on the feathers of the legs, the thick coat around the neck, and the back legs and tail. Be careful not to scratch your puppy's skin while using this tool.

Last, you might also want to get a soft-bristle brush; natural bristles are often softer. This brush helps pull out the dead hair yet is also soft on the puppy's skin. Use it after you've used both the pin brush and the rake to get out the last of the shed coat and to add a shine to the new adult coat.

Cleaning His Ears

One downfall of your puppy's gorgeous upright ears is that standing up like they do, they seem to attract dirt. Because of this, they need to be cleaned regularly.

To clean your puppy's ears, you need either some cotton balls or small gauze pads; two or three for each ear is usually enough for one cleaning. Some ear cleaner is necessary, too. This can be a commercial ear-cleaning solution, mineral oil, or witch hazel.

Sit with your puppy facing you, ideally with his head in your lap. Dampen one cotton ball or gauze pad, and squeeze out the excess fluid. Hold one ear flap in your hand to keep it still, and with the other, gently wipe the inside of the ear flap from the inside out. When one cotton ball or gauze pad is dirty, set it aside and dampen a clean one. When the ear flap is clean, gently swab the inside of the ear, cleaning all the folds. Never try to reach inside the ear canal, and never use a cotton swab to clean down in the ear canal. When one ear is clean, repeat the process on the other ear.

> ### TIPS AND TAILS
>
> If the ear is red and inflamed, if it has a waxy buildup, if he's shaking his head or pawing at his ears, or if there appears to be a discharge from the ear, call your veterinarian right away. Don't clean it first because your vet will want to see the problem.

Social Skills

Your puppy is at a fun age right now. He's had quite a bit of socialization, and he's developed a bond with you so he trusts you. The two of you should be enjoying each other's company.

However, your puppy is still teething, so his gums and jaws may still bother him a little. This means he may still be having some fearful moments—after all, discomfort can be worrisome to him.

The Jolly Routine

Can you act? Have you ever wished you could appear on stage? Well, even if you haven't, sometimes you're going to have to put on an act for your puppy.

When he's worried, especially if he appears to be afraid of something specific, you can use a jolly routine to work him past it. To do the jolly routine, simply use a happy voice and relaxed body language to talk your puppy out of his worry. Think of yourself as your puppy's cheerleader.

Now, this is not for those instances when your puppy is truly panic-stricken over something. In those cases, move your puppy away from what he perceives as danger and help him calm down. Then on another day (or two or three), you can gradually desensitize him to whatever caused the fear. To do this, you could walk him up to the scary thing until he reacts, take a step or two back, let him relax, and gradually move closer to it. Desensitizing your puppy is a slow process that you should never rush.

However, if your puppy is worried but not truly fearful, talk to him in a happy voice, and if possible, reach out and touch the item he's worried about. Pat the parked motorcycle, picnic bench, or balloon. Let him see that you aren't afraid of it, and that'll help him fear it less. Play bow to him as another puppy would to invite him to play. Reach your hands high and then bring them down to your knees. Smile and bow again. If your puppy follows your invitation and walks up to the scary thing, praise him and tell him what a wonderful, special puppy he is!

Understanding Your Puppy's Body Language

Your German Shepherd puppy may not be able to speak English, but he's still pretty good about showing his emotions. Here are some things to watch for:

Confident: A calm, confident puppy will stand relaxed. His legs will be under him but not stiff. He'll be looking at everything around him but probably not staring. His tail will be relaxed and perhaps wagging. His ears will be facing forward but moving according to the sounds he's hearing.

Concerned: A concerned puppy will still be standing upright, but he may be staring at whatever concerns him and then looking away, staring and then again looking away. His tail will probably be still, too.

Cautious: A cautious puppy may reach forward to sniff something that concerns him, and his head will be reaching forward. His front legs, however, will be braced and stiff under him and his back legs will be stretched out behind him. His ears will probably be back and his eyes wide open. His tail will be low.

Fearful: A truly fearful puppy will look away from the thing that frightens him and try to avoid it. He will turn his head away, squint his eyes, and may even lower his back legs into a squat. His tail will be down and may even be clamped to his back legs.

> ### TIPS AND TAILS
>
> If your puppy urinates, or lies on his back with his paws in the air while turning his head away, he has been pushed too far. Immediately get him away from the situation that has frightened him.

Stressed: A stressed puppy—perhaps he feels pushed into something he's not ready for—will yawn, or yawn while looking away from you. He may back away from you while looking another direction. He'll give many tongue flicks— his tongue coming out of the front of his muzzle to touch his nose and then going back into his mouth.

Keep in mind there's a balance between socializing your German Shepherd puppy and helping him through new situations while at the same time maintaining and building his confidence. If your puppy is really frightened by something or a situation, and you can't alleviate that fear, his confidence could be dashed. So learn to watch your puppy and respond to his body language by giving him what he needs at that moment, whether it's rescuing, praise, or the jolly routine.

Working on Social Skills with Kids

As your puppy gets bigger, he may try to take advantage of smaller children in his life. After all, he used to be smaller than them but because he's growing so much more rapidly than children do, he's larger and stronger now.

At this age, puppies act out in different ways. Some try to jump on the kids and knock them down. Others prefer to chase the kids and bite at their legs. Some puppies will even lie on top of the kids. Not all puppies purposely try to take advantage of kids, but at this age it's pretty common.

Some experts try to explain these behaviors by saying the puppy regards the kids as littermates, and that's certainly possible. It really doesn't matter what the puppy is doing or why. He simply needs to understand that these actions are not allowed.

First of all, be sure you supervise your German Shepherd puppy whenever he's interacting with the kids. Don't send your puppy and kids all out in the backyard by themselves. German Shepherds are awesome dogs, but puppies are puppies and will try to get away with anything and everything they can.

When you're supervising the kids and your puppy, let him play while dragging the leash. Then if he gets too excited, you can grab the leash and interrupt his play. Tell him, "No bite!" or "No jump!" as you pull him away from the action. Let him calm down a little before you let him go play again.

The children must have some rules, too. When playing with the puppy, they are not allowed to wrestle with him, run and scream, or tease him. Instead, play should be calm and gentle. They can play hide and seek, letting the puppy find them. Or they can throw the ball for him. If the play gets too loud or rowdy, the puppy needs to be somewhere else.

> **TIPS AND TAILS**
>
> If your children have friends over playing, it's even more important that the play is calm, quiet, and supervised. If the kids wrestle and scream, your puppy may think one of "his" kids is being attacked and may bite the other child.

Behavior

Much of your puppy's behavior this month will be similar to last month's. He will go back and forth between being brave and being worried. This is normal, so don't be concerned that your puppy has an unstable personality. The mood swings tend to continue until the worst of teething is over.

Your German Shepherd puppy is curious and interested in exploring, yet for the most part, he's content to stay close to you. He's still very much a puppy with a short attention span, and he's easily distracted so it's important you keep this in mind while training.

During Month 5, you're going to start to see glimpses of the dog your puppy will grow up to be—not physically so much, but mentally. German Shepherds love a challenge, and it's your responsibility to keep that wonderful mind busy and out of trouble.

Understanding the German Shepherd Mind

German Shepherds were originally designed and bred to be versatile working dogs who could protect a home and farm, work for law enforcement and military, do search and rescue and tracking, and any number of other jobs. Today they're still one of the most commonly used breeds in these occupations, as well as in drug detection and service and guide-dog work.

One thing you may be noticing about your puppy is that he likes things a certain way. He may get upset when the furniture is rearranged and will investigate all the changes. He likes his schedule for food, walks, play time, and training. All these things should be occurring on schedule when they're supposed to happen. This doesn't mean there can never be changes in your house, but do have a giggle or two watching your puppy after you make those changes.

At this age, your puppy will also be noticing things around him. He may pay attention to someone who looks different or is wearing a different kind of hat or sunglasses. When he sees something new, he may not react by retreating in fear or barking, but he will notice the different things. Use these opportunities for continued socialization. Ask the person with the hat, "My puppy is concerned about your hat. Would you take it off so I can show it to him?" You'd be amazed how most people are more than willing to help socialize your puppy.

Your puppy is also beginning to pay attention to things he might think are dangerous. People walking too close to your car or trespassing on your property will cause him to bark. This, too, is normal German Shepherd behavior. However, because your puppy is still very young, he doesn't always know when to be protective and when not to. So distract him from unnecessary barking, ask him to pay attention to you, and praise him for that attention.

At some point during this month, you may see him becoming a little more reserved with strangers. This, too, is normal. When your puppy is all grown up, he will be standoffish with people he doesn't know. After all, German Shepherds are very different from Labrador Retrievers or Golden Retrievers, both breeds known for being very social. But socialization is still important this month, so if your puppy is standoffish with someone, use your jolly routine and encourage him to meet the new person.

> ### TIPS AND TAILS

When he's feeling a little standoffish, your puppy's body language will show it. He may stand back a little or right next to you. He may even lean up against you. His head will be up and his ears erect, but his ears may move or twitch. His eyes will look toward the person and then look away. His tail will probably be still, too.

German Shepherds have a reputation for being one of the most loyal of dog breeds. They have—and they will again in the future—given their lives for their owners. Although we hope your German Shepherd will never have to make that horrible decision, this month you'll sense a deepening in the bond you share with your puppy. That bond, that connection, is what creates the loyalty your adult German Shepherd will have toward you.

Last month your puppy was your shadow. Now he's watching you more, listening to you, and hanging a little closer to you. You'll find he's choosing to be with you rather than do something else. It's a wonderful feeling to know your dog worships the ground you walk on.

"Oh, No, He's Bored!"

Your German Shepherd puppy's active, intelligent mind is a wonderful thing, and he's capable of learning so much. But there is a down side to this mind: he can easily get bored, and a bored German Shepherd can be a bad puppy!

Liz's first German Shepherd, Watachie, was exactly this age when boredom hit. He was her first dog, and she didn't know anything about dog training, dog behavior, the stages of puppyhood, crate training, or limiting a puppy's freedom. One day while she was at work, he got bored and stripped all the fabric and stuffing off Liz's sofa. The floor was covered with 18 inches of fabric and filler while the sofa was stripped down to the 2×4 frame and springs! So believe us when we say a bored German Shepherd puppy can be a bad puppy.

A bored German Shepherd can dig holes in your backyard—deep holes—uproot small trees, dig up your sprinkler system, dismantle your fence, destroy the inside of your house, torment the family cat, and bark incessantly. And that's just the tip of the iceberg. There's so much more he can do if he sets his mind to it. German Shepherds aren't just smart, they're also problem-solvers. They think about things and then experiment to see what works and what doesn't.

It's important to remember that your German Shepherd puppy isn't doing all these things to "get back at you" for leaving him alone. Nor is he destroying your sofa because you got mad at him yesterday. This is all about excess energy, a very smart mind, and boredom.

> ### TIPS AND TAILS
>
> Bored German Shepherds can also develop lick granulomas. These are open sores, usually found on the ankle or wrist, caused by repetitive licking. Although these are often triggered by a skin problem that itches, a bored dog often continues licking long after the skin problem is resolved.

There are several things you can do to combat boredom in your German Shepherd puppy:

Exercise: Be sure your puppy gets a chance to run and play before you have to leave him alone. If that means getting up half an hour earlier every day, well, that's the price of having a German Shepherd.

Training: Obedience training that's fun yet structured is very important. Practice training your puppy every day.

Challenge his brain: Teach him some tricks, and play scenting games (more on this coming up) to give him more to think about.

Limit his freedom: Don't allow your puppy unlimited freedom in the house. He's much too young for this and will only get into trouble. When you can't supervise your puppy, crate him.

Food-dispensing toys: Use toys that dispense treats or food to distract him. (See the "You and Your Puppy" section later in this chapter for more about these toys.) Give him one of these toys in his crate as you get ready to leave him alone.

Dog walker: If you're going to be gone for several hours, especially if your normal workday has you gone all day, hire a dog walker or a teenage neighbor to come let your puppy out, play with him, and take him for a walk. If you have a neighbor's teen-ager come help, perhaps he or she can take your puppy out a couple times a day.

The problem of potential boredom is going to continue on into adulthood. However, if you establish a routine of alleviating it, you can prevent the problems associated with it.

Talk to the Paw

At this age, German Shepherd puppies can be funny creatures. He's your shadow and well bonded to you, he's learning to watch your every move, and he wants to crawl under your skin so he can be ever closer to you. Yet at the same time, you may ask him to do something for you and he'll give you attitude.

This can be really annoying, especially when it happens more than once, but don't take it personally. In a couple months, he'll be hitting adolescence, and that really will be annoying. This is minor stuff right now.

However, that doesn't mean you should ignore it. Instead, put on his leash, grab some treats, and practice his obedience skills. Don't be rough, or loud, or mean. Instead, show him you are a good, kind, and fair owner, but you won't allow him to give you that kind of attitude.

Behavior Myths Debunked

A variety of dog-behavior misconceptions can threaten your relationship with your German Shepherd puppy. It's important you know what is myth, urban legend, or internet deception.

Here are some common myths you're bound to see or hear about:

My German Shepherd is bad because he's angry: Bad behaviors don't happen because your German Shepherd is mad at you. There are many reasons for behaviors you might not want to occur, including boredom, lack of exercise, lack of training, inconsistency with training, and even a poor diet. But anger is not one of those reasons.

I want my German Shepherd to be good for me, not for treats: Treats are a training tool, just like a leash or collar. However, psychologically, they can be very important because in a dog's world, the giver of food is important.

My German Shepherd is aggressive because he's dominant: The word *dominant* in relation to canine behavior has been so overused in so many different contexts, it's hard to determine what it means anymore. Rarely are dominant dogs aggressive. Most aggressive dogs are actually fearful or anxious.

My German Shepherd is aggressive because he was abused: Far too many dog owners allow frightening, aggressive behaviors to continue unchecked because they don't want to subject their dog to more trauma. However, not as many adopted dogs have been abused in their previous homes as most owners believe. Instead of being abused, the dog was more likely not socialized properly.

If you have any concerns about your German Shepherd puppy's behavior, do some research, but also talk to a respected dog trainer, behavioral consultant, or veterinary behaviorist. Many different factors affect canine behavior, including genetics, early experiences, present experiences, and health issues.

> **TIPS AND TAILS**
>
> Asking for help doesn't mean you've been a bad owner. It means you are wise enough to realize you need some help.

Bad Behaviors Are Not Outgrown

Don't make excuses about your puppy's undesirable behaviors by saying, "He'll outgrow them." Rarely does a puppy outgrow bad behaviors.

Your puppy jumps on people because he wants to greet them, and jumping gets a reaction from them. He chews on things because his gums hurt and chewing is fun. He chases the family cat because she runs from him. He digs up the backyard to bury a toy or to find the sprinkler pipe. All these things produce a reward for him, whether that reward is attention from people or a few moments of fun for him.

Dogs repeat actions that produce positive results. That's why you praise your puppy during training and give him a treat. If he has any kind of a positive result from his bad behaviors, he's not going to outgrow them. In fact, it's much more likely that if he continues having fun, those behaviors will turn into bad habits.

This is especially true with bad behaviors associated with boredom—all the more reason you need to address boredom before it turns into a bigger problem.

Training

Although training began with your puppy when he came home with you, this month your German Shepherd puppy's brain is like a sponge. He'll soak up everything you teach him. Just be sure to keep your training sessions short and fun. Show him what to do, help him do it, and praise and reward him for doing it.

When he figures out that cooperating with you makes him happy, he'll be begging to do things for you. You'll find him sitting in front of you offering behaviors—giving you a paw to shake, sitting prettily in a nice sit, lying down, or anything else he can think of. Take advantage of this willingness, and teach him this good behavior gets rewards.

Household Rules

In the previous section, we discussed the importance of not allowing bad behaviors to continue because they don't just disappear as your puppy grows up. Instead, if they're the least bit rewarding for your puppy, they'll turn into bad habits rather than go away.

The same applies to behaviors around the house. Do you want a big German Shepherd underfoot in the kitchen? Are you going to want him lounging on the sofa? Would you prefer that he wait at open doors rather than dash through every time one is opened?

What household rules you decide to establish depends on you, your family, your house, your household routine, and so much more. What's comfortable for one family might not be right for yours. However, it's important that everyone in the house agrees to the household rules and enforces them uniformly. If one person ignores the rules and encourages your puppy to break them when no one else is around, your puppy will be confused. If, for example, your teenage son allows your puppy to get up on the sofa with him, your puppy will try to get up with other people, too. Consistency is important.

Here are some suggestions for household rules:

No dog in the kitchen: Do you want your German Shepherd in the kitchen? If you have a big kitchen and like to feed him here, that's fine. But if you have a small kitchen and a big dog will be underfoot and a trip hazard, you might want to keep him out. Use your obedience training to stop him at doorways; sit and stay works well. Then if he steps inside the kitchen, stop him and move him back to the doorway.

Stay off the furniture: If you don't mind his being on the furniture now because your stuff is old, think ahead to the time you'll get new furniture. Will you want him to stay off the new stuff? If so, keep him off now, too, because it's very hard to change the rules later.

Wait at doors and gates: This really could be a safety issue because a dog who dashes out doors and gates could get hit by a car or scare a salesperson. Or he could knock you down in his hurry to get out. Have your puppy sit and stay at every door or gate. Then, after a few seconds, either give him permission to go outside or not.

Ignore the trashcans: This rule could save your German Shepherd puppy's life some day. Trashcans are attractive to puppies because they often have food or other interesting-smelling things in them. However, they can also have things that could make your puppy sick or hurt him. Plus, he makes a huge mess knocking over a trashcan and rummaging through it. Use the "leave it" exercise to teach him to ignore trashcans.

> **TIPS AND TAILS**

To teach "Leave it," you need a full-to-overflowing kitchen trashcan with something smelly on top, like an empty tuna-fish can. Put your puppy on his leash, and walk him past the trashcan. When his nose goes to the trashcan, quickly turn the other direction, using the leash to turn him away, too, as you tell him, "Sweetie, leave it!" Praise him when he turns toward you, saying, "Yeah, good to pay attention to me!" Repeat this several times. Later, when he understands, train with other distractions.

One very important part of teaching household rules is to reward good behavior. Puppy owners get so focused on saying "no" to their puppy that they often forget to acknowledge good behavior. Your puppy has to be praised for good behavior, or he will regress. After all, "No, no, bad dog," is still attention from you, even though it's not fun attention. You don't want him working for negative attention; you want him trying to get those positive rewards from you.

When you see him sniff the sofa, look at it, and then lie down on the floor, praise him. If he walks past the overflowing kitchen trashcan and looks away from it as if it weren't there, praise him. When he sits at an open door and looks at you for permission, praise him. When he picks up his toy rather than your shoe, praise him. When he watches the cat amble down the hallway and doesn't chase her, praise him.

Although interrupting bad behavior has a place in puppy training, your rewards are much more powerful. So watch him and praise him for his good choices.

Teaching "Down" and "Stay"

When your puppy learns to lie down when asked and hold still, he gains more self-control. You can ask him to stay away from the dining room table while everyone is eating so he's not begging under the table. You can have him lie down and stay at your feet when company comes so he's not jumping on your guests. The "Down-stay" is a good exercise for helping your puppy control himself.

Here's how to teach the "*Down*":

🐾 Have your puppy on leash and hold the leash in your left hand. Have a treat in your right hand.

🐾 Ask your puppy to sit, and praise him when he does.

🐾 Let him sniff the treat in your right hand and then move the treat slowly from his nose to his front paws, letting his nose follow your hand. As his nose comes down, move the treat forward.

🐾 As he lies down, praise him, "Good to down!" and give him the treat.

🐾 If he's wiggly, rest your left hand (with the leash) on his shoulders to steady him.

🐾 When you're ready for him to get up, pat him on the shoulder and tell him, "Sweetie, release!"

When you've practiced the down for a week or so and your puppy is doing it well, add the stay just as you did last month with the sit exercise. In the beginning, remain next to your puppy when you tell him "Stay" just in case he pops up. He shouldn't have any trouble, though, because he's already practiced it with the sit.

"Down" means lie down, and therefore shouldn't be used to ask the puppy not to jump on you. Keep in mind each command you teach your puppy should have only one definition.

The hand signal for the down-stay is an L shape—moving a treat from nose to toes brings his head down and then moving the treat forward gives him body room to lie down. Later, when his training is much better, you will be able to simply make a downward motion with your hand for him to lie down.

Playing a Scenting Game

German Shepherds are well known for their amazing sense of smell. Although usually not considered as good as Bloodhounds, German Shepherds are still amazing in their ability to follow a trail or find someone or something hidden. The numbers of dogs of this breed who are or have worked as law enforcement, drug detection, and search-and-rescue dogs is testament to the breed's ability.

Even if your German Shepherd puppy is going to be a treasured family pet rather than a professional working dog, he can still learn to use his nose. In fact, scenting games are great fun.

Here's a fun game for you to play with your German Shepherd puppy:

🐾 You will need six paper cups and a handful of really good, smelly treats. Pieces of a hot dog or some Swiss cheese work well.

🐾 Put your puppy on his leash, and sit on the floor with him.

🐾 Let him sniff one of the treats and then place it on the floor while he's watching you. Invert one of the paper cups over the treat so the treat is hidden.

🐾 Tell your puppy, "Find it!" and encourage him to knock over the cup to get the treat. If he's hesitant, tip the cup slightly so he noses under it to get the treat.

Do this several times and then take a break. Go play with your puppy for a few minutes so he relaxes and clears his brain. Then come back and repeat the first few steps again.

🐾 Then, right next to the cup with the treat, place another cup upside down on the floor but without a treat under it. Encourage your puppy to find the treat.

🐾 When he can do that, add another cup. Then another.

If your puppy begins to get discouraged, go back to one cup, encourage him with lots of praise, and gradually work back up to multiple cups.

You can also play this game with empty flower pots, small plastic bowls, or small buckets. When your puppy is doing well, you can shuffle the cups or bowls to make it more challenging for him. You'll be amazed at how good your puppy's nose is once he learns the game.

Talking to Your Puppy

As your German Shepherd puppy bonds more closely with you, as he is this month, make it a point to talk to him, and not just when you're asking him to do something. Instead, talk to him as if you're teaching someone a new language. German Shepherds are capable of learning to understand a huge vocabulary, but you have to talk to him for that to happen.

Here are some tips for when to talk to your puppy:

🐾 When he has to go outside to relieve himself, ask him, "Do you have to go *outside?*" Put the emphasis on the word outside. Then walk him to the door.

🐾 Go out with him and ask, "Do you have to go?" Praise him when he relieves himself.

🐾 When you give him a cookie or treat, emphasize the word *cookie* or *treat*.

🐾 As you feed him, ask if he's hungry.

Then teach him a word or phrase for going for a walk, riding in the car, staying in the car, getting out of the car, going to the front yard, going to the backyard, or going to his crate. And that's just the beginning. Challenge him to learn more words as he grows.

The more you talk to your German Shepherd puppy, the more he'll pay attention to you, tilting his head, trying to understand. It's wonderful.

Dealing with Mistakes

Mistakes happen. It's just a part of life with a puppy because there's no such thing as a puppy who hasn't made a few mistakes—or an owner who hasn't, either! Your puppy is going to chew up something, dig up a favorite flower, or dump over a trashcan. One day you'll get frustrated and yell at your puppy even if you know shouldn't. So what *should* you do when this happens?

First, it's important to understand why these things happen. Boredom is certainly one thing. A lack of exercise is another. A lack of mental stimulation and training can also play a part. Mistakes also happen because your puppy is a canine and you're human. You and he are two different species, and miscommunication will happen.

Puppies also chew many of your favorite items—the television remote control or your cell phone—because you touch those items often. They are covered with your hand oils and smell like you. That's also why your puppy might chew your shoes and socks.

But the most common reason why puppies get into trouble is because they are puppies. They don't know all the rules yet, and they have a short concentration span so even when they're in the process of learning those rules, they sometimes forget. They're easily distracted and so when playing with a toy, if they walk past the kitchen trashcan that has something good in it, they're going to check it out.

If your puppy makes a mistake, think before you do anything. If he's still in the midst of the problem—he's still in the trash—you can interrupt that activity with a sharp verbal, "Ack! No!" Then take your puppy by the collar and put him in his crate while you clean up.

Don't shake him. Don't scream at him. Don't push his face into the trash. Don't make him do a sit stay while you clean up.

Being overly harsh to your puppy is not going to teach him anything except, "Don't get caught next time!" Being this rough will also damage your relationship with your puppy.

Instead, look upon this as a learning tool for yourself. How did your puppy get into trouble? Was he unsupervised? Was the trashcan overflowing? Had the puppy gone for a walk this morning? Had someone played with him recently?

> **TIPS AND TAILS**

If you come upon a problem and your puppy has already left the scene, don't say anything to him. It's already too late, and punishment after the fact never works. If anything, it's your fault because you weren't supervising your puppy.

Preventing problems from happening is much more effective dog training than trying to do something after the problem has already occurred. Teach good behaviors, and build good habits. Look upon mistakes as something you need to address rather than punishment for your puppy.

You and Your Puppy

You're probably madly in love with your puppy by now, and that's wonderful. He's handsome, a sponge for learning what you want to teach him, and you're having a great time training him.

What might be hard for you, as it often is for many German Shepherd owners, is to balance training, guidance, and play. There's so much to teach your puppy—so much guidance you need to provide—that sometimes owners forget that a puppy this age is still very much a puppy. He's still a baby, and he still has a short attention span.

Train in very short sessions, and break up the sessions with some play time. For example, practice sit and praise, sit and praise, sit and stay, and then release your puppy and throw the ball for him a few times. Then practice a few downs and down stays and play ball again. Not only does this give him a chance to learn in a manner he's capable of doing, but it also gives you and your puppy a chance to have fun while you're doing it.

Understanding His Prey Drive

Experts who choose dogs for work—whether it's law enforcement, search and rescue, or other occupations—evaluate the dogs in many different areas depending on the job to be done. One thing they look at in particular is the dog's *prey drive*. Many consider this a strong clue as to whether the dog will be willing to work hard.

> ### DOG TALK
>
> **Prey drive** is the dog's instinct to chase moving animals or things, such as when a wolf chases and catches a small animal (prey).

You can see this in your puppy when he chases the ball you throw across the room or backyard or when he chases the family cat. German Shepherds have varying levels of the prey drive, usually from moderate to strong.

A German Shepherd with moderate prey drive can be an awesome family pet. He'll want to chase balls and toys, and he'll want to learn and work for you. Yet he can be taught not to chase kids and cats. A German Shepherd with a strong prey drive would be better in a working home because he'll have more trouble controlling himself.

You can use your German Shepherd puppy's prey drive to your advantage while teaching him. If chasing a ball is great fun for him, use that as a reward. Chasing the ball is also great exercise, so when you want to tire him out, play that game.

Giving Your Puppy Some Alone Time

Even though you may enjoy your German Shepherd shadow, you need to be without him once in a while. Not only do you have things to do that don't require a nosy German Shepherd puppy tagging along beside you, but he needs to be able to be by himself, too. German Shepherds bond so strongly to their owners that if they're not taught to be alone, they can easily develop *separation anxiety*. Once a dog has developed this, it's extremely difficult to solve.

> ### DOG TALK
>
> **Separation anxiety** is a behavioral problem that shows itself as extreme stress when the dog is left alone. Dogs suffering separation anxiety can bark excessively; become destructive; and/or try to escape from their crate, house, or yard.

Hopefully, you've been using the crate as your puppy's bed at night. Continue to do that, even if he hasn't had any accidents. Not only does the crate help him develop bowel and bladder control, it also separates the two of you a little, even if his crate is in your bedroom.

Continue to use the crate during the day, too—not for extended periods of time, but when you have to run to the store or do some errands. Although taking him places for socialization is important, don't take him with you all the time. Strive for a balance. He needs to stay home alone once in a while, too.

Food-Dispensing Toys

Food-dispensing toys make raising a puppy—especially a bright, intelligent puppy like your German Shepherd—much easier. These toys hold food or treats that, while your puppy plays with them, shake out bits of food. The food is good, of course, but by dispensing it in tiny bits, the puppy is motivated to keep playing.

One of the first commercial food-dispensing toys was the Kong. This hard, hollow rubber toy looks like a snowman, with three round shapes stacked one on top of the other. Fill a Kong with good treats, like slices of carrot, bits of apple, some cubed cheese, or pieces of meat. Then block off the end with some peanut butter. Put your puppy in his crate, and give him the Kong. He'll be amused and busy for half an hour. If he gets too good at emptying the toy, freeze it before you give it to him.

If you look at the toy aisle at your local pet store, you'll see many different types of food-dispensing toys. When you choose some, be sure they're large enough your

German Shepherd can't swallow them and sturdy enough he can't chew chunks off and potentially swallow the pieces. Many dog-toy manufacturers label the toys for "heavy" or strong chewers. Choose these because, even if your puppy is just getting his adult teeth this month, he's going to be a strong chewer soon.

When using these toys, fill them with good food and not junk. Avoid the commercial treats full of artificial dyes, colors, flavorings, sugar, and salt. You can use some of his dog-food kibble once in a while, but if you really want to keep him distracted, use some good, healthy food like carrot slices, bits of apple, mashed banana, chunks of cheese, or some pieces of cooked meat instead of his kibble. Just remember, too much may upset his stomach.

Protecting Your Puppy

Your puppy is getting bigger—in fact, he's already larger than adult dogs of many other breeds. However, he's still very much a puppy, mentally and physically.

Because he's so big, some people may attempt to treat him roughly. He needs your protection to be sure this doesn't happen. Don't let people wrestle with him, because that teaches him to fight people and to use his strength against them. You want him to cooperate with people, not fight. In addition, when people wrestle with him, they may frighten him. Again, that's not right or fair. He should be able to trust the people in his life. Some people like to finger-fight or face-fight. With their hands, they mess with the puppy's face, as if tempting him to bite. Unfortunately, this is so annoying, many puppies will bite. And then there are the people who claim to be experts in everything concerning dogs and they want to show you how to train your German Shepherd. Maybe they do know what they're doing, although most don't!

Remember, this is *your* puppy and he needs *your* protection. If anyone attempts to do anything with your puppy that you know is wrong or you're not comfortable with, stop it. Don't let it happen. If that means you need to grab your puppy and walk away, do it. You can always explain yourself later, if you even want to do that.

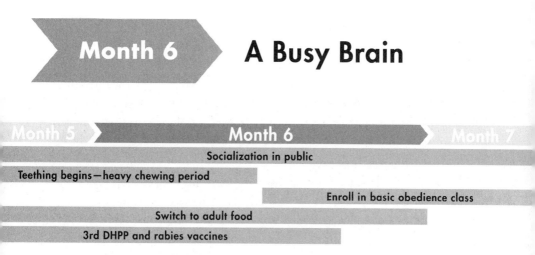

Month 5   Month 6   Month 7
                        Socialization in public
Teething begins—heavy chewing period
                                              Enroll in basic obedience class
                Switch to adult food
        3rd DHPP and rabies vaccines

This month, which encompasses weeks 21 through 24, is a busy one for your German Shepherd puppy. She's still growing; she's still tripping over her own paws; and her adult coat is coming in nicely, although some of her puppy coat remains. Shedding continues to be an issue as her adult coat comes in, so grooming is important this month—as it will be for the rest of her life.

Health care and training are the primary focuses this month. You'll continue to give her preventative medicine as well as take her to the vet to be screened for potential health problems. In addition, training is important this month to keep your puppy's brain challenged as well as to prevent problem behaviors.

Physical Development

Your puppy is still far from grown up, but her proportions are looking more like an adult German Shepherd's and less like a puppy's. By the end of this month, she'll most likely be between 50 and 58 pounds, with males a little heavier than females.

Your puppy is using all of her senses well now, although she's still figuring out how to process the information she's getting from them. Her concentration isn't yet that of an adult German Shepherd's. For example, her nose is sensitive enough to follow a track on the ground, but she may not have the mental concentration to follow it to completion.

The Eyes and Vision

For years, we've been told dogs are colorblind. Although dogs don't see color the same way people do, it's not quite true that they're colorblind. Dogs have fewer cones in their retinas than people do, so although your German Shepherd puppy can see some colors, she sees them differently from how you do.

Dogs tend to see gray best—many shades of gray—like what you'd see while watching a black-and-white television. But they also recognize yellows and blues. They don't see reds and greens well due to a lack of cells that "see" these colors.

Your German Shepherd puppy has more rod cells in her eyes than you do so she can see better in lower light levels than you can. You can probably see evidence of this when you take her outside to relieve herself in the evening. She doesn't need a flashlight; she can see quite well, while if you don't have a flashlight, you'll trip over the flowerpot near the back door.

Your puppy has a much wider field of vision and sees moving objects better than you can. However, your puppy's ability to focus—to change the shape of the lens of her eye—is not as good as that of people, and although it will improve some, her vision won't ever be as good as yours. A person with excellent vision has 20/20 vision. Your puppy probably has the equivalent of 20/75 to 20/80 vision.

The Ears and Hearing

The most important sense for most people is vision; for your puppy, her hearing is much more important. Your German Shepherd puppy has very acute hearing, can hear higher frequencies, and can hear things we can't even think about detecting. Most people hear between 20 and 20,000 *Hz* while your German Shepherd puppy hears between 67 and 60,000 Hz.

> ### DOG TALK
>
> **Hz** is the abbreviation for *Hertz*, the unit of measure used for sound and electromagnetic waves. It was named for Heinrich Rudolf Hertz, who proved the existence of these waves.

Your German Shepherd puppy's large, erect ears act as a funnel, catching and directing sound vibrations to her ear canal. Her ear canals are proportionally much larger than those of people.

The upright ears, the muscles that support them, and their ability to move help your puppy determine where sounds originate. You have to move your head to locate sounds while your puppy just swivels her ears.

The Nose and Smell

As you know, your German Shepherd has a large muzzle and nose. What you might not realize is that her nasal cavity runs the length of her muzzle and is divided down the middle so that each nostril has its own passageway for air and scent.

These two areas have many nerves—many more than people have—and the nerves connect to the olfactory center in your puppy's brain. This portion of the brain is estimated to be 40 times larger than the same part of the human brain. That shows how important the sense of smell is to your puppy.

As your puppy inhales, odors dissolve in the moisture present on her nose and inside her nasal passages. Signals are then sent to her brain. Your puppy's acute sense of smell can detect and sort through numerous scents she inhales at the same time. Although her concentration isn't the best right now to follow a complicated scent, each time she sniffs, her skills get better. Within 6 months to a year, her scenting abilities will be awesome.

HAPPY PUPPY

Your German Shepherd doesn't have a good sense of taste, especially when compared to yours. However, don't feel bad for her because her sense of smell more than makes up for it. She can actually tell more about the food she's eating from her sense of smell than you can with your sense of taste. Feeding her food with a good aroma will attract her more than bland food.

Health

Preventive health care is important for your puppy's long-term health. The heartworm preventives you talked to your veterinarian about last month are a good example, as are preventive flea treatments and vaccinations. These can help ward off future health problems, and your veterinarian can tell you about any others that would be a good idea in your region.

Health-care screenings can identify potential problems as well as congenital defects your puppy might have been born with but that you haven't yet noticed. As with most health concerns, early identification is important because veterinary care and management can often lessen the impact the health problem might have on your puppy—depending, of course, on the problem.

German Shepherd Health Challenges

Unfortunately, German Shepherds, as a breed, are susceptible to a number of different health challenges. Your puppy might not develop any of these, but knowing what the problems are, recognizing the symptoms, and working with your veterinarian are all vitally important. Then, should you see any signs or symptoms, you and your veterinarian can create a plan of action. (Health problems that are not common in puppies but may affect older German Shepherds are discussed in Month 12.)

Bloat: Bloat is the common name for gastric dilation volvulus. In this disorder, fluid and gases become trapped in the stomach, which has twisted or rotated. Emergency surgery is needed because as the stomach twists, the blood flow is cut off and tissues will die.

Bloat has several potential causes, one of which appears to be genetics. Eating only one meal a day is also a factor, as is eating very fast. Avoiding strenuous exercise immediately after eating is recommended to reduce the risk of bloat. Symptoms include a distended abdomen, vomiting, restlessness, and biting or pawing at the belly.

Congenital heart disease: German Shepherds can develop a couple congenital heart defects. Both are serious.

One is patent ductus arteriosis. When your puppy was a fetus, the ductus arteriosis, a blood vessel, enabled blood to bypass the lungs because they wouldn't be used until after birth. This blood vessel is supposed to close after birth. However, sometimes it doesn't close or doesn't close completely and blood continues to bypass the lungs. Left untreated, heart failure can occur. Surgery can repair it.

Subvalvular aortic stenosis is a restriction of the blood flow from the left ventricle of the heart to the aorta. When the opening to the aorta is narrow, the blood can't move at a normal pace. The muscle fibers of the heart where the blood flow is reduced will thicken, and heart failure can result.

Your veterinarian will need to evaluate your puppy before recommending any treatment.

Exocrine pancreatic insufficiency: Although not specifically a disease in puppies, this disorder can appear at just about any age in German Shepherds and usually appears before 4 years of age. The first symptom of this is a puppy or dog with a good appetite who is not gaining weight. In addition, the dog will be passing large, soft, foul-smelling stools that may be lighter in color than normal. Watery diarrhea can also occur, as can vomiting.

Blood tests will confirm the diagnosis. Treatment consists of a digestive enzyme supplement given at each meal for the rest of the dog's life. The vet might also recommend changes in diet and food.

Hip dysplasia: This is an abnormal hip joint characterized by a loose joint where the ball of the femur fits into the hip socket. Because of this loose joint, as the dog moves, the ball of the femur will move in and out of the joint, causing even more damage. Arthritis then forms, and the joint becomes painful.

A variety of things are thought to lead to hip dysplasia, including genetics, too-rapid growth, and too much heavy impact from repetitive exercise such as jumping. The first symptoms often appear during the sixth month of life and may be as subtle as a lack of desire to jump in the car. Other symptoms include limping or favoring of the affected rear leg. If both rear legs are affected, the puppy may shift her weight back and forth. The puppy may also move with both rear legs together—bunny hopping—and she may refuse to jump.

X-rays can determine the extent of the dysplasia and whether or not arthritis is already present. Treatment options vary depending on many factors, including how well the dog is coping, the dog's overall health, how significant the damage is to the joint(s), and the owner's budget. Your veterinarian will explain management, medical, and surgical options to you. If your German Shepherd is diagnosed with hip dysplasia, you're encouraged to keep her lean to reduce the weight on her hips, but at the same time, be sure she gets enough exercise to keep her muscles strong.

> ### TIPS AND TAILS

Genetics plays a part in the development of hip dysplasia, so potential breeding dogs should have their hips x-rayed and certified through either the Orthopedic Foundation for Animals (OFA; offa.org) or PennHip (vet.upenn.edu/pennhip).

Elbow dysplasia: German Shepherds can also develop elbow dysplasia. Like hip dysplasia, this is a disease of the joint that usually appears between 4 and 8 months of age.

First symptoms may include stiffness in the joint. Sometimes the puppy just isn't eager to play. Limping usually follows. As with hip dysplasia, treatment options vary according to the degree of damage to the joint, the dog's overall health, and whether or not she has already developed arthritis.

The options for hip dysplasia are also available for elbow dysplasia, including management, medical, or surgical options. Potential breeding dogs should be x-rayed and certified through OFA.

Osteoarthritis: Arthritis is usually due to damage to joint tissues, through trauma or malformation or because of the dog's own immune system. The result is soreness or pain, inflammation, fluid buildup in the joint, cartilage destruction, and a restriction of movement.

Arthritis doesn't usually appear in puppies of this age, but we must mention it because if hip or elbow dysplasia is present, arthritis will follow unless the initial problem is addressed. Medical options for arthritis are available, including drugs, but the puppy must also be managed with the disease in mind. That includes keeping the puppy's weight low so the joint isn't stressed and monitoring exercise (some but not too much).

Panosteitis: This is a very painful inflammation of the long bones of the legs or shoulders. If a German Shepherd puppy is going to develop panosteitis, it usually occurs when she's growing very rapidly, such as this month or in the next few months. Some German Shepherds have been known to develop it as late as $1\frac{1}{2}$ to 2 years of age.

Panosteitis may affect just one bone in one leg, or it may occur in multiple bones or legs. It's worse during periods of rapid growth and will go away on its own as growth slows. However, it's very painful, so treatments of analgesics and anti-inflammatory drugs are usually recommended.

Panosteitis can be diagnosed by x-ray. The causes are not known for certain, but it's thought to have a genetic connection. Diets high in calories and protein and over-supplementation of minerals are also thought to be factors.

Dealing with Mange and Mites

Mange is caused by mites, tiny insects that live on and in the skin. There are several different kinds of mange.

Sarcoptic mange: Often called scabies, this mange is caused by a tiny, spiderlike mite and causes severe itching. Sarcoptic mange must be treated under a veterinarian's supervision. It's very contagious and *is* transferable to people and other pets.

Chyletiella mange affects puppies and is often called walking dandruff because the mites can be seen moving under flakes of skin. This may or may not cause itching. Flea preparations often prevent mite infestations, but once infested, treatment usually consists of several baths over 6 to 8 weeks with pyrethrin shampoo. The mite can also be transmitted to people.

Demodectic mites: These mites are transmitted to puppies from their mothers, but an outbreak of mange usually doesn't occur until the puppies are under stress, such as during teething. More males seem to get it than females. There also appears to be a predisposition or inherited tendency for these mites, but exactly how that happens is unknown. During an outbreak, your puppy's skin is red, scaly, and infected, with hair loss. Veterinary care is needed because this can be serious. These mites are not contagious to people.

If you see any thinning of the coat, red skin, or your puppy is scratching and itching, call your veterinarian. Your vet can diagnose the problem and recommend treatment. She can also let you know whether the problem is contagious to other pets or your family.

Combating Dangerous Insects

At this age, your puppy is busy exploring hers world. She may stick that big nose of hers in a crack between firewood logs or down a hole. Unfortunately, doing so means she's a prime candidate for insect bites and stings. Both can be frightening as well as painful for your puppy.

Ants: More than 22,000 species of ants inhabit every continent of the world (except Antarctica). Most ants bite and have amazingly powerful bites for their size. Fire ants also have a toxin that can cause an allergic reaction in many dogs.

If your German Shepherd is bitten by fire ants, she needs immediate veterinary care. Call your veterinarian before leaving for the clinic because he might want you to give your puppy a Bendadryl first. He may also want you to go to the nearest emergency clinic.

Bees: There are more than 20,000 species of bees, and although not all of them sting, many do. Plus, most of those that do sting can cause an allergic reaction in your puppy. In addition, Africanized bees are very defensive of their territory, and when they perceive a threat, many will come to the hive's defense, so multiple stings are common.

If your puppy is stung just once, scrape out the stinger, give her a Benadryl, put ice on the stung place, and watch her. If the stung area swells a little and her face or throat do not, she'll probably be fine. However, if she appears in distress—pacing and uncomfortable—or if she has any swelling around the face or throat, get her to your veterinarian.

If your puppy is stung multiple times by Africanized bees, she's going to need immediate help. Give her a Benadryl, and go directly to your vet or the emergency clinic, whichever is closer.

Scorpions: Scorpions tend to be more common in warmer climates, but with more than 1,750 species worldwide, they also cannot be called uncommon. These eight-legged, clawed insects have a large stinger at the end of their tail. The venom is poisonous, although only 25 species are considered deadly. Many only sting when stepped on or disturbed in their hiding spots.

If you see the scorpion that stings your puppy, get a good look at it so you can describe it to your veterinarian. Call before heading to the vet's clinic because he might want you to give your puppy a Benadryl.

If you can safely catch the insect that stung your German Shepherd, do so and bring it to the veterinarian's clinic so the veterinarian can identify it. This can help his plan the course of treatment.

Black widow spiders: These spiders with a red hourglass on the underside of their abdomen are well known throughout North and South America. However, not all black widows are black, and not all have a red hourglass. Some are brown; some may have red spots, or yellow and white markings. These spiders readily bite and are potentially lethal.

If your puppy is bitten, she needs immediate veterinary care. Call your veterinarian and go directly to his clinic if he doesn't recommend the closest emergency clinic.

Wasps: There are more than 100,000 species of wasps (sometimes called yellow jackets or hornets) worldwide, and although they normally don't swarm to protect their hive, they do readily sting, especially when disturbed.

Wasp stings are quite painful and often trigger an allergic reaction in dogs. If your German Shepherd puppy is stung, give her a Benadryl immediately. Put ice on the sting, and if there's no swelling, she'll probably be fine. If you see any swelling, especially around her face or throat, call your veterinarian immediately.

The vast majority of insect bites and stings are annoying and can be painful but are not potentially deadly. However, a few can pack quite a wallop for your pup. So pay attention, watch for a reaction, and contact your veterinarian if you have any doubt at all as to what's going on with your puppy.

A Word on Joint Supplements

At this age, your German Shepherd puppy is growing rapidly and is probably pretty active. For these reasons, and because joint problems are, unfortunately, fairly common in the breed, it's a good idea to provide some nutritional support for her joints now to help ward off problems later.

Glucosamine, either as glucosamine chondroitin or glucosamine sulfate, is one of the most recommended remedies for arthritis. It helps the body repair damaged cartilage, and it has anti-inflammatory properties.

Before adding any supplements to your puppy's diet, talk to your veterinarian. Not only do you want to avoid upsetting your puppy's diet with supplements, it's also important to know how much to give your puppy.

Many foods, including kelp, salmon, papaya, blueberries, broccoli, and sweet potatoes, have natural anti-inflammatory properties. Natural supplements with anti-inflammatory properties include yucca, nettle, licorice root, alfalfa, and parsley. Work these foods and natural supplements (the latter with your vet's approval) into your pup's diet.

Nutrition

If you've been feeding your German Shepherd a commercial puppy food, you can switch her to a balanced protein-based food for all life stages this month. This can help keep her growth even and ideally prevent some health issues related to high-calorie, high-fat foods.

In Month 4, we talked about anorexia and pica, two potentially serious eating disorders. There's one other eating issue we need to discuss, and unfortunately, this one is a fairly common problem with German Shepherds: overfeeding.

Overfeeding—Don't Do It

Food is love, right? Well, not necessarily. Some German Shepherd owners overfeed their dogs, and although their reasoning can be understandable, it's often misplaced.

Most German Shepherd puppies of this age are long, lean, and lanky—and they should be. This is the stage of growth they're going through. But many owners get concerned about their pup's lean body appearance and try to feed the puppy more so she fills out.

Unfortunately, a puppy of this age who is fat is much more likely to develop joint problems, including elbow and hip dysplasia, than a puppy who is kept at a leaner weight. Overfeeding by itself doesn't cause dysplasia, but the extra weight puts stress on the joints and can escalate joint damage.

In addition, as mentioned in previous chapters, a German Shepherd who eats too much food at any given meal is also apt to have soft stools. This isn't true for all German Shepherd puppies, of course, and overfeeding isn't the only potential cause of soft stools, but it is true for enough puppies that it's worth mentioning. So if you add a little more to a particular meal to increase calories and your puppy has soft stools that night or the next morning, you overdid it.

Use the information in Appendix B to keep an eye on your puppy's weight. Using the growth and body-condition assessment there is actually a better way to watch her weight than using the scales to get a numerical weight. Her weight by numbers is going to constantly change because she's still growing. However, if you watch her body shape, how much meat she has on her ribs, and whether her tummy has a nice tuck up (or waist), you'll have a better assessment of her overall shape.

The Finicky Eater

Most German Shepherd puppies of this age are good eaters. They are active, burning calories, and need food for growth and exercise.

The breed does have a reputation, however, for being finicky eaters. Many German Shepherds simply don't enjoy eating like other breeds do. Labrador Retrievers, for example, can be eating machines and will eat anything, anywhere, at any time. German Shepherds are not like this, and, in fact, when treats are used as a part of training, finding a good treat to motivate your puppy can sometimes be a challenge.

The owners of German Shepherds can, however, make this tendency worse. Envision this scenario: your German Shepherd puppy is lean, as she should be, but you're concerned about her weight. So you try increasing her food, but because she's not hungry enough to eat all of it, she leaves some in her bowl. Now you're really concerned and add some different food. Now you've got her attention, and she eats the new food but leaves her old food in the bowl. Uh oh, a new problem! So you make more changes.

German Shepherds are smart dogs. Very quickly your puppy learns that you'll keep switching foods or adding new foods if she doesn't eat her old food. You have just created a finicky eater.

Creating a Good Eater

To help teach your German Shepherd puppy to be a good eater for the rest of her life, you need to build some good habits sooner rather than later. These are both for her and for you.

As we discussed in earlier chapters, feed your puppy on schedule, twice a day, in a quiet place in the house. Don't change her schedule, and don't change where you feed her. German Shepherds are creatures of habit and dislike changes.

Feed your puppy a good-quality commercial food or homemade diet that has a good smell to your puppy, is nutritious, and contains quality ingredients.

Feed your puppy about an hour after exercise, after she's relieved herself, and not immediately after a nap. A sleepy puppy isn't interested in eating, nor is a puppy who has to relieve herself. But a puppy who is awake, who has had some fun playing, and who has relieved herself will want to eat.

Hand-feed your puppy about a quarter of her meal, and praise her as she takes it from your hand. When she's excited about eating, place her bowl on the floor. This not only helps her want to eat, it also strengthens the bond between you.

> ### HAPPY PUPPY
>
> Hand-feeding your puppy a portion of her meal is not spoiling your puppy. It's solidifying the bond you two have. You are giving her good food directly from your hand and praising her for it. That's wonderful for building a great relationship with your puppy.

If you have another dog, feed your puppy in her crate. Some puppies will refuse to eat if they feel the older dog is a potential threat. The other dog can't take your puppy's food away from her, or even threaten to take it away, if she's in her crate.

Don't continually change foods or add new ingredients to your puppy's food. Constant changes may tempt your pup to eat, but they can also create the anticipation for new foods. Then when new foods don't appear, your puppy won't eat what she's served.

If your German Shepherd has become a finicky eater and you're concerned, schedule an appointment with your veterinarian. Have a thorough examination done, including blood tests if your vet feels they're called for, to determine if there's a reason for your pup's lack of appetite.

Grooming

This month let's talk about shedding because although you haven't seen the worst of it yet, you will. As your puppy loses more and more of her puppy coat and that adult coat comes in—complete with the dense undercoat—she is going to shed. It's a fact of German Shepherd life. But there are ways to deal with it to make life more livable.

Shedding and Your Puppy

Shedding is normal for German Shepherds. Your pup will shed some hair constantly, all year round, and you'll see heavier shedding twice a year. The timing of this heavy shedding varies depending on your climate, but generally it occurs in the spring and fall.

> ### TIPS AND TAILS
>
> Some health problems can cause excessive shedding or hair loss. These include thyroid disease, autoimmune disease, problems with the adrenal glands, or hormones. If you see a difference in your German Shepherd's shedding, talk to your veterinarian.

Brush your German Shepherd regularly, at least twice a week, throughout the year. Brushing removes dead hair, is good for your puppy's skin and coat, and also keeps her coat cleaner.

During the worst of shedding, brush daily. If, during heavy shedding, you see big clumps of hair falling out, don't worry. The undercoat often comes out in big clumps.

When you brush, use a pin brush, moving in the direction the hair grows. Start at her head, and move down your puppy's body to the tip of the tail.

Use a rake to get through the thick coat, especially around her neck, on the back of her legs, and her tail. Be careful not to scratch her skin with the rake.

Use a natural-bristle brush after you've used the other brushes. You can brush both in the direction the hair grows and against it to get out all the remaining loose hair.

If possible, especially during the worst of shedding season, brush your German Shepherd outside. This not only helps keep some of the hair out of the house, but any hair you don't pick up will be used by the local birds to line their nests.

Dealing with Hair in the House

There will be German Shepherd hair in your house; it's a fact of life when living with this breed. German Shepherds do everything with flair, and that includes shedding—and they do it very well. But you can do a few things to keep it at least slightly under control.

First and foremost, invest in a good vacuum cleaner designed to handle dog hair. The Dyson Animal or Dyson Ball have both gotten an enthusiastic thumbs-up from numerous German Shepherd owners. No matter what brand vacuum you use, use it often. Vacuum the carpet, the floors, the walls (yes, dog hair sticks to walls), and the furniture. If you develop a routine and vacuum everything often, the hair in the house will be decreased substantially.

Change or clean the filter in your vacuum cleaner often, too. How often depends on the machine you have, so check the owner's manual and change or clean it more often than recommended. After you've done this for a few months, you'll be able to figure out how often it needs to be done to keep up with the dog hair.

> ### TIPS AND TAILS
>
> When you're vacuuming the floors, walls, and furniture, or cleaning or replacing filters, you're picking up more than just hair that's been shed. You're also picking up dirt that's been tracked or carried in as well as dander (shed skin cells). That's a win-win.

Upgrade your furnace or air conditioner filter, and change it every 2 months normally and every month during shedding seasons.

To help keep hair off your clothes as much as possible, keep your closet doors closed at all times. This won't stop all the hair from reaching your clothes, but it will help. Large-size lint rollers work well for dog hair. Have some at home to use before you leave the house, and keep some in your car so you can keep the hair off your clothes before you go into work.

To protect your furniture, you can use slip covers or throw blankets over each piece of furniture you want protected. Use materials that are easily washed. That brings up another point: be sure you clean your dryer lint catcher often, too.

Your home furnishings can make life easier … or more difficult. If you're due to replace your carpet or some furniture, choose materials that are easily cleaned. You may also want to choose colors that don't show the hair as much so you aren't bothered until it's time to vacuum.

Social Skills

Your puppy's social needs are constantly evolving. She's no longer a baby puppy, but she's not yet an adult. She's very much at an in-between stage, physically and mentally.

She needs your guidance to work through this often-unsettling period in her life. Teach her what's expected of her in her interactions with people, with other dogs, and in different situations throughout her life.

Living with Humans

Although your puppy was born with the ability to bond with people, nothing in her genetics tells her how to live with people. Your puppy only knows how to be a dog, in general, and specifically a German Shepherd.

She will be intensely loyal, she's intelligent, she has great scenting abilities, and she can hear very well. With the socialization she's had, she can relate well to other dogs. But transferring this dog knowledge to people can be confusing.

Some dog owners say dogs think of people as funny dogs, but that can belittle dogs' intelligence. They know very well we aren't dogs. However, they only know what it's like to be a dog; that's simply how they think.

For example, dogs sniff other dog's genitalia. That's normal because that's where scent glands are, and dogs identify each other by their scent. People, however, don't like to be sniffed in personal places, so it's up to you to teach your puppy that's not acceptable.

If she goes to sniff you in the crotch, turn away from her and use a sharp voice, "No sniff!" If she likes to sniff guests or people she meets outside the house, have a leash on her. When she goes to sniff, turn her head away, and say, "No sniff!" When she sits to greet someone, praise her, "Good!"

Your German Shepherd may well be confused in other ways and need your help to cope. For example, she's not going to understand when kids wrestle, play, run, and scream. Give her some space away from the children when they're playing roughly or with exuberance. Don't leave her alone with the kids.

She also won't understand when you discipline a child. She might try to get between you and the child, perhaps even growl at you if the child is crying. Don't yell at her. Instead, put her away when you must discipline the child. Likewise, she'll get upset if you and another adult in the household have a loud disagreement. Again, she may try to interfere.

German Shepherds are loyal, affectionate to their people, and protective. Your puppy, at this age, is also mentally immature and not yet able to make good decisions. She needs your help so guide her, let her know what she's doing right, and interrupt her when she makes a mistake. No matter what, don't get angry.

Correcting Unsocial Behavior

If your puppy displays unsocial behavior in public, don't be overly upset. She's young and immature mentally, even though physically she's looking more like an adult. She's going to make mistakes, and sometimes she's going to embarrass you.

German Shepherds are protective; that's a breed trait. Sometimes at this age, puppies decide they have to protect their people from all strangers. So if your puppy stares at someone and begins barking, simply distract her by turning her away from that person, and tell her, "Sweetie, leave it!" When you can get your puppy's attention again, tell her, "Sweetie, watch me. Good!" Praise her for paying attention to you.

In the future, when you see your puppy begin to stare at someone, turn her away and distract her before she begins barking. Then praise her for her attention on you.

If you notice she's uncomfortable with strangers petting her, that's fine. She's had a lot of socialization up to this point and has been friendly to people. But many adult German Shepherds prefer strangers not pet them, so if your puppy is reaching this point in her development, that's fine. Just tell people no, you'd rather they didn't pet her.

Has your male German Shepherd puppy started lifting his leg to urinate? Is he trying to mark every upright object? Many puppies begin to mark at this age so they can tell the world they were there at that location. However, there's absolutely no reason why he needs to mark frequently and many reasons why he shouldn't. This can turn into a really bad habit quickly, so tell your puppy to relieve himself and then, when he tries to sidle sideways into position to mark, tell him, "That's enough," and turn him away.

> ### TIPS AND TAILS

> You may notice that at times your male German Shepherd puppy's penis is protruding outside of the sheath. Don't assume he's sexually excited. It simply means he's excited; there may be no sexual emotions at all.

What else does your puppy do that you'd rather she didn't? Use your training skills to prevent it from happening. Then distract your puppy from her focus, transfer her attention to you, and reward her for that attention.

Behavior

As your puppy continues to get bigger, stronger, and more coordinated, she's going to be more athletic. She's going to try some things she may not have tried before or take a second shot at something she wasn't successful at previously. Plus, as she begins to mature mentally, she might be thinking more and doing more problem-solving.

The end result is that you're going to see more behaviors you consider problems. None of these is a problem as far as your puppy is concerned, but they're behaviors you're not going to want her to continue.

Playing Too Roughly

Your German Shepherd puppy is, at this age, a big puppy. She's getting heavier by the day and has huge paws and big teeth, and when playing with other puppies, she's going to use all these. If she's too rough with another puppy, that puppy will cry and then either stop playing or growl and snarl at your puppy. It's very clear communication that your puppy was too rough.

You also need to let your puppy know when she's too rough with you. But first, carefully consider the games you play with your puppy. Don't wrestle with her, because this teaches her to use her strength against people. Don't wave your hands in her face; that teases her and one day she'll bite out of frustration.

Instead, play retrieving or hide-and-seek games. These are good exercise and fun for both of you. As a bonus, at the same time you're playing, she's doing something for you—bringing back the ball or toy or finding a hidden toy or person.

If, during a play session, she does get too rough by jumping on you, charging you, running into you, or grabbing you with her mouth, stop the play immediately. Say sharply, "Hey! That's too rough!" Then walk away. Go inside if you were both in the backyard. Or if you were inside, take her to her crate. Don't punish her, yell at her, or continue to scold her. Instead, stop the game and separate the two of you. This will make more of an impression than anything else.

Jumping on People

Your puppy jumps up so she can greet people face to face, and because most faces are above her, up she goes. However, bending over to put your face at her level isn't going to work, either—you might end up with a big German Shepherd nose in your eye. If she's excited enough to jump, she's too excited to control her enthusiasm.

Many techniques are taught to stop puppies from jumping up on people. One technique says to knee the dog in the chest when she jumps up, while another recommends grabbing her front paws and holding on tight. Still another says to turn your back on your dog when she jumps on you.

The bad thing about most of these techniques is they teach the puppy that jumping on people is bad or isn't fun, but the techniques don't teach the puppy what to do instead. After all, she's jumping for attention, so how is she to get that attention?

By teaching your puppy to sit and sit still, you're teaching her self-control. When she can sit still for petting, she can then get the attention she wants but without hurting anyone or getting muddy paws all over the person.

The next time you come home, try this: greet your puppy with empty hands. Put down your purse, briefcase, groceries, or dry cleaning. As your German Shepherd puppy dashes toward you, grab her collar as you tell her, "Sweetie, no jump!" Then help your puppy sit, "Sweetie, sit. Good!" Continue to pet and praise your puppy as she sits. After she calms down, release her.

> ### TIPS AND TAILS
>
> Don't ask guests to make your puppy sit for greeting. They may not do it well, or they may let your puppy get away with jumping. Instead, have your puppy on leash and have her sit before you let your guests pet her.

The first time you do this won't change her behavior, and neither will the second, third, or fourth time. But with repetition, sitting will become a habit until one day you find your German Shepherd dashing toward you and sliding to a sit in front of you. When she does, praise her!

Digging in the Yard

German Shepherds can dig. They can dig big, wide, deep holes, and they take a great deal of pleasure in digging. They dig to find gophers, to bury bones, to create a nice bed outside, and just because they like to do it.

If you have a puppy who likes to dig, the first thing you need to do is find a place in the yard where she can dig to her heart's content and it won't bother you. Maybe there's a place behind the garage. Then create a spot—like a sandbox—by digging up the dirt and breaking up the clumps. Frame it off with boards if you want. To introduce your puppy to this spot and show her it's okay to dig here, bury some toys and treats. Then bring her to this spot and tell her, "Where's your toy? Get the cookie!" Point at the half-buried toy or treat. When she digs, praise her, "Yeah! Good girl, get the toy!"

Keep refreshing this spot and taking your puppy to it. With repetition, she'll go to it on her own.

> ### TIPS AND TAILS
>
> If you come home and find a huge new hole in the backyard, don't yell at your German Shepherd, drag her to the hole and shake her, or do anything else to punish her. Punishments after the fact don't work. Instead, start taking her to her spot again and praising her for digging there.

Dashing Out Open Doors

Does your puppy look upon every open door or gate as an invitation to run? Dashing through open doors or gates is a dangerous habit. Not only can your puppy become lost, but she also can end up hit by a car or scare someone walking past your house.

Teaching your puppy to wait nicely at doors isn't difficult. Here's how:

❧ Begin by having her on leash so she won't dash away during your training session.

❧ Walk her up to a door, and close it.

❧ Ask your puppy to sit within arm's reach of the door. Praise her for sitting, tell her, "Sweetie, stay," and open the door.

❧ If your puppy moves from the sit stay toward the door, or if she dashes through the door to the end of the leash, tell her, "No." Bring her back to her original spot, have her sit stay again, and close the door. Repeat the exercise.

❧ When she will hold her sit stay for a few seconds with the door open, praise her, release her, and walk her away from the door.

On subsequent training sessions, practice at a variety of doors and gates. Then make it more difficult by having her sit stay, opening the door, and stepping through the door yourself while holding the leash.

> **TIPS AND TAILS**

Once you start this training, be sure you always stop your puppy at doorways and gates. If you're going to walk your puppy through that door or gate, have her sit, praise her, and then release her—or give her permission—to walk through.

Barking Barking Barking Barking Barking

German Shepherds—puppies and adults—can be barkers. They bark when they play, and they bark when they're lonely. They bark at strange noises and at people walking past your house. To make matters worse, German Shepherds have a big bark.

Very few neighbors appreciate a dog who barks too much. Your German Shepherd puppy doesn't have to bark to the point your neighbors complain. Teach her when she's allowed to bark and when she needs to stop. This requires clear communication on your part.

When she's playing and wants to bark, give her a toy and praise her for having it in her mouth, "Good girl to have a toy!" With a toy in her mouth, it's hard for her to bark, and when she does, it's muffled.

When she gets excited in the house, teach her to go find a toy. Walk her to a toy, encourage her to get it, and praise her when she does.

When the doorbell rings, let her bark a few times and then ask her to stop, "Sweetie, quiet!" Then praise her for the quiet. Don't yell at her to be quiet; she'll just think you're barking, too. Instead, use something to distract her, like dropping a book. Then praise her for the quiet.

As with other problem behaviors, problem barking is going to require consistent training. After all, your German Shepherd is barking to communicate just as you talk to communicate.

Stopping Chasing and Nipping

German Shepherds were originally herding dogs, and many still participate in herding work. That instinct to chase moving things—children, bicycles, cars, sheep—comes from this herding instinct as well as a strong prey drive. When a German Shepherd herds sheep, she uses a nip to control livestock that doesn't go where it's supposed to go.

Unfortunately, chasing people, bikes, and cars is dangerous. People can be frightened or nipped, people on bicycles could have an accident, and your dog could be hit by a car.

The first step in solving this behavior is to never allow the dog to chase. That means keeping her on leash around children, and don't let her run free where people may be jogging or riding bicycles.

Teach the leave it exercise we introduced in previous chapters. That way, when she focuses on some kids or a moving bicycle, you can tell her, "Sweetie, leave it!" and then praise her when she turns to look at you.

The desire to chase (and then nip) is a very strong one. Preventing your puppy from doing it is the best resolution for this potential problem.

Using Your Schedule

Hopefully, you have continued to use the schedule you established for your puppy when you brought her home. If you have slacked off a little, thinking the schedule was no longer important, please review it and bring it back.

A schedule provides security. Your German Shepherd puppy needs that schedule and the security it provides. When things happen as they should, at the time they're supposed to happen, your puppy (and later your adult German Shepherd) feels secure. All is right in her world when things happen as they should.

A schedule also helps her internal time clock work as it should. She eats, sleeps, plays, and relieves herself according to a schedule, and that helps prevent housetraining accidents.

> ### HAPPY PUPPY
>
> Your puppy is happiest when she's on a schedule. Without it, she may be wide awake at midnight, hungry at 3 A.M., or want to play when you're ready to leave for work. Maintain a schedule, and both you and your puppy will be happy.

A schedule also helps promote healthy growth. Your German Shepherd puppy needs to eat and sleep at regular times so she grows as she should. If your puppy is constantly being jostled—by the kids, for example—she may not get enough deep sleep. She should be allowed to eat and sleep in peace at regular intervals throughout the day.

A schedule helps your puppy learn, too. By eating well, sleeping deeply, and having the security of a schedule, your puppy will be able to pay better attention during training sessions.

Having a schedule doesn't mean everything is written in stone or that it can never be changed—after all, things come up all the time that may interfere with the schedule. However, the schedule does need to be adhered to as much as possible.

Don't Be the Problem

Sometimes your puppy isn't the problem—you are. After all, you love your puppy but you think as a human thinks, not as a canine thinks. So seeing things from your puppy's perspective can be tough.

Here are some tips to help things go smoothly:

❧ Be consistent. If you aren't, your puppy won't understand whether something is allowed or not.

❧ Use clear communication. Something is either right or wrong but never partially right or partially wrong.

❧ Set up your puppy to succeed rather than causing her to make a mistake.

- Be sure your puppy gets appropriate exercise. She should be tired when you're done. Don't ask her to jump or run too hard, though. You don't want her to hurt herself.

- Play with her daily so she gets time with you that's fun as well as exercise. Teach her to fetch, play hide and seek, or catch a ball in the air.

- Train with your puppy often, and do more than just sit, down, stay, and come. Challenge her brain, and teach her tricks. Play scenting games with her.

As your German Shepherd matures, she's going to want to be a good dog. In fact, her greatest joy will be making you happy. But now, as a puppy, she's easily distracted and amused. So help her be a good puppy.

Training

If you can figure out how to teach your German Shepherd puppy something, this month she can learn it. She still has that short puppy attention span, but her retention is better this month. If you keep her training sessions short and fun, she can learn—and she'll remember her lessons better than she did even last month.

You have many training options, from training by yourself to private training or group classes. Each form of training has its pros and cons. Keep in mind, too, that everything you do with your puppy teaches her something.

Enrolling in Basic Obedience Class

If you and your puppy enrolled in a kindergarten puppy class, also often called a puppy socialization class, you've both probably graduated by now. The next level of classes is a basic obedience class. Some trainers or training clubs also call these pre-novice or novice classes.

The differences are easy to see if you think about classes for young children. The kindergarten puppy class is like kindergarten for kids. There's lots of socialization, learning to get along with others, basic social rules, and an introduction to the concept of self-control.

Basic obedience is like first grade. There's more emphasis on self-control and learning about skills the youngster will need in the future.

Many dog owners who don't have much exposure to formal dog training tend to think of it as a boot-camp–type scenario. In years past, that might have been the case. Because of changes in training techniques, dogs today tend to approach training class with tails wagging wildly. Dogs get to spend time with their owners, receiving praise, treats, and most importantly, their owner's undivided attention.

Even though you and your puppy have begun many of the basic exercises—including sit, down, stay, come, and leave it—in class, your puppy would be expected to do them alongside other puppies and their owners. That means your puppy will have many more distractions than she's probably used to, and that can be hard. With your help, however, your puppy is certainly capable of this.

Going It Alone or with Help?

You started training your puppy when she first joined your household and have been adding to those skills each month. Many German Shepherd owners teach their dogs by themselves at home and do well without the services of a professional trainer. But sometimes dog owners need help.

Group classes are usually quite economical when compared to private training. Group classes have a set curriculum, although the instructor usually addresses individual issues, too. A group class can provide distractions you don't have at home, which provides both you and your puppy a chance to learn and work with other people and other dogs.

Private training, also called one-on-one training, can be in your home or at the training facility. With these lessons, you and your dog will meet with the trainer, and you'll have her undivided attention. Private training lessons can be centered around your puppy's individual needs. These are great if you have a variable work schedule and can't make a group class. Private training is more expensive than group training.

Behavior consultations are held by *behaviorists* or *behavior consultants*. Behavior consultations usually focus on problem behaviors.

A **behaviorist,** or **veterinary behaviorist,** is a veterinarian who specializes in animal behavior. A **behavioral consultant** is a behavior specialist, and often also a dog trainer, who is not a veterinarian.

Each of these forms of training is beneficial, depending on your needs. If you have any doubts as to what you and your puppy need, talk to your dog trainer.

Training Tips

When living with and training your German Shepherd puppy, it's important to remember she's not a fur-covered person. Even though she has become a well-loved member of the family, and at times does seem very human, she's not. Her thought processes, her view of the world, and how she responds is always going to be different.

Your German Shepherd, no matter how intelligent she is, is never going to be able to think like a human. That means you have to try to decipher what she's thinking and why she does what she does. This can be tough because you can guess how your puppy thinks, but you'll never really know for sure.

This month, continue to limit your puppy's freedom in the house and use the crate and baby gates. She might be getting big, but she's still a puppy physically and, most importantly, mentally.

Do not give your puppy off-leash freedom outside your fenced yard. She's not going to be mentally mature enough, or well-enough trained, until she's 2 or 3 years old.

Continue to try to prevent bad behaviors from occurring rather than trying to deal with them after they've happened. Preventing the bad behaviors can help build good habits, and that's your goal.

Teach your German Shepherd that "Sweetie, good!" or "Sweetie, thank you!" are words that make you happy. Say them with a smile and a happy voice. And remember that timing is very important. Praise your puppy as she does something right, and interrupt bad behaviors as they happen. Punishment after the problem behavior has already occurred doesn't work and could potentially damage your relationship with your puppy. She won't understand what you're upset about.

> **HAPPY PUPPY**

Continue trying to help your puppy succeed both in her training sessions and in her life. She learns much more from her successes than she does from her mistakes.

Training does tend to have some serious aspects. Your German Shepherd is going to grow up to be a big dog, and she could be incredibly destructive in your home or yard—and even overpower you if she wanted. This can provide a lot of motivation to be sure she's well trained.

Even with this seriousness, however, don't forget to have fun with your training. If the training is fun, you're going to be more apt to do it. And if both you and your puppy have fun, she's going to cooperate more. Plus, it's fun watching your puppy learn, understand, and do what you ask her to do.

You and Your Puppy

Your puppy is a lot of fun at this age. She's past the very young months of puppyhood when she was somewhat fragile and you had to worry about housetraining accidents and whether or not she was going to sleep through the night. This month, she's playing and learning, and you're getting to know her better.

The Frenzies

Does your German Shepherd puppy have one particular time of day when she has the frenzies? She's running and jumping and dashing and barking. One owner compared it to a saying one of her grandparents used, "Running around like her tail was on fire!" Your puppy may seem like her brain isn't controlling her body. That's the frenzies.

The frenzies can be caused by many things. Excitement is a primary cause. You may see it when you come home from work. Your puppy may have been sleeping until you got home, so when you come in the door, she's excited, happy, and full of excess energy.

Many German Shepherds don't metabolize cereal grains well, so when they eat a diet that contains large amounts of rice, wheat, corn, and other cereal grains, they have a spurt of frenzies half an hour or so after eating. These puppies often do better with a food that supplies carbohydrates from sources other than cereal grains.

Your puppy may also have the frenzies if she's not getting enough exercise, or if she's bored, or if you haven't done any training recently. If her people are busy and haven't played with her, she may decide to amuse herself.

To calm a frenzied puppy, take her outside and throw the ball so she can run. Don't try to reason with her or have her sit or lie down. She can't do it right now, and she simply needs to work off her excess energy.

Just keep in mind your German Shepherd isn't purposely being bad when she goes tearing around. Instead, look upon these activity bursts as a sign that something is going on. Either she's happy to see you, she needs more attention, or perhaps she needs a different food. So take a look at her life and see if you can figure out what's going on.

Enjoying Quiet Time

With so much going on in your puppy's life right now, it's important to create and share some quiet time with her. You need peace and quiet once in a while, and so does your puppy. The two of you can enjoy each other's company while you watch the news, check your email, or read. She'll nap quietly beside you or at your feet.

If your puppy tends to be a little calmer during certain times of the day, take advantage of those times if you can make them work in your schedule. For example, if immediately after dinner your puppy wants a nap, use that time to sit with her and check your email. Just ask her to lie down near your desk or chair, praise her when she does, and tell her stay. With practice, your puppy will come to understand that "down" and "stay" are not just for training sessions.

Some quiet times should be for both you and your puppy. Find a time that works for you, perhaps in the evening after you come home from work or just before you go to bed. Sit on the floor with her, or if your puppy is allowed on the furniture, invite her to lie down next to you on the sofa. Put her head in your lap, and stroke it, or if she rolls over to her back, give her a tummy rub.

Enjoy the quiet with no television and no music, and simply calm your soul by touching your dog. It really doesn't get any better than this.

Month 6 ▷	Month 7	▷ Month 8
	Socialization in public	
	Adult teeth are in—chewing continues	
	Enroll in basic obedience class	
	Moderate growth	
	Sexual maturity	

Your 7-month-old German Shepherd is growing out of puppyhood, but he's not yet a teenager. He's a "tween"—a little bit of both. At times, he'll be very puppyish and want to climb up on your lap like he did as a baby. But at other times he may react to life more like an adult. You'll probably see more protective actions this month.

Although these changes can be confusing—for you and your puppy—they can also be fun and are a natural part of growing up. So while you try to understand what's going on with your puppy, be sure you maintain your sense of humor.

Physical Development

During your puppy's seventh month, he's growing tremendously. He's gained about 5 pounds since last month. Males will weigh between 58 and 63 pounds right now while females generally weigh about 50 to 55 pounds.

Your puppy's body is long and lean, his legs still look long for his size, and his paws are huge. His nose looks too long for his head, and his ears are gigantic. He's clumsy and will often trip over his own paws. When he's running and playing, his legs may get tangled and down he'll go. Many German Shepherd owners call the 7-month-old gangly stage the "uglies." Over the next few months, he'll grow out of this awkwardness.

Right now, your German Shepherd puppy still has a lot of growing up to do, both physically and mentally. He won't be physically mature until he's about 2 or 2½ years old. Even then, he'll still have some filling out to do. Mentally, he'll be closer to 3 before he's grown up.

Female Sexual Maturity

Many female German Shepherd puppies reach sexual maturity during their seventh month. This can vary, however, with some females *coming into season* this month while others may mature within the next few months. Other female German Shepherds may not mature until 1½ or 2 years of age, although this is much less common.

The first signs of a female dog coming into season may be a change in behavior. She may begin mounting other dogs (male or female), or she may become touchy or grumpy. Some females become very flirty.

There are several stages of the season but the most noticeable to most German Shepherd owners is the discharge from the vulva. This can be quite messy, and many dog owners use feminine pads and a diaper-type arrangement to protect the house. Several commercial products are available, too. Just be sure the hole for the tail is big enough for her to be comfortable. If it isn't, she'll rip off the diaper in a heartbeat.

A female in season will be attractive to any *intact* male dogs in the neighborhood. In fact, when a female is in season, normally well-behaved males will escape from their yards and climb or dig their way into the female's yard. Keeping her safe is vital to preventing unwanted pregnancies.

> ### DOG TALK
>
> **Coming into season,** also called *coming into heat,* is when a female dog becomes receptive to breeding. **Intact** refers to sexually mature dogs who have not been neutered.

Although your female puppy may be sexually mature at this age, she should not be bred now, purposefully or accidentally. She's much too young physically to carry puppies to term and nurture them. She could miscarry, her puppies could be undersized or not healthy, and she might not be able to nurse them. In addition, many 7-month-old females are too mentally immature to care for their puppies. She might abandon them once they are born. Plus, a pregnancy at this age could harm her.

Last but certainly not least, some of the health clearances that should be done prior to choosing the best dogs for breeding (see Months 1 and 2) cannot be done until she's more mature. Screening for hip dysplasia, for example, is best done at 2 years of age.

Male Sexual Maturity

Male German Shepherd puppies also reach sexual maturity at this age. As with the females, though, this can vary. Some male puppies develop a little more slowly than others and will mature a little later.

With this maturity, the male puppy is producing sperm and is capable of siring puppies. Over the last couple months, depending on the puppy, the testicles have been developing and growing larger. Although this by itself doesn't mean he's fertile, it's a sign that he's maturing.

As with the female, males of this age should not be bred. Although the boys are not responsible for carrying a pregnancy and nursing the litter, they should have health clearances that are best done when they're older.

> **TIPS AND TAILS**
>
> Reputable breeders spend time studying pedigrees to choose the right breeding animals. They have health checks done, confer with other breeders, and study individual dogs. They have a veterinarian on standby when it's time for the puppies to be born, and they worry over new homes for the puppies. Breeding is not for the faint of heart.

When they become sexually mature, many male German Shepherds begin lifting their hind leg to urinate. This marking behavior comes with sexual maturity and is the often joked about, "peeing higher up the tree." This marking is a communication to other males and females, announcing his sexual maturity and laying claim to that territory.

Owners of adolescent males need to be conscious of leg-lifting and put some strict restraints on it. Some newly mature males mark any vertical surface, inside the house and outside, and it can become a severe behavioral problem. Let your tween know this is not acceptable behavior by using a verbal interruption, "Not allowed!" in a sharp tone of voice. Then take him where you want him to relieve himself, tell him to go as you did when he was a puppy, and praise him when he does.

Some male German Shepherds may have only one testicle descend into the scrotum. Unfortunately, *cryptorchidism* is known in this breed. If the testicle hasn't descended by this month, it probably won't drop. Your veterinarian will need to do surgery to find and remove the undescended testicle. If it isn't removed and is allowed to remain inside the body, it usually becomes cancerous. This surgery can be done when the dog is neutered—and he should be neutered, because dogs with this defect should not be bred.

Health

At 7 months old, your puppy has completed all his puppy vaccinations, and during that process, he's been examined by the veterinarian several times. Hopefully, your puppy is healthy and growing well. If you decided to spay your female or neuter your male, that surgery may have been done last month. If you and your veterinarian decided to wait a month or two before doing this, that's fine, too. Just mark your calendar so you don't forget, and be sure you budget for the surgery.

One of the most common threats to your puppy's health at this age is an emergency caused by an injury. Your German Shepherd puppy is curious about everything and now is big enough and strong enough to do more to get to these curiosities. He may be able to reach things that were previously out of reach. He's more active now, too, and more athletic, both of which can lead to an injury.

Some emergencies can also be caused by health difficulties or illnesses, although in general these aren't as commonly seen in puppies. Unfortunately, however, they can occur. Learning to recognize an emergency and knowing what to do about it is important. This knowledge will also give you some peace of mind, even if you never have to use it.

Debunking Health Myths

Some health myths are much too common, and they can negatively impact your German Shepherd's physical well-being. Some of these have been around for perhaps as long as humankind has shared their homes with dogs—or almost as long—while others seem to become more common with the advent of the internet. Let's see what's true and what's not:

Cold water causes bloat: Giving your German Shepherd cold water to drink will not cause your dog to develop bloat.

Raise your dog's bowl to prevent bloat: Raising your dog's bowl won't prevent bloat. In fact, elevated bowls have been shown to lead to a higher risk of developing bloat in dogs who are prone to bloat or have a higher risk for it.

Licking wounds helps treat them: Mythology says dogs can help heal their wounds by licking them. That works if the dog is licking the wound to clean it, but some dogs continue to lick a wound and make it worse—to the point of increasing the wound's size and causing an infection.

Dogs have clean mouths: The myth is that dogs' mouths are cleaner than human mouths. There are so many variables here that could be both right and wrong. How clean are the dog's teeth? Or the human's? How is the dog's overall health? Or the human's? The mouth's cleanliness depends on the animal's state of heath and how much bacteria is in the mouth.

People food is bad for your dog: Dogs have lived with humans for thousands of years, eating their people's leftovers. In fact, what makes a dry, cereal-grain kibble good for dogs? It's certainly not a natural food for dogs.

A dry nose is bad: If your puppy's nose is dry, does that mean he's sick? Perhaps it means he's running a fever, but it might also mean the humidity in the air is low that day. A cold, wet nose or a dry, warm nose do not definitively relate to anything specific.

Instead of relying on myths and internet legends for health-care advice for your dog, talk to your veterinarian. If you have any concerns at all, call him.

Recognizing an Emergency

A veterinary emergency is generally a situation in which action must be taken immediately to prevent a worse outcome. For example, if your German Shepherd puppy is vomiting but isn't showing any other distress, your vet might want you to bring him in that same day but won't stress that she needs to see the puppy immediately. However, if your puppy is bleeding and the bleeding won't stop with direct pressure, that's an emergency and you need to get your puppy to the vet's office.

Here are some potential emergencies your German Shepherd puppy might face:

Breathing difficulties: Your puppy cannot breathe, is gasping for air, or his breathing is impaired.

Choking: Your puppy is pawing at his mouth, is struggling or gasping without getting enough air, or has something obviously stuck in his mouth or throat.

Heart or circulation problems: Your puppy's heart is beating too slowly or too fast, or you cannot find a pulse.

Severe allergic reaction: Your puppy has been stung by a bee, bitten by a spider, or exposed to something that causes redness and swelling—especially around the face, muzzle, nose, or throat—and that swelling is hampering his breathing.

Bleeding: Your puppy has a wound that's causing bleeding occurring in spurts (an arterial injury) or is bleeding steadily and won't stop.

Bloat and torsion: Symptoms include drooling, distended abdomen, retching or vomiting, restlessness, and pacing.

Dislocated joint: A dislocated joint will be nonfunctional and look wrong, and your puppy won't put weight on it.

Broken limb: A broken leg may be bent and look obviously broken or wrong. But not all fractures are so obvious; sometimes the leg will look straight. It will swell, and your puppy won't put any weight on it.

Burns: Major burns that cause loss of fur, loss of skin, blackness, swelling, and blistering need immediate care.

Heat stroke: Symptoms include a body temperature over 104°F, bloody diarrhea and/or vomit, depression or stupor, difficulty breathing, increased heart rate, and red mucus membranes.

Hypothermia: An overly cold puppy may have a body temperature of less than 95°F, a slowed heart rate, stupor or unconsciousness, pale or blue mucus membranes, and extreme shivering.

Although these are the most commonly seen emergencies in young dogs, anything that threatens your puppy's health immediately could be an emergency. If you have any doubt at all, call your veterinarian for assistance in evaluating the situation.

Calm, Assess, Call, and CPR

The first thing to do in any emergency is to calm yourself. If you're in a panic, you won't be thinking clearly and your puppy will react to that. If you're emotional, he might struggle and fight your efforts to help him. So take a deep breath and calm yourself.

Then assess the situation. What happened? What caused the problem? Now look at your puppy. What is his condition?

> **TIPS AND TAILS**
>
> Knowing what's normal can help you assess an emergency. Normal temperature is between 100°F and 102.5°F. Normal respiration is between 10 and 30 breaths per minute. Normal pulse is between 60 and 100 beats per minute, with younger puppies having a faster heart rate than older puppies.

Now call your veterinarian or the local emergency veterinary clinic. They will want to know the following:

 What happened?

 Is your puppy breathing? Is he breathing with difficulty? Be able to describe it.

🐾 Does your puppy have a pulse? What is it?

🐾 What is his temperature?

🐾 Has he vomited or passed any stools? What do they look like? Did he pass any foreign objects in his stool?

🐾 Is your puppy bleeding? How much?

If your puppy has no pulse and isn't breathing, you need to perform cardio-pulmonary resuscitation (CPR). This will keep oxygen in your dog's system until you can get him to help or someone else can assist you in getting him help. Never do CPR on a dog who has a heartbeat or is breathing. You'll cause more harm.

To perform CPR, first check your dog's airway to be sure nothing is obstructing it. If he's got a ball stuck in his throat, for example, pull it out using your fingers, needle-nose pliers, tongs, or anything else you can grab it with.

Inhale a good breath, and blow into your dog's nose, cupping your hands around his muzzle to make it airtight. You can wrap his lips around his mouth and hold them with your hands to prevent air from escaping. Watch to be sure his chest rises with your exhale.

Place your hands, one above the other, over your dog's heart where his elbow touches his chest. Lean over and press downward in short bursts. Compress five times and breathe for him again.

Meanwhile, try to call for help from someone else in the house or nearby. It's tough to perform CPR or stop bleeding and also call the veterinarian for guidance all by yourself.

Your veterinarian may have additional questions depending on the circumstances. She will also provide some guidelines about restraining your puppy, what needs to be done immediately, and when and how to bring your puppy to the clinic.

Enrolling in a Pet First-Aid Class

Pet first-aid classes are a great idea for all pet owners. Not only will the classes teach you how to recognize an emergency, but they also have a canine CPR dummy so you can practice CPR skills. That alone can give you some peace of mind because you'll know what to do should something happen.

The American Red Cross offers first-aid classes for people and pets (dogs and cats). Other programs are available, too, although many are based on the Red Cross program.

To find a class near you, contact the Red Cross, your veterinarian, or a dog trainer in your area. The classes are usually very reasonable in cost and are only 3 or 4 hours long. The Red Cross class also includes a small book and a DVD.

Creating a First-Aid Kit

Liz has maintained three first-aid kits—at home, at work, and in her car—for years. In fact, it's a standard joke with her friends and family that if anyone needs anything—bandages, ibuprofen, or a cold pack—check with Liz! She doesn't mind because that's why she has them.

Liz's first-aid kits include things for people and pets, but if you already have one for people, then it's easy to put one together for your German Shepherd puppy.

A basic first-aid kit should include the following:

- 🐾 Gauze sponges and pads of various sizes to clean wounds and put pressure on a wound
- 🐾 Bandaging tape to hold gauze pads in place
- 🐾 Stretch tape or wrap to cover bandaging or to immobilize a wound
- 🐾 Antibiotic ointment
- 🐾 Benadryl for allergic reactions
- 🐾 Cold compresses to reduce swelling
- 🐾 Scissors (both round tipped and pointed tipped)
- 🐾 Tweezers (metal ones are better than plastic)
- 🐾 Disposal razors to shave hair away from a wound
- 🐾 Nail clippers big enough for German Shepherds
- 🐾 Rectal thermometer and petroleum jelly
- 🐾 Sterile eye wash
- 🐾 Antiseptic cleaning wipes
- 🐾 Styptic powder to stop bleeding from a broken toenail
- 🐾 Pen or pencil and paper to jot down information for the veterinarian or advice from the vet

It's also a good idea to have a towel or two at hand and a blanket, depending on where you live and what activities you do with your German Shepherd puppy. You can use the towel to dry off your puppy when he's wet or clean up after bleeding or vomiting. A blanket can immobilize a hurt dog or keep him warm.

You should also have a muzzle that fits your puppy. A hurt, frightened German Shepherd puppy can bite hard enough to really hurt you.

> ## HAPPY PUPPY
>
> Practice muzzling your puppy before an emergency arises. Have some treats at hand, slip the muzzle on your puppy, verbally praise him, slip it off again, and give him a treat. Tell him how wonderful he is. Then do it again. If he associates muzzling with praise and a treat, he's more apt to accept it when you need to muzzle him.

Nutrition

Right now, the adage, "If it ain't broke, don't fix it," applies. If your German Shepherd puppy is eating well, is growing nicely, and is healthy and strong, you don't need to make any changes to his diet.

However, if he's not thriving as well as you'd like, if you have some doubts about what he's eating, or if you want to look into a different food, it's important to do some research first. Let's take a look at dog-food labels, because that's where you can find some of the most important information concerning a specific food.

Who's in Charge of Pet Foods?

A number of organizations oversee pet foods. These organizations establish regulations that govern not just the making of the pet food, but also what's printed on the label. Interestingly enough, these regulations also state what cannot be on the label.

The Association of American Feed Control Officials (AAFCO) sets the maximum and minimum levels of nutrients in foods. It also makes recommendations concerning pet-food labels so information is presented in an understandable format. The Center for Veterinary Medicine (CVM), a branch of the Food and Drug Administration (FDA), specifies what ingredients they permit to be used and how the foods are to be prepared. The United States Department of Agriculture (USDA) states what can and cannot be present on labels. Individual states also have organizations or departments that govern pet foods within that respective state.

Other organizations with input into pet foods include the Pet Food Institute (PFI) and the National Research Council (NRC). The PFI is a lobbying group that represents pet-food manufacturers. As its name suggests, the NRC evaluates new and ongoing research and makes recommendations for changes.

With so many organizations involved, it's easy to see why things can be slow to change and why this field can be so confusing.

What's on a Label?

Every package of pet food must clearly show the food name, the manufacturer, and a means of contacting the manufacturer. This could be a mailing address, phone number, email address, or website.

It must also state whether this is a dog food, cat food, or a food for another animal, such a ferret or rabbit. If the food was made for a specific purpose (such as for puppies or geriatric dogs), that must also be clearly stated.

The package must also contain a nutritional adequacy statement. This shows that the food has been tested according to AAFCO guidelines, either through feeding trials or through nutritional analysis. The debates are ongoing as to which is better.

The guaranteed analysis provides the percentages of several different parts of the food. This includes the minimum amounts of protein and fat as well as the maximum amounts of crude fiber and moisture. These percentages are for the food as packaged, and although they state the amount of protein, fat, fiber, and moisture in the food, there's no assurance of the quality of those ingredients.

> ### TIPS AND TAILS

The guaranteed analysis doesn't say anything about the digestibility of the food. Substances in the food may show, through laboratory analysis, that the food has a certain level of protein, for example, but that doesn't guarantee your dog can actually digest the protein.

The dog-food label must list the ingredients in the food in decreasing order by weight. That means a meat that might contain 70 percent water is going to be heavier than another ingredient such as barley, which contains far less water, even though there may actually be far more barley (by bulk) in the food.

We've said it before, but it's worth repeating: manufacturers must follow these rules pertaining to decreasing weight, but it's still possible to mislead consumers. For example, if a food label lists ingredients as chicken, wheat germ, wheat flour, wheat middlings, and so on, you might assume the food contains more chicken than wheat because the chicken is listed first. However, by splitting the wheat ingredients into three different things, the chicken is still listed first even though there is most likely far more wheat than meat.

The AAFCO website (aafco.org) has a complete listing of ingredients allowed to be used in pet foods, as well as an explanation of what the ingredients are and are not. It's worth your time to research your dog's food.

Choosing the Best Food for Your Puppy

Choosing the right food for your German Shepherd puppy can be tough. Even people who have been studying dog food for years, as we have, are continually learning—not just because it's a complicated subject, but because things change. Research provides new information, new ingredients are allowed, manufacturing processes vary, and regulations change.

You don't have to study nutrition to choose a good food for your puppy. Just read the dog food labels, understand what they say, and if you don't understand something, contact the manufacturer and ask questions. Obviously, they are going to try to sell you their food, but you can tell if your questions are being answered or if you're not getting a direct answer.

Grooming

Grooming is an ongoing process that will continue throughout your dog's life. Although German Shepherds don't have nearly the grooming requirements some breeds have, they do need regular care. Cleaning your puppy's teeth is one of those chores, as is checking his coat for tangles and matts.

Cleaning Those Pearly Whites

Your German Shepherd's adult teeth should be grown in by this month. He may have a molar or two still working its way in, but most puppies this age will have all their adult teeth broken through the gums.

Although those teeth are beautiful and pearly white now, they won't remain that way without some care. Just as with people, the health of your dog's teeth and gums has a direct relationship with his body health. If his teeth become covered in plaque and his gums get inflamed, that inflammation can spread throughout his body.

There are a number of different ways to clean your puppy's teeth. Some people use a piece of gauze wrapped around a finger while others use a dental appliance that squirts out a strong stream of water. Many dog owners use toothpaste made for dogs. Don't use toothpaste made for people. It foams too much, and many contain ingredients that may not be safe for dogs.

Liz likes to use a child-size toothbrush to brush her puppy's teeth. As her dog grows, she switches to an adult-size brush. She wets the toothbrush and then dips the bristles in a paste made of baking soda and water. This works well for cleaning the teeth and isn't a problem should the dog swallow some of it as she works on his teeth.

> ### TIPS AND TAILS
>
> Mix the baking soda and water so the paste is about the consistency of your own toothpaste. If it's too dry, it won't stick to the toothbrush. If it's too wet, it'll run right off.

Introduce teeth-cleaning gradually because your puppy is not going to be fond of it. Because this is a grooming chore you should do at least twice a week for the rest of his life, make it as pleasurable as possible. Don't turn it into a battle.

Begin by gathering your supplies close at hand. Invite your puppy close, and give him a massage to relax him. Then, lifting the lip on one side of his mouth, simply touch his teeth with the toothbrush and baking soda. Talk to your puppy as you do so. After a few seconds, remove the toothbrush and praise your puppy. Then do it again.

Do this every night for several days, and when your puppy is calm and accepts his teeth being touched, begin gently brushing the teeth. Brush a quarter of his mouth and stop, praising him for his cooperation. When you're finished, offer your puppy a drink of water.

Very gradually, over a couple weeks, increase how many of his teeth you brush in each grooming session. If he's accepting, go ahead and do more. If he's stiff and resistant, go more slowly. Eventually, you'll be able to brush his entire mouth at one time.

Dealing with Tangles and Matts

German Shepherds aren't prone to tangles in the coat as so many other breeds are, but that doesn't mean tangles don't happen. The very soft puppy coat can tangle and *matt*, especially behind her ears and in the hair on the back of his rear legs.

> ### DOG TALK
>
> **Matts** are tangles in the hair that have turned into knots. As the knot moves with the dog, more hairs get caught and the matt grows—sometimes to the point that it pulls on the skin and causes the dog discomfort.

German Shepherds can also develop some matts when the dog is shedding and the undercoat hasn't been brushed out or when a burr gets lodged in the coat. If your dog develops allergies and is chewing and scratching, his coat can also get tangled and matted.

As you brush your German Shepherd puppy, be sure the brush goes through his outer coat and undercoat to his skin. Don't press so hard you scratch his skin; you just want to get through all of his coat rather than brushing over the top of it.

If the brush gets caught in the coat, stop, take the brush out of the coat, and look to see what stopped it. A burr or foxtail might be caught in the coat. But most likely it's a tangle or matt.

You may be able to untangle the hair with a wide-tooth comb. Brushes called matt splitters with long teeth are made specifically to work out matts.

If the matt just doesn't want to comb out, don't fight it. Pulling the hair can cause your dog to really dislike grooming, and that's a bad thing to teach your puppy. Work a dab—a very little bit—of hair conditioner into the matt with your fingers. When the matt breaks up, comb it out.

Don't leave tangles or matts in your puppy's coat, hoping they'll go away. They don't; they only get worse.

Social Skills

You German Shepherd puppy has had several months of socialization now and should be quite comfortable in his world. He's met a variety of people, heard some different sounds, walked on a number of surfaces, and smelled new things. Hopefully, he's able to handle whatever comes his way while you're by his side.

Making a Good Impression

Your puppy still isn't ready for you to slack off on his socialization, though. He's a long way from being grown up, and this continued exposure to the world only helps him as he's maturing.

This month is a great time to combine his social skills with his training. Make a point to take him out in public as you practice his basic obedience. While you're out and about, have him sit each time you stop at a curb. Ask him to lie down and stay as you get your mail from the postal box at the end of your driveway. Be sure he walks nicely with you, with no pulling on the leash. Ask him to pay attention to you when other dogs walk past. Ask him to lie down and stay as you talk to your neighbor. Have your puppy sit and stay as someone pets him. All these things can help make your puppy a well-socialized lady or gentleman.

These training sessions away from home in social settings outside his normal training routine help your puppy understand that he's expected to behave everywhere. This also gives you and your puppy a chance to show off. An owner who asks his puppy to behave himself and a well-trained young dog are the best ambassadors the breed can have.

Plus, when your puppy is well behaved, you'll be the recipient of some positive reinforcement, too. When people compliment you on your puppy's good behavior, it's a reflection of your efforts. We all need some positive reinforcement once in a while!

Introducing a New Animal

During your socialization efforts over the past few months, your German Shepherd puppy has met other puppies, some friendly adult dogs, maybe a dog-friendly cat (or an unfriendly cat), and perhaps the neighbor's pet rabbit. These are commonly found pets, and it was probably fairly easy to find these pets to introduce to your puppy.

However, there are many other animals in your puppy's world. This month, try to find a goat, sheep, horse, goose, duck, ferret, or a large pet bird to introduce to him. These are all animals he might see at some point during his life, and it's important that he learn how to deal with them.

These introductions should all happen with your puppy on leash. Ideally, the other animal's owner is restraining him. A ferret, large bird, or rabbit can be held in the owner's arms while a larger animal should be on a lead.

Ask your puppy to sit. While he's sitting, let him look at the animal and sniff toward it. When he's calm and the other animal is calm, walk your puppy toward the animal. Be sure your puppy walks calmly—no dashing, lunging, barking, or growling. If he acts up, turn him away. When he's far enough away to calm down, have him sit again.

When he can approach the animal calmly, let him sniff noses with it, if possible. Praise him. Obviously, if the other animal is stressed or agitated, be sure your puppy keeps his distance.

If your puppy and the other animal both are calm, let them sniff each other, visit, and investigate each other. Praise your puppy for his good behavior.

If either animal gets agitated, walk your puppy away again.

Never let your puppy run loose with another animal like this. The chase instinct—that desire to run after (and perhaps hunt and catch)—another running animal is very strong in German Shepherds.

German Shepherds have worked as herding dogs with livestock and can be very effective at this occupation. However, it requires some special training. If you're interested in getting your puppy involved with herding, do an internet search for stock dog trainers in your area.

As with all your socialization efforts so far, keep it upbeat, happy, and friendly. At the same time, be sure your puppy behaves herself. If it feels like this is a balancing act, you're right—it is.

Behavior

Seven-month-old German Shepherd puppies are more grown-up than baby puppies, but they're not yet adults. They are, however, on the verge of becoming teenagers—adolescents. They truly are at an in-between stage.

German Shepherds are naturally protective dogs and will protect their family, home, property, and vehicles. Many German Shepherds have put themselves in harm's way—with some paying the ultimate price—to protect their people.

Unfortunately, puppies are not yet mature enough to know when to protect and when to let you handle a situation. Often they bark, growl, and lunge toward a perceived threat without knowing whether there is really any danger present. If allowed to continue, this can turn into unsafe behavior.

So when your 7-month-old German Shepherd reacts protectively, simply tell him "Thank you" and ask him to sit, lie down, or stay. Not only will he have a hard time concentrating on that perceived threat while paying attention to you and performing obedience commands, but by asking him to work for you, he's also learning that you have the situation under control. Praise him when he does what you ask.

Dealing with Protection and Aggression

It may seem like the terms *protection* and *aggression* are just different words for the same thing, but behaviorists consider them two different behaviors.

Upon seeing an unknown person approaching his owner, an adult German Shepherd may simply step in front of his owner. That's protection. That same dog may allow a strange person in the house when his owner allows it, but the dog may keep that person in sight all the time he's there. Again, that's protection. Most people who have German Shepherds want—and treasure—this instinct. It's a part of what makes a German Shepherd what he is.

Aggression, simply defined, occurs when the dog takes the protective instinct too far and is willing to use force. The dog watching the stranger approach may step in front of his owner, but he'll also lunge toward the stranger, barking, growling, baring his teeth, and showing the willingness to bite. When that stranger has shown no signs of threat or aggression himself, the dog's reaction is too aggressive. It's beyond protection.

> ### TIPS AND TAILS
>
> Aggression is often the result of many factors. If a puppy's parents tend to be aggressive, chances are the puppies will be, too. But aggression can also result from a lack of socialization, training that has encouraged this behavior without any controls over it, environmental influences, and a lack of leadership from his owner.

An aggressive dog also often shows a willingness to use force in situations where none is required. He may growl, bark, and lunge while out on walks, when there is absolutely no threat. He may not settle down when you give permission for a friendly person to come into your home. When this aggression is combined with an immature teenage puppy, the scene is set for a potential disaster. Even an adolescent German Shepherd could cause a great deal of harm if he bites.

If you believe your German Shepherd puppy is reacting a little too strongly, call a professional dog trainer or behaviorist for some help. Don't wait. This doesn't get better by itself.

Redirecting a Protective Puppy

Most German Shepherd puppies go through a stage around this time when they become a little more protective. Your puppy might bark more at the doorbell and not settle down as quickly afterward as he used to. He may watch strangers on the street more intently than he did when he was younger. This is normal.

However, just because it's normal doesn't mean you should ignore it. You want your puppy to use those protective instincts later, when he's old enough to make better decisions. But for now, while he's still young, you want him to look to you for guidance.

For example, if you're out for a walk and something catches your German Shepherd's eye and he peers intently and growls, tell him, "Sweetie, thank you," in the tone of voice you use for praise. Follow that with, "Sweetie, watch me. Good!" Praise the protective reaction, but then redirect his attention to you and praise him for that.

At first, he might not want to redirect his attention to you. After all, his natural instincts control his behavior much more than your training does right now. But with practice and continued training, your control of his actions will get better.

Controlling an Alarm Bark

Most puppies this age bark when their protective instincts kick in. When someone comes to the door, your puppy probably barks a surprisingly deep bark. Although you want to control his actions so he doesn't overreact, an alarm bark is a good thing—as long as he stops when you ask him to be quiet.

First, decide what word or phrase you want to use to identify an alarm bark. Some people say, "What's that?" Others use a sound, such as, "Sssssss." What you use is up to you.

Then, when your puppy alerts on a potential threat and barks, tell him, "What's that? What's that?" Let him bark a couple more times and then tell him, "Thank you. Watch me! Good boy!"

You have given him a phrase to associate with his alarm barking and let him bark a couple times to help put the bark together with phrase. Then, after thanking him for the barks, by redirecting him to you with the "Watch Me," you've shown him that you are taking control of the situation.

Alarm barks should not continue endlessly. That annoys neighbors (and dog owners). Only let him bark a few times to let you know he sees or hears a problem.

Training

You've been doing a lot of training with your puppy over the last few months. He's been learning the basic obedience skills, including "Sit," "Down," "Stay," "Come," and "Leave it," and how to walk on a leash nicely without pulling. The two of you have been learning how to communicate with each other, too, and that's one of the most important training skills you can have.

Practicing His Skills Often

His obedience skills should not be used only during your training sessions. It's important to put them to use in your everyday life, too. By using these basic obedience exercises in other daily situations, you and your puppy can make them a part of your normal routine.

For example, when you teach your puppy to sit and stay when the yard gate is opened, you can prevent him from dashing out through the gate. He'll also learn to look to you for permission to go through the gate. This can help keep him safe.

Here are some other ways to use obedience exercises:

- 🐾 Have your puppy sit as you feed him so he doesn't jump up and knock the bowl out of your hands.
- 🐾 Have him sit as you hook the leash to his collar so he's not spinning in circles or jumping on you in his excitement.
- 🐾 Have him sit and stay at the front door so he doesn't dash out the open door.
- 🐾 Have him sit and stay before jumping in the car so you can spread a blanket on the seat.
- 🐾 Have him sit and stay in the car so he'll wait until you give him permission to jump out.
- 🐾 Have him down and stay away from the kitchen while you're cooking so you don't trip over him.
- 🐾 Have him down and stay away from the dining room table so he isn't begging or stealing food before, during, or after family meals.
- 🐾 Tell him to leave it around all trashcans so he learns to ignore them.
- 🐾 Tell him to leave it around the family cat's food and litter box.

> ## HAPPY PUPPY

Although many people hesitate to have their dog comply with obedience exercises, perhaps not wanting to inhibit the dog's free will, dogs—and especially German Shepherds—thrive in a situation where they are provided with guidance. They like to know what to do, when to do it, and how to do it. As long as you're fair with your training and praise your puppy for his efforts, he'll be a happy dog.

Each home, family, and household routine is different, and you have to decide which of these ideas work best for you. Once you begin thinking about ways to use these exercises, we're sure you'll come up with more.

Teaching Cooperation, Not Confrontation

An ideal training relationship between a German Shepherd and his owner is one of cooperation. The dog and owner should communicate well with each other, respect each other, and show affection toward each other. Many German Shepherd owners say it's as if their dog can read their minds.

As your 7-month-old puppy moves toward adolescence—when he may well begin challenging you—you want to emphasize a relationship of cooperation rather than confrontation. In the dog's world, an aggressive, confrontational attitude from his owner is more apt to instigate aggression from him.

To emphasize cooperation, reward your dog for his cooperation in training and in daily life. Right now, acknowledge even simple things. If you ask the dog to move out of your way, praise him for it. Tell him, "Good boy to move! Thank you!"

If you interrupt behaviors you don't want, always follow up by showing your puppy what to do instead and then reward him. If he grabs your shoe and is running around the house, interrupt that, take your shoe away from him, hand him one of his toys, and tell him, "Get a toy! Good boy to get a toy!"

Interruptions can consist of a sharp verbal command, "Ack! Drop it!" or you can use your puppy's leash to restrain him or to stop an action or behavior.

Don't ask your puppy to do anything he doesn't yet know or isn't capable of doing. Feel free to help him and then reward him, but don't set him up to fail. For example, if his sit and stay is still a little shaky, don't tell him to sit and stay at the open door, off leash, while you're carrying in the groceries. Instead, have him on leash while he's sitting and staying at the open door, and ask another family member to bring in the groceries. Set your puppy up to succeed!

If you feel yourself getting angry or frustrated by your puppy's antics, put your puppy in his crate or outside in the yard for a little while. Don't allow yourself to lose your temper. Instead, sit down and take a few deep breaths. Deal with those puppy antics later.

Introducing Stairs

If you live in a house with more than one floor or level, your German Shepherd already knows how to go up and down stairs. Feel free to skip this section.

However, if your house is all on one level, your puppy may not know how to maneuver stairs. When you keep in mind that German Shepherds have long legs and a long body, stairs can be a challenge.

If your house has a set of stairs—even just a few stairs outside your front or back door—use those before training this in a public place. Your dog is comfortable at home and will be less distracted than he will be elsewhere.

Your eventual goal is to have him go up and down the stairs slowly and with confidence. Note: *slowly.* Many dogs prefer to dash up or down the stairs as fast as they can, and that's how dogs (and dog owners) are hurt.

When introducing your puppy to stairs, have him on leash and fill a pocket with high-value treats. Walk up to the stairs, and step up on the first stair yourself. If your puppy puts one or both front paws on the stair riser, praise him and give him a treat.

Step back off the stair, take a few steps away, and repeat the first training step.

Walk away, repeat the first step again, praise him, and then go up one or two more stairs—up enough that to reach a treat in your hand he's going to need to bring his back paws up on the first riser. Praise and reward him, go back off the stairs, and walk back and repeat the last training steps.

Gradually, over several days and training sessions, add more stairs moving up and down. Emphasize calm. Don't let him dash up or down. If he does dash, use the leash to stop him. Then have him stand still on the stairs until he breathes and calms himself. Then begin training again.

You and Your Puppy

German Shepherds were not bred to spend too much time alone. In fact, they are happiest when they can be your shadow and follow you from room to room. One of Liz's German Shepherd's was unhappy every time she shut the bathroom door with him on the other side.

Cuddling him in the evening while you're watching TV is relaxing and a good way to bond with your puppy. Training him is important, as is socialization. But as your puppy grows up, there's even more you can—and should—do with your puppy.

Exercise Is Becoming More Important

The German Shepherd is an athletic breed that needs regular exercise. If you think of what the breed was bred to do—work for people—it's clear that being a couch potato is not what the German Shepherd does best.

Training, socializing, and having fun with your puppy helps keep his mind challenged, but you also need to tire his body. Exercise is going to be increasingly important as your puppy grows, matures, and becomes more coordinated and athletic.

Playing retrieving games is good exercise for him. Toss a ball or another toy, and encourage your puppy to bring it back. Let him take a rest now and then so he can catch his breath and calm down.

Running and investigating in a fenced-in area with tall grass, brush, or trees is good exercise, too. Playing with another puppy of the same age is great. Playing with a friendly adult dog who isn't too rough is wonderful. It's important to provide safe opportunities where your puppy can move his body, gain coordination, and expend energy.

However, because your puppy is still actively growing, choose these opportunities wisely. The *growth plates* on your puppy's bones won't close until he's 9 to 14 months old. Hard, repetitive exercise such as steady jogging on hard surfaces like sidewalks can damage those growth plates. Too much jumping can also cause injuries. Injuries to the growth plates can cause bone deformities later.

> ### DOG TALK
> The **growth plates** are the sections of bones where the growth occurs.

Large breeds such as German Shepherds tend to mature slowly, especially when compared with much smaller breeds. If you have questions about your puppy's growth, whether the growth plates have closed or not, or how much exercise your German Shepherd can have, talk to your veterinarian.

Playing Tug-of-War

When German Shepherd puppies play together with toys, it's not unusual for one puppy to grab the end of a toy while another puppy grabs the other end. Pulling back and forth, the puppies growl at each other, brace their feet, and pull as hard as they can.

When the puppies are just a few weeks or months old, these tug-of-war games help the puppies gain strength and balance. They also learn how to play with another puppy without losing their temper. This is such a natural game for puppies that most will invite their owners to play tug by dropping a favorite toy at their owner's feet. When the person goes to pick up the toy, the puppy will grab it, too, and growl.

In the past, dog trainers discouraged tug games because the dog is basically fighting the owner by trying to take the toy away. This was considered bad for the dog-and-owner relationship. However, you can play tug-of-war with your puppy as long as your puppy observes a couple rules: he must always drop his end of the tug toy when you ask him to do so, and he has to be careful and never grab your hand instead of the toy.

Before you begin playing tug, be sure your puppy knows the "Drop it" exercise from last month. If he's not very good at it, practice that before playing tug. When he drops any toy when you ask him to, you can begin tug-of-war games.

Choose a toy that offers a good grip for your puppy's teeth. He'll be less likely to keep changing his grip (and thereby potentially getting your hand) if the toy is easy to grab and sink his teeth into. Bumper toys (long, narrow padded toys) made of canvas make good tug toys. Thick, knotted ropes are also good.

Begin the game by offering your puppy one end of the toy, telling him, "Get it!" When he grabs it, even tentatively, encourage him, "Yeah! Good toy! Get it!" Tug gently to begin. If you're too rough or too excited, your puppy may drop the toy and back away. Instead, gradually increase the intensity of the game.

Then, after some tugging, tell your puppy, "Drop it." When he lets go of the toy, praise him. Then toss the toy for him to retrieve a few times, and offer to tug with him again.

If, during your play, your puppy grabs your hand, immediately cry, "Ouch!" and tell your puppy, "Drop it!" Then stop the game. Just take the toy and walk away. If your German Shepherd circles you, tries to grab the toy out of your hands to restart the game, or barks at you, tell him to down and stay. Or if he's really annoying you, put him in his crate or outside.

Both parts of this are important. The "ouch" is much like the cry one of his littermates might have made if your puppy had been too rough while playing. And stopping the game teaches your puppy that when he's too rough, this fun game will immediately stop. You can play again later.

Varying His Toys

Many toys are made specifically for playing with dogs. Pet-supply store shelves display a wide variety of such toys. Many puppy owners are tempted to buy lots of toys in the hopes that these will keep their puppy occupied and out of trouble.

Toys can help keep your German Shepherd puppy busy, but too many toys can also be a problem. If your puppy is always surrounded by toys, he might begin to think everything in the world is a toy, and that could include your shoes, the TV remote control, your cell phone, and anything else he finds attractive.

If you like to see your puppy play with toys and want to buy him lots of toys, that's fine. Don't give them all to him at once, though. Give him three or four each day, and put away the others. On other days, put away the first toys and bring out three or four other toys. By rotating your puppy's toys, you can keep them fresh and exciting and therefore more appealing to him.

Entertaining Your Pup with Simple Toys

Commercial toys are great, but sometimes the simplest toys can be the most fun. A small or medium cardboard box is an awesome toy. Turn the box over and open one side. Toss a treat inside, and encourage your German Shepherd to find it. When he sticks his head in to find the treat, praise him and toss in another treat.

Then turn the box right side up—open side up—and drop a handful of treats inside. Encourage him to get them. What does he do? Some puppies climb inside the box, while others grab the box and dump it over so the treats fall on the floor. No way is right; let your puppy get them any way he wants.

He can even destroy the box if you want to let him. After all, he's not hurting anything. Chewing and shredding a box isn't going to turn him into a destructive puppy; all puppies want to tear stuff up. Better he does it once in a while with your permission than any time he wants.

Just keep in mind the most important part of play is your participation. If you put your puppy outside with a box, he'll ignore the box and sit at the door looking for you. So enjoy playing with your puppy, and participate often.

Month 7	Month 8	Month 9
	Socialization in public	
	Adult teeth are in—chewing continues	
	Enroll in basic obedience class	
	Moderate growth	
	Sexual maturity	

For the last several months, you've been working hard with your German Shepherd puppy. She's housetrained, and her obedience training is going well. The family is working together to teach her household rules, and everyone is having fun playing together. All is going well.

Then sometime this month, things change. Her behavior regresses, and she acts like she hasn't been taught a thing. She ignores established rules and probably even does some growling. What's happening to your well-behaved puppy?

Behavior

In human teenagers, adolescence is the stage of growth when children transition to adulthood. They try to see if the rules their parents and teachers have set for them still apply. They challenge authority. These soon-to-be young adults cut their parents' apron strings and race toward independence.

Researchers have found that teenagers' brains go through some major changes during this period. That might explain why they're emotional and their moods swing from screaming at their parents one second to wanting hugs the next. They often make poor decisions—sometimes really bad ones. Some of their behavior is simply poor choices, yet another part is because the brain is not mature yet.

Your German Shepherd puppy's brain goes through these same physical changes, and she will exhibit many of these same symptoms. As well-behaved puppies turn into teenagers, they make poor decisions, and they're more emotional and reactive. But instead of screaming, "I hate you!" as human teenagers might, your puppy may ignore you or act like she's never seen you before.

If your puppy regularly socializes with adult dogs, you may see that those dogs have less patience with your puppy, especially if she's rowdy or pushy with them. If they growl, snarl, or knock her to the ground, don't interfere. They're teaching her.

Unfortunately, as a result of these behaviors, and because many owners don't understand canine adolescence, more dogs are turned over to shelters for behavioral problems during adolescence than any other age. Adolescence can be unsettling for puppy owners and a lot of work, but it's normal and just a passing stage of life.

Understanding Puppy Adolescence

Most German Shepherd puppies hit adolescence during their eighth month. This is an average, however, and some dogs can come into it sooner or later. One of the first signs of adolescence you'll see is when your shadow disappears. As a puppy, your German Shepherd's instincts told her to follow you because you could protect her and keep her safe. When adolescence hits, that instinct disappears.

The worst of adolescence is during the period between month 8 and 1 year. But when your puppy hits that 1-year mark, that doesn't mean she's all grown up and mentally mature. Remember, your German Shepherd puppy isn't going to be mentally mature until she's about 3 years old. But after she's a year old, the adolescence will gradually improve.

Most puppy owners take this rebellion personally, "Why is she doing this to me?" they lament. It really isn't directed at you. Rather, it's Mother Nature's way of preparing your puppy for adulthood. Even though your German Shepherd is going to continue living with you and is never going to have to live on her own as a human teenager will, your dog is still going to need to make some decisions on her own. Those might include whether or not to listen to you and cooperate, or whether to ignore a dog who challenges her to a fight. During adolescence, her brain is changing from that of a puppy to that of an adult who can make good decisions.

Bite-Inhibition Lessens

As your German Shepherd puppy moves into adolescence, she's also growing larger and stronger. This, combined with the hormones of adolescence and her willingness to challenge authority, means she'll be more casual about using her teeth. She may show less bite inhibition in her play, both with other dogs and with people.

Be sure she gets an opportunity to play with friendly adult dogs, preferably some her own size or larger who she's known for a while. Ideally, have her play with dogs she considers friends. Then, should she use too much force while playing, they will let her know with barks, growls, and snarls. They'll also put a stop to the play if she continues to be too rough.

She can also play with younger puppies or smaller adult dogs if she behaves herself. But if she starts being a bully—knocking down the other dog, biting too hard, or otherwise not playing nicely—stop the play. Leash her, and have her sit or lie down while the others finish their play without her.

When she plays with people, don't let her bite, use her strength against people, or otherwise be a bully. If she does, again, stop the game right away and leash her.

> ### TIPS AND TAILS

Be sure you continue caring for your puppy's mouth and teeth during adolescence. Clean her teeth regularly and while doing so, open her mouth to examine her mouth and teeth. This is good grooming and health care, but it also tells her you can control her mouth—a good lesson for adolescents who tend to get mouthy or bitey.

Dealing with Leg-Lifting

When adolescence hits, leg-lifting can become a problem. Your puppy may have begun leg-lifting last month or even earlier, but this month, expect to see more of it. Now that he's hit his teenage period, he wants to mark everything to claim ownership.

Intact males are the most prone to mark by lifting a leg to urinate, but neutered males will, too. To the surprise of many dog owners, some adolescent females—intact and spayed—also lift a leg to urinate.

Leg-lifting is more than simply urinating. When your puppy urinates, he empties his bladder. When he marks, he urinates a tiny splash each time, saving some urine for future marking opportunities. The goal of marking is to tell the world your dog was at here and claimed ownership of this spot. It's the dog equivalent of saying, "I was here, and this is now mine!"

Unfortunately, leg-lifting can become a problem when the adolescent desires to mark every vertical post or surface, inside the house and outside … and then every dog who follows does the same, marking on top of your dog's mark. Fire hydrants become so disgusting, fire fighters don't want to touch them. When items in the house are marked, they're often ruined, as is the carpet or flooring under the item.

Should you ever catch your adolescent urinating on you, family members, or personal items, act shocked and horrified (that probably won't be a problem!), and let him see that reaction from you. Then leash him, walk him to his crate, and close the door. Leave him alone for a while. When you do let him out, keep him on a leash in the house and closely supervise him.

While out on walks and out in the house, discourage leg-lifting. At the beginning of your walk, tell him to relieve himself and then praise him. When he begins to sidle sideway to get into position to lift his leg, use the leash and/or your voice to interrupt him, "Ack! Not here," and move on.

Resource Guarding

Many adolescent German Shepherd puppies begin showing the tendency to guard things they treasure. You puppy might growl if anyone approaches her food or tries to reach for her toy. Or while she's lying at your feet, she might growl if someone approaches you.

Although many breeds have the tendency to guard resources—things they think are good—this is a strong trait in German Shepherds. Protecting your valuables is, after all, one of the breed's jobs. However, although your teenage puppy can protect your valuables from trespassers and robbers, she shouldn't growl at you or family members. That is unacceptable.

To prevent inappropriate *resource guarding,* practice "Leave it" with a variety of different objects she shouldn't have, from the trashcan to the family cat. At this point, don't use an object she's guarding. Instead, practice with many different items so she understands that if she's told to leave it, that thing isn't hers. Use lots of praise and rewards while practicing this so your teenager learns that this exercise is an opportunity for lots of praise. You don't want this to turn into a battle.

Resource guarding is a natural behavior that causes the dog to guard things she likes, including her owner, food, toys, and other things that are important to her. This is an unsafe behavior because a dog who's guarding may bite to defend that item.

Once something is in your German Shepherd's mouth, it's too late to teach her *not* to grab it. Now you want to teach her to spit it out, and the easiest way to do that is to trade her the thing you want—your sock, for example—for something even better she wants—her tennis ball or food.

If, for example, she picks up one of your socks, here's what to do:

❊ Pick up her treasured tennis ball and tell her, "Sweetie, ball!" and show it to her.

❊ If she still has the sock, walk toward her as you show her the ball. Don't say anything about the sock.

❊ When you approach her, hold out the ball.

❊ If she spits out the sock, let her have the ball as you tell her, "Sweetie, drop it! Good."

When she understands the exercise and the words "Drop it," begin using them often, trading one thing for another.

If your German Shepherd begins guarding things seriously, growling and snarling as you try to trade her for something else, and you're concerned, call a dog trainer or behaviorist right away. Don't hesitate and hope the behavior will resolve itself, because it won't. Without intervention, it will get worse.

Surviving Adolescence

Even though this is a very natural stage of life and there's nothing you can do to rush your puppy through it, you're also not helpless as you sometimes struggle through puppy adolescence. You can make things easier for yourself and your puppy as she moves through this stage of life.

Here are some suggestions:

❊ Be patient. She will eventually grow up.

❊ Laugh a lot. Her behavior may be so different at times you'll have to either laugh or cry. Laughing is better.

❊ Set her up to succeed. Help her do what's right and what you expect of her. Be sure you praise and reward her for good behavior.

❊ Prevent bad behaviors. As much as reasonably possible, prevent her from making bad decisions.

❊ Be consistent. Expect her to follow the social, household, and behavior rules you've already established.

Don't make excuses. Don't let her get away with bad behavior simply because her brain is in a muddle.

It's very important that you pay attention to your puppy's behavior during this time and respond to it. If you ignore some bad behaviors and excuse them due to this adolescence stage, your puppy could continue to repeat these behaviors and you could end up with a poorly behaved adult German Shepherd.

> **TIPS AND TAILS**

When you feel like your puppy is pushing all your buttons quite successfully and you can feel yourself getting angry, put her in her crate and give yourself some time away from her. Getting angry doesn't solve anything, so relax, calm yourself, and deal with her again in a little while.

Physical Development

Your puppy is going through many changes during this month. She's getting bigger, and her proportions are looking more like an adult's. Female puppies especially look almost grown up at this age. Males still have more growing to do, but even their proportions are better and less gangly now.

Her adult teeth are usually all in, although her last molars may still be working through the gums. Your puppy can still be having some teething pain—those big molars can make your puppy really uncomfortable—so continue offering her ice and frozen food-dispensing toys to soothe her sore mouth.

During adolescence, the differences between males and females become more apparent. Males are larger, and have been since puppyhood, but now the differences are more than just size. A male German Shepherd has a broader head, wider chest and shoulders, and heavier legs than the females.

Females are more feminine and slender. Even with being slender, though, the females are still strong and agile. There's no impression of weakness in your female German Shepherd.

Intact male German Shepherd adolescents produce testosterone at several times the rate an adult male does. This high level of testosterone can create a number of problems, including aggressive behavior, fighting with other male dogs, leg-lifting, roaming, and mounting.

Health

Adolescence, by itself, doesn't cause any health problems, but some do show up as a by-product of this age. Sometimes rapid growth, combined with a genetic predisposition, can cause a puppy to develop painful panosteitis (more on this coming up).

You might also notice some changes in your puppy's sleep patterns. During puppyhood, she slept quite a bit. In fact, most of her growth occurred while she was asleep. But she's not going to be sleeping as much now.

Growing Pains

In Month 7, we discussed panosteitis, an inflammation of the long bones, usually in the legs or shoulders. Not all German Shepherds develop this, but unfortunately, it's not uncommon. It can occur during the puppy's seventh month or at any time during adolescence. Panosteitis is very painful, and most dogs have a significant limp as they try to ease the pain in the affected limb.

If your puppy is spayed or neutered this month, she'll be in some pain after the surgery. Your puppy may also suffer from the pain of an injury because German Shepherd puppies this age are becoming more athletic yet are still clumsy. Your puppy may trip and hurt herself while running after a ball. Worse yet, she may not look where she's going and run into something.

Each puppy handles pain differently. Some are stoic and show pain only when it reaches an extreme level. Often the owners of such dogs aren't aware their dog is in pain because she hides it so well. Other puppies cry at the slightest discomfort.

It's important to know your individual puppy and know how she handles pain. Does she get quiet and go curl up away from everyone? Does she come to you and become very clingy? Does she whine, cry, or whimper? Does she limp or does she tough it out? If you learn how your puppy handles minor aches and pains, you'll be better prepared to recognize when she really does hurt.

> ### TIPS AND TAILS
>
> If your dog is in pain, muzzle her before you try to determine what hurts. Dogs who hurt will bite. Your dog won't purposely try to hurt you, but biting is a self-defense mechanism triggered by pain or panic. Turn back to Month 7 for tips on muzzling your puppy.

Don't give your puppy any over-the-counter pain medications without first consulting with your veterinarian. Although buffered or coated aspirin is usually safe for short-term pain relief, it can have significant side effects, including severe gastrointestinal upset and potential bleeding. If your veterinarian recommends aspirin, give it in 5- to 10-milligram doses per pound of body weight. And give it with food, hidden in a bit of cheese or meat. Have two pieces; give the one with the pill first while displaying the second one. Your puppy will swallow the first one quickly to get the second piece.

Changing Sleep Habits

When your German Shepherd puppy was about 12 weeks old, she routinely slept 18 to 20 hours each day. Not only did she sleep at night, but she also took naps routinely during the day.

Gradually, she has slept less and less, but this month, as adolescence kicks in, her sleeping habits are changing to those of an adult. As she grows up, she won't sleep more than about 12 hours in each 24-hour period.

An adult who isn't in a crate at night will sleep, patrol the house looking for danger, sleep again, and get up to patrol. In the crate, your puppy may wake up, but because she can't get up to check for danger, she'll go back to sleep.

During the day, your puppy will still nap, but those naps will be shorter. In addition, she won't sleep as soundly during the day. Do you remember how you could walk through a room and your baby puppy wouldn't wake up? That won't happen now. If you walk into a room where your adolescent puppy is napping, her eyes will immediately pop open, and most likely she'll also jump to her feet to see what you're doing.

Nutrition

Treats play a part in your German Shepherd puppy's nutrition, as does everything else she eats. It's important to take these extras into consideration so they don't upset the nutritional balance of her diet. As a general rule, everything you feed your puppy that's an add-on to her normal diet, such as treats, should not exceed 10 percent of the calories of her food.

For example, an 8-month-old German Shepherd who weighs about 65 pounds and is moderately active should eat about 2,000 calories per day. All her treats, then, as well as anything added to her normal diet, should not exceed 200 calories per day.

Training with Treats

Most training techniques used today, including the ones we teach in this book, recommend using good treats as a part of the training process. The treats are used as a lure to help your puppy do as you ask, and they can also serve as a reward. When used with verbal praise and petting, treats can provide motivation for your puppy to cooperate with you.

To be effective, your puppy must like the treats, so the best ones tend to have a very good smell to attract your puppy's attention. After all, smell is more important to your puppy than taste.

Training treats should also be small. A small tempting treat is actually more effective than a larger one. With the small treat, your puppy wants more. Plus, with smaller treats you can give your puppy more treats without exceeding her caloric limit.

> **HAPPY PUPPY**
>
> Vary the treats you give your puppy. That way, you can use different treats throughout the training session or use different ones for different sessions. Your puppy won't know what to expect, and that will help keep her attention. The calorie count you're allowed with different treats will vary depending on what dog food you use as well as what kind of meat you use as a treat.

German Shepherds can have a sensitive digestive system. They tend not to take changes well, and they can develop an upset stomach or diarrhea if given a large number of unfamiliar treats. If you use several treats that contain good ingredients—healthy foods such as meats, cheeses, and vegetables—and vary these same treats over several days, your German Shepherd's system should be able to keep up.

It's usually a good idea to avoid many of the commercial treats that contain additives, artificial flavorings and preservatives, sugar, and salt. However, if you prefer using commercial treats, read the ingredients carefully and avoid treats with a lot of additives and junk foods.

Avoid foods such as greasy or spicy foods, or foods high in salt or sugar, that could upset her gastrointestinal tract. Instead, use good foods such as cooked meats, cooked yams, cheese, or carrots. The following table offers some suggested healthy treats for a growing German Shepherd along with the calorie counts of each.

Food	Amount	Calories
Carrots, sliced	½ cup	25 calories
Popcorn, popped, plain	1 cup	80 calories
Yams, cooked, cubed	½ cup	80 calories
Cheese, Swiss, cubed	¼ cup	125 calories
Cheese, American, cubed	¼ cup	132 calories
Cheese, cheddar, cubed	¼ cup	133 calories
Chicken, gizzard and heart	4 ounces	150 calories
Beef, liver, cooked	**¼ cup**	**198 calories**

Feeding Chew Treats

Throughout the last few months, especially during the teething process, we've recommended you give your puppy things to chew on. Ice cubes, for example, contain no calories and aren't going to affect your puppy's diet or gastrointestinal system.

Several commercial treats can be good for your puppy to chew on, both to satisfy her need to chew and also to help keep her teeth clean. When choosing treats, remember your puppy—even though she isn't full grown yet—has large, strong jaws and teeth. Choose treats that she can't immediately break up and swallow, and that will provide her with some chewing pleasure time.

Here are some to check out:

Bully sticks: Also called *pizzles,* these are long, dried sections of the male steer or bull's anatomy. They are low fat and high in protein. For a German Shepherd puppy, don't get the smaller sizes; the minimum size should be 9 inches long and then supervise your puppy when she's chewing on the bully stick (or any of the other chew treats mentioned here). Be sure she doesn't try to swallow a long section.

Moozles: These are dried beef snouts. They are high in protein and low in fat. These aren't as hard as bully sticks, but they do require some chewing.

Snoozles: These pig snouts are also high in protein and low in fat. As with moozles, they're not as hard as bully sticks but are good chewing.

Water buffalo tendon chews: Dog chew and treat manufacturers are responding to customer requests for treats from different sources, which are particularly good for dogs with allergies. Water buffalo treats are lower in fat than beef and pork, and are also high in protein.

As with any other commercial dog food or treat product, when you look at new chew treats, read the label. If at all possible, choose American products that must adhere to FDA and AAFCO safety requirements. Know what the ingredients are, and avoid those treats with too many additives.

Preventing Begging

German Shepherds can be funny dogs. Your adolescent may at times be a poor eater, turning up her nose at food she normally eagerly eats. Or she may eat but leave some food in her bowl. Perhaps she's finicky about training treats. But when you have a roast-beef sandwich and potato chips, she'll be at your knee drooling.

You shouldn't allow begging because it's very easy for simple drooling and begging to turn into a bad habit. Begging while you're eating often turns into pushier behavior, such as pawing at your leg or stealing from your plate, the table, or kitchen counters. It also can lead to trashcan–raiding.

Your dog begs because it's often self-rewarding behavior: the dog begs and receives tasty food. It's just like training: the dog does something and then receives a reward.

To prevent begging, first of all, never feed your German Shepherd puppy from your plate or from the table. If you have some leftovers you'd like her to have, save them and add them to her meal later. But don't give them to her as you eat or from where you normally eat.

Also, should she come up, sit, and stare at you with those big, dark eyes while you're eating, leash her and walk her away from the table. Teach her an alternative behavior by asking her to lie down and stay. Then go back to your meal. She can't beg while holding the down and stay as you asked. If she doesn't hold the stay, calmly walk her to her crate, close the door, and leave her there until you finish your meal.

> ### TIPS AND TAILS
>
> It's important that the family all agree that begging is not to be allowed. If one person continually feeds your puppy from the table or drops her scraps in the kitchen, your German Shepherd will continue to beg.

Grooming

This month, let's talk about bathing your puppy. You may have already bathed her several times over the last few months, but as her coat grows in, bathing her will be a little different. Of course, her growing size adds some difficulty, too.

German Shepherds are pretty much wash and wear. Keep them clean and brushed, and all should be well. They can have a few skin issues, including allergies, so it's a good idea to keep a close eye on your puppy's skin.

Rub-a-Dub-Dub

Usually, German Shepherds do well without a lot of baths. Dirt tends to come out of their coat nicely when they're brushed regularly. However, if your puppy gets really dirty—maybe she's been playing in the mud—then she'll need a bath.

Always brush your puppy thoroughly before getting her wet. Not only will the brushing remove a lot of the dirt before the bath but it will also get rid of any hair that has loosened up to be shed. Less coat on your pup means less coat to wash. Brushing also helps you find any tangles or matts. If you don't get rid of those before you wash your puppy, they grow exponentially when they get wet.

If you're going to bathe your puppy during the summer, you can use water from the hose and wash her outside. However, you can count on getting as wet as she will. If you think the water from the hose is too cold for you, it's also too cold for your puppy.

Many people bathe their German Shepherds in the shower and just climb in, too. This is great if you have a handheld showerhead. The bathtub is probably the easiest place, though, because you can sit on the edge of the tub as you work on your puppy.

Hundreds of dog shampoos are available. To choose one for your German Shepherd, look for one that's safe for puppies and doesn't have too strong of a scent.

> ### HAPPY PUPPY
>
> Your puppy has a very good nose, and if the shampoo leaves behind a strong scent, she's apt to go outside as soon as her bath is done and roll in something to deaden the scent.

If you just want a simple soap and aren't interested in scents and conditioners, and if your puppy doesn't have any skin issues, dishwashing soaps can work. Groomers often use plain Dawn or Joy because these soaps cut through dirt and oils without leaving any residue behind. Plus, they rinse out of the coat easily.

Before you bathe your pup, you'll want to create an easy-rinse mixture. To do this, mix about 1 cup white vinegar with 1 gallon warm water. Using this mixture after shampooing helps rinse out all the soap and calm her skin after the bath.

Here's how to bathe your puppy in the bathtub:

☙ Run the water until it's a comfortable warmth for you. Put a nonskid matt in the bottom of the tub.

☙ Leash your puppy, invite her into the tub, and praise her when she gets in.

☙ Put a cotton ball in each ear.

☙ Begin wetting down your puppy, starting behind her ears, working down her neck to her back, down her sides and toward her tail. Wet her head and face last.

☙ Apply the soap or shampoo, again beginning behind her ears and working down and back toward her tail, getting her face soapy last.

> ## TIPS AND TAILS

Your puppy will dislike most having her face wet and washed, so leave those areas until last to keep her happier. Plus, if she has any fleas, getting her soapy around the neck first will keep the fleas from running to her ears and face.

☙ When she's all soaped up and scrubbed, rinse her face first and then begin rinsing from behind her ears toward her back and down. Thoroughly rinse all the soap out of her coat. Any soap that remains can cause itching.

☙ With your puppy still in the tub, and beginning behind your puppy's ears, dribble the vinegar mixture into her coat, working it in with your fingers as you do it. Be sure you get it all over in her coat.

☙ Rinse again. You don't have to be as thorough this time; if a little vinegar remains in her coat, it's okay.

☙ Tell your puppy, "Sweetie, shake," and blow lightly in one ear. When she shakes, praise her.

You'll need at least a couple thick bath towels to get most of the water off her. Rub and rub some more with the towels, asking her to shake in between each toweling. She can air dry (in a warm spot if it's cold outside) to get fully dry.

When your puppy is dry, she'll need to be brushed again. Bathing the coat loosens any remaining dead hairs, so she'll lose a lot of coat after each bath.

Scratching and Chewing

Your German Shepherd puppy will scratch if she has an itch. However, if the scratching continues and she bites at herself, something else is going on.

Allergies: Allergies show up in the skin in several different ways. If your puppy licks her paws after playing in the grass and her belly is also red, she may be allergic to grass. As strange as this seems—a dog allergic to grass!—it's not that unusual. Or if your puppy constantly licks her paws and chews at the base of her tail, she may have food allergies. Talk to your veterinarian if you suspect your puppy may be suffering from allergies.

German Shepherd pyoderma: A dog with pyoderma develops sores over her back, hips, and rear legs that drain pus and fluid. She'll need veterinary care to treat it. This may have an inherited tendency, although allergies and fleas can exacerbate the condition.

Hot spots: These moist, oozing, red, and swollen patches of skin are often caused by itching allergy spots or fleas. The dog will itch and scratch repeatedly, and the wound will appear very rapidly—often within hours. If untreated, the painful wounds grow and can become several inches in diameter. Hot spots require thorough cleaning, veterinary care, and medication.

Impetigo: This shows itself as pus-filled blisters that pop and scab over on the abdomen and groin. These are often caused by bacteria. A puppy who is dirty is more apt to get this. The puppy will need cleansing baths, clean living conditions, veterinary care, and medication.

If your teenager is scratching and it seems to either be continuing or there's an underlying skin condition, call your veterinarian. She can diagnose the problem and get your puppy started on treatments.

Social Skills

Adolescence brings with it so many changes, so it shouldn't be a surprise your German Shepherd puppy's social skills are affected this month, too. You may find that your puppy barks at people when out on a walk or in a public place. She may lunge to the end of the leash to bark menacingly at another dog.

Many owners of adolescent German Shepherds have questioned who this monster is on the end of the leash. This dog can't be their previously wonderful, well-socialized puppy.

Don't blame yourself when she's unsocial to people, dogs, or other animals during this stage. Her behavior doesn't mean you did a poor job socializing her. Rather, her behavior simply reflects the stage of development she's going through right now.

When She's Unsocial Toward People

When your adolescent was younger, she was happy to greet people. Her body language was happy and wiggly, and she happily went up to people and invited petting.

Now, during month 8, she's more standoffish. She's not always happy about strangers approaching and may bark at them. If they continue to approach, she may growl or duck behind you. She is no longer the social butterfly she once was. Strangers are no longer just people she doesn't know; now they're also potential threats. Last month, we explained that these protective instincts were developing, and now, during adolescence, they are in full operation.

> **TIPS AND TAILS**
>
> To be sure your adolescent remains safe and social to people, continue taking her places. Don't force her to greet strangers, but be sure she continues to go places with you so she constantly sees people she doesn't know.

Use her obedience training to help her behave herself. Watch her body language and learn what she does just before she lunges and barks. When you see she's on the verge, distract her, turn her away, and redirect her attention to you before she erupts in barking. Praise her when she does pay attention to you.

Protect your puppy from herself. If she's feeling particularly antisocial on any given day, don't force her to visit with people. When you're out on a walk, tell people not to pet her. When guests come to the house, leash your puppy and have her lie down at your feet while you're sitting and talking to your guests. If people are actively moving around, put your puppy in her crate in a back room. Don't force her into a situation where she may make a stupid mistake.

All the socialization you did with your puppy has not been in vain. It helped build a good foundation for your puppy, and that foundation is still valuable. When your puppy works her way through adolescence, you'll see those socialization skills reemerge. Plus, without that socialization, adolescence would have been much worse.

When She's Unsocial Toward Dogs

As an adult, your German Shepherd is not going to like every dog she meets, just as you don't like every person you meet. Some dogs will be annoying to her, or threatening, and some may just be too pushy. Don't expect her to like all other dogs.

This dislike is going to be more evident this month, not just because your puppy is an adolescent when her brain is so volatile, but also because she's growing up. German Shepherds are, as a breed, cautious with strangers, and that applies to canine strangers as well as human ones.

Your dog will have certain dog friends she really likes. These may be neighbor dogs or friends from her puppy and basic obedience class. Most likely, these are dogs she sees on a regular basis and has been able to establish and maintain a friendship with them.

> **HAPPY PUPPY**
>
> Dogs follow strict rules of social interactions that communicate clearly what the individual dog's intentions are. Body language, including postures and movements, and sounds are uniform through all breeds and help prevent miscommunications and misunderstandings. As long as the dogs are playing happily, with tails wagging wildly, you can let them have fun.

However, at some point during adolescence, your dog may be a little short-tempered or impatient, and a squabble may break out. This may just be some growling and snarling and never move beyond the verbal. Unfortunately, sometimes these squabbles do turn into fights.

There's often no rhyme nor reason to dog fights, but intact males tend to be quicker to fight, especially with other intact males. Intact females will fight with other females, intact or not. And males rarely start a fight with a female and often won't respond if challenged by a female.

If your dog has been in a dog fight with another adolescent dog of the same sex and about the same size, and no one needed to go to the veterinarian, don't panic. That means both dogs had good bite inhibition, and during adolescence, that's good news.

However, if your adolescent puppy is challenging many dogs, no matter what their sex, and the size of the dog doesn't matter to her, you may well have a problem. This doesn't mean you have a bad or poorly behaved dog, but you do need some help to figure out what's going on. It's definitely time to call a behaviorist for an evaluation.

If a dog fight happens, don't try to grab the dogs' collars. You might get bitten because most dogs try to grab their opponent's neck or face. Instead, ask for help. You and the other person should grab the dogs' back legs, lift the legs, and pull the dogs away from each other. Keep the legs elevated until the dogs stop trying to get to each other. Then leash the dogs and walk them away.

While your puppy is going through adolescence, remember that her brain isn't working well, so limit her playtime to the dogs she already knows well. Don't go to the dog park and turn her loose with unknown dogs—that's setting her up for failure because she might start a fight. If she doesn't start the fight, she might be willing to answer a challenge she would have otherwise ignored when she was younger.

Continue taking her places where she will see other dogs, but just don't turn her loose to play. Dog-training classes are a great way to continue her exposure to other dogs. Even if she can't play with other dogs, she needs to continue to be around them, so don't isolate her.

A Canine Good Citizen

The American Kennel Club (AKC) began the Canine Good Citizen (CGC) program more than 20 years ago. At the time, Liz and her husband had German Shepherds, and they knew well what breed discrimination was. People would see their German Shepherds and, without knowing the dogs, assume they were aggressive.

The CGC program was designed to recognize responsible dog owners and well-behaved dogs. The exercises pertain to real-life skills—things you and your dog probably do every day. When the dog is able to pass all 10 exercises, she is awarded the title Canine Good Citizen and can have "CGC" listed behind her name. The program is open to all dogs, purebred or mixed breed, registered with the AKC or not.

The exercises include the following:

🐾 The dog, with her owner, allows a friendly person unknown to the dog to walk up and greet her owner.

🐾 The dog, when with her owner and approached by a friendly person, allows that person to pet her.

🐾 The owner shows responsibility by making sure the dog is clean, healthy, and well groomed.

🐾 The dog and owner can go for a walk, and the dog is under control.

🐾 The dog and owner can walk through a crowd, and the dog is under control and doesn't pull or wrap the leash around people's legs.

🐾 The dog and owner can demonstrate that the dog knows and will do a sit, down, and stay when asked.

🐾 The dog comes when called.

🐾 The dog behaves politely around other dogs and does not lunge or bark at another dog.

🐾 The dog does not panic to a visual or sound stimulus, such as a jogger or a flapping trash bag.

🐾 The dog can be left with another person for 3 minutes. For example, perhaps you need to use the restroom while out on a walk and your neighbor holds the leash.

The CGC has become so popular, many landlords now require it as a condition of allowing a dog in a rental home. Some insurance companies offer discounts for dogs who have passed the CGC, and many therapy dog organizations use the CGC as a test for potential therapy dogs. To find a CGC evaluator in your area, go to the AKC's website at akc.org.

Training

Training is always an important part of life for this intelligent breed, but it's even more vital now. Human teenagers test boundaries, challenge authority, try to gain some independence, and eventually gain that freedom. Canine teenagers do the same thing, but you want your puppy to look to you for guidance rather than strive for independence.

Group classes are a great idea now to help keep your teenager working for you around other people and dogs. Even if your puppy has already attended a basic obedience class, enroll in another one. The exercises will be repeated, but the class will provide you and your teenager a chance to work with distractions in a controlled situation. Then continue practicing those skills out in public, in a variety of situations, and at home.

Using Her Training

When your puppy is in the worst of adolescence this month, back off from teaching a lot of new exercises. When her brain isn't functioning at its best, trying to focus on new things would be asking too much of her. However, you can work on exercises she already knows and emphasize those in your daily routine.

Start by refreshing her skills with those exercises. You can even reteach them to polish her skills. Plus, some refresher training with praise and treats keeps the training fun and helps the two of you work together.

Emphasize using these skills when they're needed, especially when her adolescent behaviors show up. For example, she learned the "Watch me" exercise several months ago, and ideally, you've been using it regularly to help her pay attention to you. One day, you're out on a walk and your puppy sees another dog walking toward you. You know she's been more reactive toward other dogs recently, so to prevent this, have your puppy sit and face you. Ask her, "Sweetie, watch me!" Praise her when she does. If she ignores you and turns toward the other dog, use the leash to turn her back toward you, have her sit again, and ask her to watch you again.

If she's still ignoring you, use the leash to give her a pop on the collar—snap and release—as you let her know she has ignored you enough, "Ack! That's enough!" Again, turn her toward you. Hold her collar so you can help her control her own actions.

> ### TIPS AND TAILS
>
> When working with dogs, aggression begets aggression. If you get aggressive toward your dog, chances are at this time in her life she will respond in the same manner. So if you need to interrupt bad behaviors, do so calmly. Don't lose your temper or get violent.

The more you use your puppy's training skills, the better they will become and the more second nature to her. You want her to look to you for guidance on how she should behave or react in any given situation, and her training will help with that.

Giving Your Puppy Permission

Another way to teach your teenager to look to you for guidance is to give her permission to do things. As you teach this, you can also deny her permission.

For example, your German Shepherd puppy needs to go outside to relieve herself and has come to you, gotten your attention, and gone to the door to the backyard. When you follow her to the back door, ask her to sit. Praise her for sitting. Then take hold of her collar and tell her, "Sweetie, wait," as you open the door. Let her wait for a few seconds and then release her, "Sweetie, release. Okay, go outside." As she goes outside, praise her.

Just the act of having her wait for a few seconds helps teach self-control—an important skill right now because if she's sitting and waiting, she's not dashing out the door as soon as it opens. She's also not running into your legs and knocking you down. Plus, by waiting for your permission, she's looking to you for guidance: "Okay, can I go outside now?"

You can do the same thing in other situations:

🐾 Have her wait before jumping in the car. Perhaps you want to spread a blanket in the car before she jumps in.

🐾 Have her sit and wait when she's inside the car as you open the car door. You want to hook up her leash before she jumps out.

🐾 Have her wait when you set down her food bowl so she doesn't jump up and knock the bowl out of your hands.

🐾 Have her sit and wait at the gate when you open it.

All these situations have been discussed in previous chapters as examples of using the basic obedience exercises. But now they're also important for teaching self-control in adolescence as well as looking to you for permission to do things she wants to do.

Just as you give your teenager permission to do things, you can also deny it. Tell her no, she can't go out the front door, she can't jump in the car, and she can't have your leftover sandwich. By either giving or denying permission, you are teaching your puppy that she is to look to you rather than simply doing what she wants to do.

Mistakes Are Experiments

When your teenager makes a mistake—and she will—don't assume she's challenging you personally. She may be testing her boundaries, sure, but her behavior is not a personal attack.

What's more likely happening is a scientific experiment. Kate Abbott, a dog trainer in Vista, California, says dogs are like scientists. When they ask a question (via their behavior) and they get an answer, they ask another question.

So when your teenager tries one variance of behavior and you don't like it, she'll try something else to see what you have to say about that. She's experimenting: "Is this right? Or how about this?" The brighter, more intelligent the dog, the more questions she might ask.

You need to answer each of your teenager's questions very clearly. If, for example, you ask her to sit and she continues to stand, tell her, "Ack! Sweetie, sit," and help her do it. Don't continue to say, "Sit, sit, sit, sit," until she finally does it. Ask her once and then help her do it. Use clear communication.

You can have fun with your training—keeping it as positive as possible—while continuing to enforce your rules. When the training is happy and fun, your German Shepherd puppy is more compliant. If you're angry, she's more apt to fight you.

Or if you ask your dog to sit and she lies down, do the same thing. Tell her sit and help her do it. After all, you didn't ask her to lie down; you asked her to sit.

Clear communication won't make adolescence go away—nothing but time will do that. But communicating well with your dog can ease some headaches. So let your dog know what you want her to do, and help her do it. Should she make a mistake, let her know and then help her do what you asked her to do. When she does it, reward her for cooperating.

You and Your Puppy

The adolescence stage is a challenging one for both you and your German Shepherd puppy. When your puppy is driving you nuts, she isn't doing it on purpose. Remember, most of the time she isn't thinking much at all. She's simply reacting to her hormones and instincts.

You, however, are doing a lot of thinking, and at times you may wonder if you brought home the wrong puppy. Maybe you should have chosen a different breed. You may question yourself about all sorts of things, including whether you made mistakes in raising her. It's hard not to follow this line of thought when your puppy is a teenager—after all, the parents of human teenagers question themselves, too. They just ask different questions.

The relationship you've built with your puppy over the months since you brought her home is her anchor right now. Even though she may push you, ignore you, and challenge your authority, she is well bonded with you and loves you as only a German Shepherd can.

Think of yourself as your teenager's parent, and act like one. Provide her with guidance and limits, and help her be a good puppy as you both work through this stage of her life together.

In Search of a Leader

Socialization in public

Adult teeth are in—chewing continues

Ready for more advanced training

Moderate growth

Sexual maturity

Your German Shepherd puppy came into adolescence last month and is still in it now. In fact, month 9 through about 1 year will be the most trying for you because your puppy will be physically strong and active as well as mentally willful. These things, combined with his intelligence, make for a potentially challenging few months.

This month, your leadership becomes even more important. During adolescence, your puppy challenges authority, so if you don't provide the leadership he needs, he may decide you're no longer important. Without your leadership, he could continue to look to you for food and affection but may ignore any of your requests for cooperation. And that's not what you want.

Behavior

Adult dogs are excellent teachers for puppies. Your puppy's mother or an adult dog in your household instinctively knows how to coach your puppy. In fact, adult dogs assume a natural leadership role toward younger dogs. That is, if you don't interfere. By learning how an adult dog instructs and leads a puppy, you can become a better leader for your own German Shepherd.

Your adolescent's behavior will vary widely this month, from puppyish and adorable to adult and elegant, from bravery to bravado, from unsocial and standoffish to social butterfly—all with moments of fear mixed in. At times, you'll find yourself standing still, looking at this German Shepherd, and wondering who he is and what happened to your puppy.

Take a deep breath. This, too, shall pass, and you might as well enjoy it as much as you can. Laugh at him, enjoy the process, and know that in just a few months you'll be seeing a change.

Being a Good Leader

Both human and canine teenagers need good *leaders*. Not just because the teenage brain isn't working well right now, but also so the teenager has a guide for learning how to grow up.

A **leader** is one who guides or commands, a guiding force as part of a team. A leader is one who is looked up to.

John Rosemond, family psychologist, said it best: "Effective leaders are in complete, unflappable possession of their authority. They maintain their cool, purposeful confidence in the face of anything and everything. They can't be disarmed." Although he was writing about the parents of human children, it applies to the owners of puppies, too.

Adult dogs communicate very effectively with puppies and adolescents. When all is going well, the adult is warm and affectionate, plays with the younger dog, and when sleeping, the adult and the younger puppy touch each other. Their relationship is wonderful to watch.

Yet, should the puppy or adolescent push the adult too far, the result is also very clear. The adult gets very still. She stands up on her toes, making herself taller, and turns her body toward the adolescent so her increasing size is obvious. She holds her head up and may lift a lip over one canine, baring it. She'll also make a deep rumble.

If the teenager wilts and shrinks, accepting the correction, the adult will hold the pose for a few moments longer to be sure the communication is understood. Then it's all over. The adult doesn't walk around grumbling for hours, and she doesn't hold a grudge. The communication is clear and concise.

As a human leader for your teenager, you can use some of the adult dog's examples. For example, use eye contact with your puppy. When you can see he's thinking about misbehaving or is getting too rowdy, make eye contact with him and don't smile when you do it. And stand up tall. Don't stoop low to your teenager during this stage of his life. When you pet him, lean over him.

Use your voice, too. When he's beginning to make a mistake, use a deep voice to tell him, "That's enough!"

But at other times, silence is golden. When your puppy is not necessarily making a mistake but is acting out or just being obnoxious, sometimes eye contact and silence is the most effective way of communicating. After all, your puppy is used to either praise or a verbal interruption, but silence can be unsettling.

Don't hold a grudge. When your puppy accepts your guidance, let it be over. That doesn't mean you have to love on your puppy right away—in fact, it's better if you don't. Let him think about what happened.

Always enforce your rules. Don't let the hassles of adolescence cause you to slack off on household and social rules you've already established.

During adolescence, it's important that you continue to be warm and affectionate with your puppy. A good leader is. Just don't praise and pet your puppy immediately after you've had to interrupt bad behavior or a teenage challenge.

Continue to prevent bad behaviors when possible and help your puppy do what you want him to do. When an adolescent challenge arises, think of how your puppy's mother would have handled it.

> **TIPS AND TAILS**

If your teenager puppy growls at you for any reason, don't turn that challenge into a fight. You might lose, and you don't want him to think fighting you is allowed. Stay calm, use his leash to move him away from the situation, and quietly put him in his crate until he calms down.

It would be nice if all you had to do was love your dog. Unfortunately, love isn't enough. You may be providing your German Shepherd with the best food, lots of toys, and top-notch veterinary care because you love him, but that doesn't mean he's going to be a good dog.

Use your leadership skills to help your dog, but don't try to be his best friend at this point. He is, over the coming months, going to be a better friend, but during adolescence, he needs your leadership more than your friendship.

Instead, have a vision of the dog you want your puppy to grow up to be. Liz wanted her first German Shepherd, Watachie, to grow up to be like Rin Tin Tin. She had a vision of the wonderfully well-trained heroic dog. But you know what? Watachie grew up to be even better than Rin Tin Tin. And even more important, Watachie was *her* dog.

Nothing in Life Is Free

One of the easiest ways to ensure your German Shepherd doesn't go through life with a sense of entitlement is to teach him that nothing in life is free. That means he needs to do something for everything he wants.

If he wants a treat, he needs to sit first. If he brings you a toy to throw, he can sit first. He can sit for his meals and while you hook the leash to his collar so you both can go for a walk.

As he matures, though, a single sit may not be enough. He may need to sit, lie down, and then come back up to a sit. He can sit, down, sit, down, and then sit again. Teach him some tricks and have him sit, shake a paw, lie down, and roll over.

Use lots of praise during these sessions, and finish by giving him what he wants, if it's appropriate. It it's not the right time for his meal, for example, or his walk, then don't give it to him. Just praise him for his efforts and release him.

Dealing with Temper Tantrums

Teenagers—both human and canine—tend to think the world revolves around them and they want what they want *right now*.

Canine teenagers can't put their thoughts into words, but their actions convey their thoughts. Your German Shepherd puppy wants to play when he wants to play, and if you're busy, that has no meaning for him. He wants to eat when he's hungry and go outside on his schedule.

> ### TIPS AND TAILS
>
> German Shepherd puppies have a big nose, and they aren't afraid to use it. When your puppy wants attention, he may come up and poke you in the leg or in the behind, or lift your arm with his nose. He can poke you once—maybe he needs to go outside—but if that isn't the problem and he's just trying to get your attention, tell him to knock it off and lie down.

At times, your teenage German Shepherd might throw temper tantrums when things don't go his way, barking, jumping up and down, and otherwise acting like a spoiled puppy. Teenager puppies tend to throw temper tantrums if these behaviors worked well for them in puppyhood. They also throw tantrums when they feel they deserve something and it's not appearing as desired. Some tantrums can even escalate into mouthing and biting.

If your teenager has a temper tantrum, don't scream at him, fight with him, or try to make him behave. During a temper tantrum, his brain isn't thinking; he's simply reacting.

It's important not to get aggressive with your puppy when he's throwing a temper tantrum. Don't grab him and shake him, push him to the ground, or sit on him. In dog language, aggression begets aggression.

Instead, be quiet, and take hold of either his collar or his leash. Then walk him to his crate and quietly put him in it. Close the door and walk away.

If you're not at home and a crate isn't available, walk him away from the scene of the temper tantrum and have him sit, lie down, and stay. Then be sure he does it and have him remain there until he calms down.

After the tantrum is over and your puppy has settled down, don't try to apologize to him or pet him and love him. And also don't hold a grudge or mutter threats at him. Instead, keep calm and be matter of fact. The temper tantrum is over and so is your reaction to it.

Working Through Fear Aggression

When your German Shepherd teenager is afraid, especially in a social situation, his fear could escalate into aggression. This usually happens when he feels he has no way out of the fearful situation. He might be on leash and is being forced to remain where he is, or it might happen when someone corners him such as in the veterinary exam room.

The first step is to recognize when your puppy is afraid and then identify what's causing his fear. When you know what the situation is, you can do something about it.

For example, if you realize your puppy is fearful in the vet exam room, ask the veterinarian if, for that visit, you and your puppy can go to the back of the clinic in the hospital area where there's more room. That way your puppy won't feel as trapped and confined as he might in the small exam room.

Then, later, make a few trips to the vet clinic without an appointment and sit in the lobby, giving him treats and letting the staff give him treats.

After several visits, ask the staff if you can walk him into an empty exam room. With the door open, you and the staff can both give him treats.

Over several more visits, he can then get up on the exam table, lie down on the table, and get some treats with the door closed. The staff can pet him, touch him all over, and even give him a belly rub. A plan of action such as this takes time, but it's well worth the effort.

You can use a similar plan to work through other fearful situations, too. What's important for your dog to understand is that you will help him without putting him into a situation where he feels the need to panic. When your puppy panics, he's no longer thinking.

Physical Development

During your puppy's ninth month of life (weeks 33 through 36), he's about 70 to 80 percent of his adult size. Dogs this age probably weigh between 60 and 70 pounds, with females being on the lighter end of the range.

All 42 of his adult teeth are in now, and the problems associated with teething have stopped. Hopefully, any destructive chewing he started because of teething discomfort hasn't turned into a problem behavior. If you're still seeing some chewing, prevent it from happening as much as possible and keep him supplied with acceptable things to chew.

Getting Lots of Exercise

Your adolescent is more coordinated now and is tripping over his paws less and less each day. He's getting faster when he runs, his stamina is increasing, and he plays longer and harder. The latter is good because exercise is important this month. He needs a chance to play every day and play enough to become tired.

The growth plates on his long legs and shoulder bones haven't closed yet—and won't close until he's 1 to 1½ years old—so continue to restrict hard, repetitive exercise. No jumping or running on hard surfaces, for example, and no repeated jumping even on softer surfaces.

Playing retrieving games is great right now. Just let him stop and breathe every once in a while so he's not continually running. Throw the ball or toy low, too, so he doesn't jump high in the air to catch it. The hard-jarring repetitive motions are what most commonly damage the growth plates, although a single traumatic injury can also hurt him.

> **TIPS AND TAILS**
>
> Combine play and training by throwing the ball for your dog several times and then asking him to lie down and stay for a few minutes. Then repeat. This breaks the exercise session and challenges his brain at the same time.

Increasing Bowel and Bladder Control

Your German Shepherd puppy's bowel and bladder control are better now, too, and he can generally hold off going outside for 6 or 7 hours. This is *possible,* but we don't recommend you make him wait that long as a regular routine, except maybe at night.

Asking him to hold it too long on a regular basis can result in health problems, including urinary tract infections and constipation.

Hopefully your puppy is still crated when you have to leave him alone, so just be sure he's had some exercise and has relieved himself before you put him in his crate. Then pay attention to the time and either let him out yourself or arrange for someone else to let him out in a few hours.

> **HAPPY PUPPY**
>
> Your German Shepherd puppy will be happy in his crate as long as this practice isn't abused. He can spend the night in his crate, and a few hours here and there throughout the day are fine, but don't leave him in there all day. When you do put him in his crate, give him a food-dispensing toy or a treat and praise him.

Health

Most German Shepherd puppies this age are healthy. Any congenital problems have been discovered, hopefully, and the puppy vaccinations are finished. Your puppy is already spayed or neutered, or you and your veterinarian are just waiting until your puppy is a little older to do the surgery. Overall, everything is looking good.

The primary health problem with puppies of this age is an injury. Although any type of injury can happen—from a bruise to a cut—the most common tend to be injuries of the paws or legs.

When Your Puppy Is Limping

If you see your puppy run into something or trip and flip over, you'll know exactly what happened. But sometimes he's having so much fun and so much adrenaline is coursing through his system, he may not even react when he hurts himself. Therefore, you may not even know anything's wrong until he's relaxed after the exercise and gets up limping.

If you see your puppy limping, do some detective work and try to figure out as much as you can:

    ✧ Was your puppy running around the yard? Was he chasing the ball? Did anyone in the family take him for a walk or a run?

❧ Have someone walk your puppy slowly and watch his steps. Where does he appear to be sore? Is he limping on one leg or holding up one leg? Or do multiple limbs appear to be involved?

❧ Massage the shoulder or hip, leg, and paw of the leg you suspect is hurt. Does your puppy react at any specific spot? Compare the potentially hurt leg with the opposite leg. Do the same exam on both legs to find a difference.

When examining your puppy, don't use only your eyes; let your hands feel for differences in your puppy, too. For example, if you think his left front leg is hurt, place your hands on both front legs and gently rub them both at the same time. Feel the sameness or differences between the two legs. Is there a bit of swelling on the injured leg that's not on the other leg?

Once you've found out which leg is hurt, see if you can determine what the problem is. Here are some possibilities:

Broken leg: If his leg is broken, your puppy won't put any weight on that leg. It may also be misshapen or deformed and will be swollen. A broken leg is usually obvious.

Sprain: A sprain is an injury to a ligament. If your puppy has a sprain, he may or may not put any weight on the leg depending on the severity of the sprain. If he does put weight on the leg, he'll limp. There may also be swelling with the sprain.

Strain: A strain is an injury to a muscle or a tendon. As with a sprain, the puppy may or may not put any weight on the injured leg. There's usually swelling.

Infection: A cut on a leg or in a paw, an imbedded foxtail, or another injury that causes a break in the skin can become infected. Sometimes the skin will be healed from the original injury while an infection builds in the underlying tissues. An infection will be red, hot, and sore. Most puppies will lick the infected area, and he'll probably limp if the infection is in the paw but may or may not limp if the infection is in another part of his leg.

When you think you've narrowed down the injury or have eliminated one or more potential problems, call your veterinarian as soon as you can. A broken limb needs immediate care, but all these problems require veterinary care as soon as possible.

Keeping Up with His Energy and Stamina

You'll probably see an increase in your puppy's energy this month. He's sleeping less now than he did when he was younger, and he's more active. He may pester you for attention or beg you to play with him—sometimes to the point of dropping a ball or toy in your lap.

Although his play invitations may be cute initially, they'll get old very quickly. If you respond and play with him each time he asks—or even most of the time—he's going to take advantage of you.

So rather than playing with him every time he asks, ask him to do something else instead, such as *puppy push-ups*. This way you're giving him the attention he wants, but you're working both his mind and body, on your terms.

> **DOG TALK**

Puppy push-ups consist of having your puppy sit when you ask, then lie down, then sit, then lie down. Have him do just a couple repetitions at first. As he learns to do push-ups, he can do more reps at a time.

Your puppy's stamina is also increasing as he gets stronger. When he was younger, he might have been tired after a half-hour play session, but this month he'll still be going strong after an hour. Although he needs the exercise and time with you, don't think he needs to be exhausted after every playtime. Far too many injuries occur when the puppy is overtired because he no longer pays attention to where he's going or what he's doing.

Many owners of an adolescent German Shepherd report that their puppy sometimes plays hard and then stops as quickly as if they had hit a wall. This is an adolescent characteristic. Where adult dogs might work, rest, and work some more, the adolescent runs and runs and runs until he can't run anymore. He crashes, sleeps, and is ready to go again.

If you find one day that your puppy seems to have low energy, pay attention. Although German Shepherds can have a lack of energy during major growth spurts, most of the time a marked lack of energy is often related to a health problem. Many diseases have a lack of energy as a symptom, as does an infestation of parasites or heartworms. It can also be the result of an inadequate diet.

If the lack of energy is accompanied by other symptoms, note those and call your veterinarian. If the only symptom is lethargy, watch your puppy for a couple days and see if he returns to normal. If he doesn't, call your veterinarian.

Nutrition

This age isn't the time to make any changes in your puppy's food. He still needs a good-quality protein-based food appropriate for all life stages. If he's been doing well on his present diet, continue feeding as you have been.

Determining His Caloric Needs

Adolescent puppies generally have 1.25 times the caloric needs of adult dogs the same size. So if your puppy weighs 70 pounds right now, let's compare him to a 70-pound adult. The adult, if active and not sedentary, needs between 1,800 and 2,100 calories a day. Based on those numbers, your adolescent needs 2,250 to 2,625 calories a day.

For comparison, the National Research Council recommends that an adult dog who weighs 70 pounds and has an average activity routine should eat 1,768 calories per day. An adult dog who weighs 90 pounds and is also at an average activity should eat 2,135 calories per day. As you can see, a 20-pound difference in the dog's weight makes a big difference in calorie needs.

Active dogs need even more calories because they burn so many more. An adult dog who weighs 70 pounds and is active needs 1,800 to 2,100 calories per day. A 90-pound, active, adult dog needs 2,200 to 2,500 calories per day.

> **TIPS AND TAILS**
>
> What constitutes an active dog is not well defined. If your German Shepherd puppy patrols the backyard several times a day, plays hard regularly, is participating in training, and is not as apt to take a nap in the sunshine as other puppies, consider him active.

These amounts are averages, and each dog is different. Continue to monitor your puppy's body condition (see Appendix B), and adjust his food according to his needs, feeding him two meals a day. If he prefers one meal over another, feed more at that meal. However, don't feed to just one meal a day. Your puppy may well eat too fast or too much at that one meal, which could lead to vomiting or potentially bloat.

Putting Your Overweight Adolescent on a Diet

If you're feeding your German Shepherd puppy a commercial food for all life stages or a puppy food, be aware that the feeding guidelines on the package are simply that: guidelines. If you feed the amount recommended, your puppy could potentially end up overweight. Again, it's important to monitor his body condition and feed him what he needs rather than what the package recommends.

Not many German Shepherd adolescents are overweight; most are too active to be heavy. However, if you evaluate your teenager's body condition using Appendix B and you feel he's overweight, you can adjust his diet.

Don't simply cut his food significantly or you'll have a hungry—and very unhappy—teenager. He may then decide to eat the cat's food, steal food off the kitchen counter, or raid the trashcan.

Instead, cut his food very slightly each day and add extra fiber to make him feel full. For example, for the first week of his diet, cut his food by $\frac{1}{4}$ cup and replace that with $\frac{1}{4}$ cup cooked or steamed green beans. At the end of the week, evaluate his body condition. If he's lost some weight, continue without making any additional changes.

If he doesn't appear to have lost any weight, decrease his food by $\frac{1}{3}$ cup instead and again add that amount of green beans. Feed him this way for another week and then evaluate the results.

> **HAPPY PUPPY**
>
> High-fiber foods most dogs enjoy include green beans, wax beans, grated zucchini, grated squash, puréed pumpkin, and broccoli florets. Before you feed these, lightly cook or steam them so they're more digestible.

During this time, extend your walks, play sessions, or exercise. Weight loss for dogs is the same as it is for people: fewer calories in and more calories burned equals weight loss.

Grooming

Your German Shepherd teenager doesn't need any major grooming (and far less than many other dog breeds), and other than his shedding, none of the grooming chores are extreme. That's one of the wonderful traits of this breed!

Some grooming chores should occur on a regular basis all year around, of course, including wiping the sleep from his eyes, cleaning his ears, cleaning his teeth, and brush-ing his coat. You may need to clean under his tail once in a while and perhaps trim the hair back there. This is especially important for lush-coated dogs. When your German Shepherd gets dirty, a bath may be in order. Other than that, grooming is easy.

However, there are a few things to keep in mind as the seasons change. These vary according to where you and your dog live. Obviously, winter grooming needs in San Diego are very different from those in Chicago.

Grooming in the Spring

After a winter inside when the house was heated, your German Shepherd puppy's coat is apt to be dry. Be sure he's eating a good diet with natural fats (such as from meat) to help him grow a healthy coat.

The first thing to be ready for come spring is shedding. All German Shepherds shed in the spring, but if you live in a cold climate and your dog grew in a thick win-ter coat, he's going to shed a lot as spring arrives. Daily brushing is a great idea, with a pin brush first, and then a rake, and followed by a natural-bristle brush.

> ### TIPS AND TAILS
>
> Dyson has created a handy grooming brush that attaches to a vacuum cleaner hose so as you brush your puppy, the loose hair is sucked up. It's best to introduce this gradually so he accepts it. Without using the brush, turn on the vacuum. Stand a few feet away, and give your puppy a few treats. Turn off the vacuum, and praise him. Repeat this several times. Then brush your puppy with the vacuum hose attached to the brush but with the vacuum off. Praise him again. Do this a few times over several days and then, with some good treats, brush him with the vacuum on. If he's nervous, keep the session short, and praise and reward him after. Gradually work up to a full brushing session.

In many parts of the country, the first ticks show up in the spring as soon as weather warms up. Don't forget to examine your puppy often, especially after he walks in tall grass or brushy areas.

Spring is also the time to start your dog on flea, tick, and heartworm medications if you took him off those preventatives during the winter months. Your veterinarian may want to do a heartworm check before prescribing new medications.

Grooming in the Summer

Parasites are one of the biggest challenges during the summer months. Your German Shepherd should remain on the flea, tick, and heartworm medications, depending on where you live and the pests in your area. Talk to your veterinarian about whether you need to be concerned about any of these.

Protect your puppy from mosquitoes during the summer, too. Some citronella spray or a natural pest repellent often works well. Pay particular attention to his face, paws, and ears, but know a mosquito can get to his skin anywhere if his coat is parted.

One of the common complaints German Shepherd owners mention during the summer is fly bites on their puppy's ears. Flies will bite the tips of his ears, and with repeated bites will draw blood. This attracts more flies, and pretty soon, the ears are being eaten by the flies.

Some German Shepherd owners use repellent sprays to keep the flies away, but most German Shepherds hate sprays in their face. The most recommended product that's effective and also easy to use is SWAT, a pyrethrin-based ointment that both repels and kills flies. It's made for horses, but it's safe for dogs, too. Simply rub the ointment on his ears and anywhere else the flies are biting. It helps heal wounds as well as repel the flies.

> **TIPS AND TAILS**
>
> You might see hot spots on your puppy during the summer due to allergies or a wound that he won't stop scratching. Remember, they require veterinary care and medications to heal.

As grasses and weeds dry out in the summer heat, watch for seeds that can torment your German Shepherd. Foxtails, burrs, and other seeds are made to catch fur as an animal walks by—that's how the seeds are dispersed. Unfortunately, when they get caught in your German Shepherd's coat, they can work down into his skin, create matts in his coat, and lodge between the pads of his feet. Just as you check him for fleas and ticks, check him for grass and weed seeds, too.

Grooming in the Fall

Depending on where you live, fall grooming needs can be a continuation of summer's. Keep an eye on your puppy's coat, and watch for fleas, ticks, and especially grass and weed seeds. Be on the lookout for fly bites on the ears, too, because they can still be a problem, especially during a fall heat wave.

Fall is also a prelude to winter, and your German Shepherd will begin shedding again. This time, he's losing his summer coat and growing in his new winter coat. This shedding usually isn't as heavy as his spring shed, but it's still impressive.

Many German Shepherd owners like to bathe their dogs in the fall, especially once the shedding has begun in earnest, because the bath loosens all the dead coat. When your puppy has dried after the bath, you can brush him and really get out a lot of the dead coat.

Grooming in the Winter

In many parts of the United States, fleas and ticks disappear during most of the winter months, as do mosquitoes and flies when the weather is colder. That relieves some grooming chores. However, winter brings with it some additional concerns.

If your community puts down salt or other products to melt ice or keep sidewalks and streets safe during winter weather, be sure to wash your German Shepherd's paws when you get back home. Don't let him lick his paws before you wash them because many of these products can be harmful.

> **HAPPY PUPPY**
>
> Look into dog boots for your German Shepherd. These protect his paws in the winter from both the ice and the products used to melt the ice on streets and sidewalks. Use lots of treats, praise, and patience as you teach your puppy to wear these boots.

When your German Shepherd puppy comes in from outside when there's snow on the ground, check his paws for balls of snow and ice between his pads. These can form quickly, and they hurt. If you see him licking his paws, this may be what's going on.

If your German Shepherd's coat appears to be drying out because of the dry air in your home, add some flaxseed oil to his food. This nutritious oil will help keep the coat healthy. If you find your skin drying out, too, you may want to use a humidifier to add moisture to the air and help you and your dog, too.

Social Skills

As your puppy's adolescence continues, so should the work you began last month with his social skills. His attitude this month is probably much like it was last month … if not a little worse.

He may be unsocial toward both unknown people and other dogs, so continue taking him out in public, especially to a dog-training class, and make him behave himself. Don't expect him to be the social butterfly he was earlier in puppyhood, but do require him to be well behaved.

Introducing Mother Nature

Your German Shepherd adolescent is being somewhat unsocial right now, but he still needs to get out of the house. So this is a good time to introduce him to Mother Nature. Hopefully, he's already been for walks in different places and has had an introduction to the world around him.

Make a concerted effort this month to find some different places where you and your teenager can enjoy the world around you:

🐾 If you live near an ocean, go to the beach with your puppy. Let him sniff the sand and seaweed and splash in the waves. Play tug-of-war with a long piece of seaweed. He may even want to swim.

> ### HAPPY PUPPY
>
> Liz's second German Shepherd, Michi, loved to swim in the ocean but didn't feel Liz was capable of being safe in the water. Every time Liz went in, he would push or drag her back to the beach. He was happiest if he was swimming and Liz just watched.

🐾 Visit a forest. Your German Shepherd's nose will work overtime with all the smells there. Trees, underbrush, and wildlife will amaze him.

🐾 Go for a walk in a meadow. The grasses, flowers, and sunshine will refresh both of your souls.

🐾 Find a shallow river or creek nearby. Splash in the water, look for fish, or find a crawdad for your puppy to investigate.

While you and your teenager check out all these new things, keep him on leash. He's not mentally mature enough yet to be allowed off-leash freedom, especially in new situations and places like these. But don't worry; you're not spoiling things for him by keeping him on leash. Instead, you and he can share all these new things together because you're closer to each other.

Keeping him on leash and close to you also keeps him safer. You can watch for bees that might sting him or snakes that would do him harm. You can help him make better decisions, too.

Teach your puppy to wear a doggy backpack. Because he's still growing, you're not going to ask him to carry much weight in the backpack, but he can carry a couple of water bottles, a foldable water bowl for his use, and some doggy bags.

Helping Him Through Fearful Moments

Adolescents can have fearful moments even if they're no longer in one of the traditional fear periods we discussed in earlier chapters. These fearful moments don't mean your German Shepherd isn't brave; instead, they're a sign that he's smart and recognizes when something is potentially amiss.

Fear is a survival tool. If a human or canine becomes fearful in certain situations, that person or dog is more likely to make a better decision that could lead to survival. A dog or person who is overly brave might get himself hurt.

If your German Shepherd is uncertain or fearful in a situation, just stop, ask him to sit, and let him observe and think about what's going on. As the two of you watch and your teenager muddles through his worries, he knows you're by his side and you're not going to let anything happen to him.

During other fearful moments, you can help your German Shepherd teenager succeed. For example, the first time Liz took Michi to see a redwood forest in northern California, Liz wanted to walk on top of a fallen redwood. Michi, however, was only 9 months old and was cautious about this idea. So Liz encouraged him to jump up on this huge log, and they just sat there, side by side, for a few minutes. Then Liz stood up and as she did, so did Michi, but they just stood still. Gradually, over an hour or so, they began moving while Liz talked to Michi, encouraged him, and praised his bravery when he began walking the log.

If Liz had forced Michi to walk along the log without giving him a chance to get used to it, he may have panicked and jumped, hurting himself. Or he may have followed Liz, but as he did, his fears might have escalated.

By helping Michi do what she asked, but also by giving him time to get used to their new adventure, he was able to work through his fear. Plus, he learned again he could trust Liz, something all dogs need to feel with their people.

Training

German Shepherds are intelligent working dogs, bred to do a job. Keep this in mind as your teenager pushes all your buttons this month.

As he tests his limits and tries to amuse himself by doing some strange things—perhaps rearranging the pile of firewood in the backyard or herding the family cat—don't get into the habit of repeatedly saying, "Sweetie, no." His name isn't "Sweetie-no-bad-dog," and you don't want him to think it is.

Focus on helping him do what is right rather than allowing him to make mistakes. That means you to have to be sure the house and yard are still puppy-proofed (or adolescent-proofed). Be sure he gets plenty of exercise and training opportunities so both his body and mind are challenged.

Continuing Using the Crate

Even though your puppy is getting big and looks more like an adult German Shepherd every day, remember, he's not all grown up yet. At 9 months, he's still mentally immature and isn't yet making good decisions, so don't stop using his crate. If you allow him too much freedom right now, he might start urinating in the house. He probably wouldn't be breaking housetraining but instead would be marking, claiming things as his own.

Destructive behaviors can also rear their ugly head this month if you give your puppy too much freedom. He may decide to chew on things that are heavy with your scent such as the television remote control, your shoes and socks, or your cell phone. Crating your teenager when he's not being supervised can prevent these behaviors.

When your puppy isn't in his crate, continue to keep him close to you. When he's feeling rebellious, he may try to distance himself from you, but don't allow it to happen. Close doors, keep him leashed to you, or use baby gates. This, too, can prevent bad behaviors.

> **HAPPY PUPPY**
>
> Even though your teenager's brain is a muddle of emotions and thoughts, keep his training as positive as possible. Yes, interrupt bad behaviors, but also put more focus on preventing bad behaviors and teaching your puppy how to succeed.

Making "Come" Fun

"Come" is an important exercise and one you'll use with your German Shepherd all his life. You want him to think coming to you is the absolute best thing he can ever do.

Remember, never call your German Shepherd to you to scold or punish him. Always keep it fun, exciting, and rewarding. Praise him for coming, pet him, and give him a treat or a toy. And never call him to come in a situation where he'll ignore you. Do something else instead, such as, "Sweetie, cookies!" Or walk up to him and leash him.

To keep the come fun, play games while you practice the come exercise. Not only will your dog have fun but so will you, and when you have fun, you're more apt to practice it.

If several people live in your household, everyone can practice "Come" with this game:

🐾 Hook up a 20-foot-long leash or length of rope to your puppy's collar. Tie a bean bag to the handle end of the leash. Everyone should have some treats in their pocket.

🐾 Have everyone form a circle. One person can begin the game by holding the puppy's collar. That person should then toss the bean bag to someone across the circle.

🐾 The second person then calls the puppy, and praises him and gives him a treat when he comes. If the puppy doesn't come directly across the circle, the second person uses the leash to be sure the puppy does come without any detours.

🐾 The second person then tosses the bean bag to a third person, who calls the puppy.

Five minutes of this game, with everyone calling and cheering on the puppy, is fun. At the same time, this game teaches the puppy that he needs to listen to everyone in the house.

Teaching "Stand and Stay"

When your puppy was younger, most of the emphasis in his training was on teaching him self-control. Often that meant having him sit, down, and stay. These exercises required him to be aware of his own actions and to hold still. Now, though, even in adolescence, he should have a good idea of what self-control is and what "Sit," "Down," and "Stay" mean.

The "*Stand and stay*" exercise is very nice and builds on the skills you've already taught your German Shepherd. You can use "Stand and stay" at the veterinary clinic so your vet can examine your puppy. Or you can use it when you're brushing your dog. If you're out for a walk in bad weather, you can ask your puppy to stand and stay rather than sit so he stays cleaner.

> ### DOG TALK
>
> "**Stand and stay**" means remain upright with all four paws on the floor and hold still.

Teaching your dog to stand isn't difficult—other than he may be confused because so much emphasis has been put on sit and down. But the stand and stay is a little harder because when your puppy is standing, it's so easy to take a step forward. And then another step forward ….

Here's how to teach the stand and stay:

🐾 Have your puppy on leash, hold the leash in your left hand, and have some treats in your right hand.

🐾 With your puppy on your left side, let him sniff the treat in your right hand, and move your hand forward so he gets up and follows it.

🐾 After he steps forward, gently place your left hand under his belly to keep him standing and prevent him from sitting. Tell him, "Sweetie, stand," and give him the treat. After he eats the treat, release him and praise him.

🐾 Repeat several times and then give him a break and play with him Then try it again.

🐾 When he's standing well and not trying to sit, tell him, "Sweetie, stay." Initially don't go anywhere—remain standing by his side—because he may associate "Stay" with either the sit or the down. Just have him stand and stay a few seconds and then praise and release him.

Teaching the Emergency Down

When you taught your puppy to lie down, you asked him to sit first and then lie down. There was a purpose to this. If he was sitting, to have him lie down, you just needed him to lower his front half.

But sometimes you may want to him lie down immediately. Perhaps you drop a glass to the floor and it shatters. You want your puppy to immediately lie down and stay so he doesn't step on any of the glass.

This quick down and stay is called the emergency down, but to save your puppy from some confusion with a second "Down" you'll tell your puppy, "Sweetie, place!"

Here's how:

🐾 Have your puppy on leash, and have some treats in your right hand.

🐾 Walk forward with your puppy by your left side at a fairly brisk pace.

🐾 As you're walking, place your left hand on your puppy's shoulder. Bend over, hold a treat in front of his nose as you tell him, "Sweetie, place," and take the treat in a motion to the ground in front of him. Make a line from your puppy's nose to the ground. Don't have him stop and sit; just go straight down to the ground.

🐾 Your hand on the puppy's shoulder can help keep him from getting back up or from fighting you, but don't use the hand on his shoulder to push him into the ground; that's too rough.

🐾 Praise your puppy and then release him.

> **TIPS AND TAILS**

Walking briskly helps make this exercise easier. If you're walking slowly, your puppy may brace against you. However, when moving quickly, that momentum can help him move right into the down.

Practicing, Practicing, and More Practicing

We can't emphasize it enough: you need to practice your German Shepherd's training skills. Your dog has to have what's called *behavior rehearsals* so he can learn what you're teaching him. He has to practice those skills over and over and over, with positive reinforcements, until the behaviors become habits.

> **DOG TALK**

Behavior rehearsal means practicing a new behavior, with guidance, so it can be learned and then performed as a normal behavior.

When you're teaching your dog different skills, such as obedience training, he has no idea why it's so important to you. So you need to practice these new skills with him and reward him for doing them right on a regular basis.

You and Your Puppy

Your German Shepherd is an adolescent now, but remember that adolescents are still puppies. Your German Shepherd is quite immature mentally. He's definitely not a grown-up even though he's beginning to look like one.

One of the biggest mistakes many German Shepherd puppy owners do right now is treat their adolescent like an adult. Unfortunately, the puppy is going to get into trouble. He's going to get distracted and run from his owner and ignore her calls to come. He may challenge an adult dog and end up in a fight. He could chew up an expensive cell phone. It's worth repeating: he's going to get into trouble.

Keep in mind he's still a puppy. And he's going to be one for several more months yet. Remember, too, that any bad behaviors during adolescence are not personal attacks on you. They may be directed at you because you're the adult, or they may seem like they're directed at you just because you're the closest. There's often no rhyme or reason to teenage behavior.

Your emphasis with your puppy this month should be on developing your leadership skills. Concentrate on providing your teenager with guidance and leadership. Remember that good leaders are kind, they're caring, and they communicate clearly when they have a message to convey.

During all this adolescent stuff, and with all the new rules, don't forget to have fun with your puppy. To like your puppy, you need to have some fun with him. And he needs to have fun with you to like you. All work and no play makes for a dull dog and an unhappy dog owner. Neither of you wants that.

Socialization in public

Adult teeth are in—chewing continues

Ready for more advanced training

Moderate growth

Your German Shepherd puppy is still an adolescent this month (weeks 37 through 40), and she's going to show some typical teenager behaviors. She may be loving and affectionate one moment and ignore you the next. As we've mentioned in previous months, sharing your home with a canine teenager requires patience and a sense of humor.

At the same time, though, your German Shepherd is ready to work. In fact, she needs work. A job or two helps keep her brain challenged, focused, and out of trouble. Working together is also good for your relationship. It helps build that bond between you, which comes in especially handy when your teenager frustrates you.

Training

Training is an excellent way to exercise your *adolescent*'s brain. She needs to think about things, what to do and what not to do, and the best way to do that right now is by continuing to learn. Training can also become one of her jobs.

Finding What Motivates Him

It's time to re-evaluate the motivators you're using for getting and keeping your German Shepherd's attention. When she was a young puppy, it was probably quite easy to get her attention with food treats. But she's changed a lot over the past few months, and what motivates her may well have changed, too.

Ideally, your voice as you praise her should be a good motivator. If you can say, "Sweetie, good job! Thank you!" and her head comes up, she looks at you, and her tail wags wildly, you know that's a good motivator.

An **adolescent** is one who is immature, past puberty but not yet an adult.

You're going to need more than just your voice for those adolescent times when she's more distracted than normal. Try some different food treats so you have a few choices. The ideal treats are small, they have a good smell, and your dog can eat them quickly.

Think outside the box when it comes to treats. You've probably been using some bits of meat and cubes of cheese. But how about pieces of apple slices, slices of baby carrots, or bits of cooked sweet potato? Try some dry kibble cat food, maybe with a fish flavor.

Vary the treats you use from day to day and training session to training session. Your puppy will be more excited if she has no idea what treat you have until you begin your training session.

Your German Shepherd may be motivated more by toys than food. A tennis ball tossed in the air for your dog to catch can create some great enthusiasm. A tug toy is also good for building excitement.

Try some different things to see what excites your dog. Then use a few of those things as rewards during your training sessions.

Enrolling in Class ... Again

You and your dog have probably attended a kindergarten puppy class as well as a basic obedience class. Hopefully the two of you were successful in these classes and learned a lot.

You may want to repeat that basic class this month, especially if your teenager has been pushing your buttons with her adolescent escapades. Repeating the class doesn't mean she's bad. It just means she's an adolescent and needs the work.

When you both repeat the class, learning the basic skills doesn't have to be the focus of your attention. You both know those skills, so now you can spend more time working on bettering those skills—making the sit quicker and nicely by your side, for example, or making the down neat and quick rather than sprawled all over. Plus, if your German Shepherd has been showing some less-than-desirable behaviors during this month—such as jumping on people or barking inappropriately—you can work on those problems during training.

If you feel that repeating a basic obedience class would be too much of a repetition, talk to your trainer and get her recommendation. She can evaluate your dog and let you know which class you should attend.

Training for Life

Your training shouldn't be limited to just training class and practice sessions. Some dogs learn the lesson that training means these skills apply only at certain times and in certain places. That's a bad lesson for your dog to learn because then she'll assume that all other times are open for other behaviors.

To prevent this, practice anytime, anywhere, especially those times and places where you want your adolescent to behave himself. Here are some examples:

🐾 When you're waiting for the water for your tea to heat, ask your dog to sit, down, sit, down, and stay.

🐾 When you take the trash outside, ask her to sit at the door and stay.

🐾 Ask your dog to come across the living room and sit in front of you.

🐾 Have her come to you down the hall and sit in front of you.

🐾 While you're out on a walk, ask her to sit and stay at each curb. Then give her permission to walk with you.

🐾 When you go down the block to talk to your neighbor, ask your teenager to sit while your neighbor pets her.

When you practice these skills often and in different places, they become second nature to your puppy. She's also less apt to challenge you as much when the exercises are practiced often.

Teaching "Heel"

In Month 4, you learned how to introduce your puppy to walking on a leash without pulling. Constant pulling is annoying. Plus, she has what's called an *oppositional reflex*: pulling leads to more pulling and then even more—it's a vicious circle. Your German Shepherd adolescent doesn't have to pull. There's no reason why she can't learn to walk nicely on the leash. It just requires some training, practice, and self-control on her part.

This command is the "*Heel.*" When your German Shepherd heels, her job is to maintain her position by your left side no matter where and how you walk. That means if you get caught out in the rain and need to jog back to the house, your puppy should maintain that position beside you. If you're walking through a crowd, she still needs to maintain that position. When she heels, she is to pay attention to you and stay in the heel position.

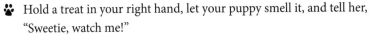

DOG TALK

Oppositional reflex causes the dog to push against force. If you pull on your dog's leash, she will pull back. It you push her, she will push against you. "**Heel**" means your puppy should walk by your side with her shoulder next to your left leg. She needs to maintain that position no matter what the distractions.

The difference between the no-pull exercise in Month 4 and the heel this month is your puppy's level of self-control. In her fourth month, she had enough concentration that you could keep some slack in the leash but only enough that if she got distracted and dashed to the end of the leash, she'd get pulled back. You probably had to remind her several times about the tightness of the leash.

At 4 months, your puppy was too mentally immature to learn and perform the heel. Plus, even if she did learn it—and some owners do teach the heel at a younger age—it would have been difficult for her to concentrate for long. However, now, in her tenth month, there's no reason why she can't develop enough concentration to heel with you.

Here's how to teach "Heel":

🐾 Leash your teenager and have her sit by your left side. Have a pocketful of high-value treats.

🐾 Let your left hand hang naturally by your side. Gather the leash so most of the slack is taken up but it's not tight. If the clip of the leash is hanging loose, that's good.

🐾 Hold a treat in your right hand, let your puppy smell it, and tell her, "Sweetie, watch me!"

🐾 When you have her attention, tell her, "Sweetie, heel," and begin walking forward.

🐾 When she's walking with you, doing the "Watch me," praise her, "Good girl! Yeah!"

🐾 If she gets distracted, use that treat to get her attention again.

🐾 After about 10 steps, stop and have her sit. Praise her when she does.

🐾 Repeat these steps several times and then stop and take a break to play with your puppy for a few minutes. Then repeat the steps again.

▶ TIPS AND TAILS

Use your voice as a training tool to tell your puppy what to do, praise her, and interrupt bad behaviors. Use treats to lure her and reward her. Use the leash to be sure she stays close to you.

Don't get into a pulling war with your puppy; that will cause her to fight you even more. Instead, focus on helping her succeed by using these steps.

If she's determined to pull, simply turn and walk the other direction. For example, when she pulls forward, without any warning to her, simply hold the leash so it doesn't pull out of your hands, turn around, and walk the other direction. When the leash tightens, she's going to turn to see what happened. If she catches up with you, dashes past, and tries to pull again, turn around again. It may take a few repetitions before she decides to pay more attention to you. When she does, praise her.

Gradually, over several weeks, extend the distance you ask her to heel before giving her a break. If she gets distracted, can't seem to maintain focus, or is having trouble with the heel, back up a few training steps. Stop, repeat the initial training steps, and reteach her. Vary your treats, making sure you have a high-value treat for the lure and reward, and give her plenty of verbal praise to motivate her.

Also, don't be in a hurry to stop using the treats. Consider them a training tool, just like your voice and the leash. You won't have to use treats forever, but they are an important part of the training process now and through adolescence.

Making "Heel" Fun

Heeling in a straight line all the time can be boring for you and your teenager with a short attention span. So when she understands the heel, add some variation to it:

🐾 Heel 10 feet at a fast pace, turn around 180 degrees, heel 10 feet, stop, and have your dog sit.

🐾 With your dog heeling, jog, walk a normal speed, walk slowly, and jog again.

🐾 Place two outside trashcans about 10 feet apart, and heel in a figure-eight pattern around the cans. Stop and ask your puppy to sit when you're between the two cans.

🐾 Have your German Shepherd heel, stop, sit, go forward again at the heel, stop, and down. Heel forward, stop, and have her stand.

These are just a few suggestions. We're sure you can come up with some variations of your own. Just mix it all up so you and your dog stay focused, entertained, and enjoy your training sessions together.

Preparing for Off Leash

One of the goals many German Shepherd owners have is off-leash control. And who can blame them? The idea of their dog working without a leash is exciting! Unfortunately, most owners try to train their dog off leash too soon, when their puppy is still an adolescent, and the training backfires because she's not ready.

Teaching your German Shepherd to work for you without a leash is two-pronged: you want to instill in her the desire to work for you and you also want to teach her she has no choice.

To build that desire to work for you, you have to work on motivation. Find those treats or toys or tugs that really get your German Shepherd excited. And learn to use your voice to get her amped up to do something—anything—for you. Keep that motivation high as you train with her. Keep her on her tiptoes, watching you, with her tongue out, eyes bright, and tail wagging. If she's getting bored and distracted, either you lost your motivation or your training session was too long.

> **HAPPY PUPPY**
>
> To practice your verbal praise, start talking to your dog using a happy voice. Your goal is to have her wag her tail; make her dance; and have her wiggle, dance, and bounce all over. The power of your voice is amazing, but you have to know how to use it.

To teach your adolescent that she has no choice, continue training with the leash throughout her adolescence. Make working for you a habit so she's no longer challenging or testing you. Vary the leashes you use, too, so no particular leash means cooperation. Use a 6-foot leash, a 4-foot leash, and a short traffic leash. And have a leather one, a nylon one, and perhaps even a makeshift rope leash. The idea is that she cooperates with you no matter what.

Don't try training your dog without a leash for at least 6 to 8 more months—and longer, if at 1½ she's still mentally immature. If you try too soon, she may decide to dash away from you and then you'll have to refresh her training from the very beginning to get that idea out of her head.

Practicing Stepping and Jumping

Your teenager is coordinated enough now to begin learning how to step and jump with some grace. Up to now, she's probably scrambled up into the car or dashed up and down the stairs with great glee … but no coordination.

Unfortunately, this lack of coordination often leads to injuries, and because teenagers tend to hurt themselves enough as it is, you should do all you can to prevent harm from befalling your pup. There are several exercises you can do to help your teenager be aware of her legs and feet, how to use them, and where to place them.

For the first exercise, you'll need four or five long sticks, broomsticks, or 2×4s. Place them on the ground, parallel to each other, and about 18 inches apart.

With your teenager on leash, simply walk up to the sticks and walk over them. If your puppy steps over the sticks without knocking into them, praise her. If she trips over them, ignore her. Do this several times, using verbal encouragement and even a few treats as motivation.

When she can do that well, elevate one end of each of the sticks. If you have a couple extra 2×4s, place them under one end of the sticks so the end is 4 inches off the ground. Again, walk over the sticks so your puppy picks up each foot and steps over the sticks. Praise her when she does. Repeat several times.

Then walk quickly or even jog over the sticks. You can step over the lower end and have your puppy jog over the higher end. Again, praise her when she shows some thought and coordination.

Throughout several training sessions over a couple weeks, gradually increase the distance between the sticks to about 4 to 6 feet. At the same time, increase the height of the sticks to about a foot high. Run alongside the sticks so your puppy can jump them but you don't have to. Praise her enthusiastically when she does so.

> **TIPS AND TAILS**
>
> Don't raise the sticks any higher than 12 inches, and keep the training sessions short. Higher jumps with hard landings and repetitive jumping can damage your puppy's growth plates. Remember, those won't close for several months. Practice on good footing such as grass, carpet, or any padded flooring so your puppy doesn't slip.

Practicing Climbing

Climbing also takes some coordination. This training exercise is a little harder to set up, but if you can find something for your dog to climb when out on hikes, that would work just fine.

Look for a steep, short bank, like above a retaining wall. With your dog on leash, encourage her to climb it. You want her on leash so you can help her if she needs it or, more likely, to save her should she get her legs tangled up with each other. She can also clamber up on a boulder, on the trunk of a fallen tree, or up several levels of a retaining wall.

Never ask her to do this by herself without your help. At this age, she would be more apt to hurt herself. Always be close to your adolescent, with a good hold on the leash, and help her climb. As with any other training, you want her to succeed at this, not hurt herself.

Continuing the Crate

You might be tempted to put your adolescent's crate away until you get your next puppy. After all, your teenager hasn't had a housetraining accident in a long time. But don't do it.

Continue using her crate for several more months. Not only does the crate continue to give her her own spot—a place of refuge—but it also helps prevent problem behaviors now, as it has the past several months.

Just as your adolescent isn't mentally mature enough to train off leash, she isn't mature enough for complete freedom of the house when you aren't supervising her. She may have a few days when she behaves herself, but then one day she'll have too much energy or she'll be bored and she'll chew on something she shouldn't. Or she'll empty the trashcans or eat the cat's food. She'll find something to do that she shouldn't be doing.

So use the crate to keep your teenager out of trouble when you can't supervise her. She should still sleep in the crate at night, too.

Physical Development

As your puppy grows and looks more adult and less like a puppy, she's also looking more like a German Shepherd. You may have noticed that although all German Shepherds share some characteristics, they don't all look exactly alike. Some dogs are larger than others, and some have heavier bodies. Colors vary, too, as do coat lengths.

However, there is an ideal German Shepherd. The German Shepherd breed standard is what keeps a German Shepherd looking like a German Shepherd rather than, say, a Greyhound.

The German Shepherd Breed Standard

The German Shepherd Dog Club of America was founded in 1913 and incorporated in 1916. The purpose of the club was—and is—to promote the breeding of quality German Shepherds and to promote the working aspects of the breed, especially as a law-enforcement, military, herding, and service dog. For many years, the club has also promoted events for the breed, including dog shows and working events, and offered prizes for those events.

Most importantly, the club, which is also called the parent club, maintains the breed standard. This written description of the ideal German Shepherd is the guideline for the breed. Breeders can compare their breeding stock to the standard and then strive to produce a more perfect dog. Judges for conformation dog shows can study the standard and then choose those dogs who best compare to the standard as winners.

The standard applies to adult dogs. Several characteristics, including the depth of the chest and even the dog's color as an adult, won't be fully developed in your puppy at only 10 months or even 1 year. However, let's take a look at several of the most important points of the standard. You can find the complete breed standard at the AKC's website: akc.org/breeds/german_shepherd_dog.

General appearance: The German Shepherd is first and foremost an athlete. She must be strong, agile, and well muscled to perform the jobs she was bred to do. She should look well balanced, with no part of her outweighing another. Males must look masculine, and females must look decidedly feminine.

Temperament: The ideal German Shepherd is one who is ready, willing, and eager to do what is asked of her. She is a working dog above all else, confident, eager, and alert. She is not fearful or shy or cringing, while at the same time she is not aggressive or dangerous, either.

Size: Males should be between 24 and 26 inches at the withers, the point of the shoulder. Females should be between 22 and 24 inches.

Proportion: These dogs are longer than they are tall. Length is measured from the point of the breastbone to the rear edge of the pelvis. The ideal proportion is 10 to 8.5, length to height.

Head: The head is in proportion to the body. Males have a larger, more masculine head, while females have a more feminine one. The head is strong, the skin is tight, the muzzle is long, and the topline of the muzzle is parallel to the topline of the skull. The eyes are medium sized, almond shaped, and very dark. The ears are pricked (upright) with a moderate point and are positioned so the opening of the ears is forward. The nose is black. The jaws are strong, and the mouth contains 42 teeth. The front teeth meet in a *scissors bite*.

> **DOG TALK**

A **scissors bite** is where the inside of the top front incisors meet the outer side of the bottom front incisors.

Neck, body, and back: The neck is strong, muscular, and in proportion to the rest of the body. When excited, the head is carried high, but normally the head is carried forward and slightly higher than the shoulders. The body gives the impression of strength without bulkiness. The point of the shoulders is higher than the back and slopes downward to a straight back.

Chest: The chest is deep and is carried well down between the legs. There's ample room for the lungs and heart, yet it's never barrel shaped. The shape of the chest should allow for free movement of the front legs.

Front legs: The upper arm joins the shoulder blade at a right angle. The front legs are straight with an oval bone rather than round. The pasterns are strong and provide spring to the dog's steps. The dewclaws can be removed but normally are not. The feet are compact with well-arched toes, thick pads, and short, dark nails.

Hips and rear legs: The thigh is well muscled, and the upper thigh and lower thigh form as close as possible to a right angle. Dewclaws on the rear legs should be removed. The rear feet should be the same as the front feet.

Tail: The tail is long, with the last vertebrae reaching to the dog's hocks, and carried low. The coat is bushy and thick.

Coat: The coat is a double coat of medium-length fur. The outer coat is dense, with the hair straight and lying close to the body. A slightly wavy or wiry texture is permissible. The head, legs, and paws have a shorter coat. The back of the legs has a slightly longer coat.

Gait: The German Shepherd has a smooth, ground-covering, effortless trot. The standard goes into great detail as to how this trot is to be performed, including how the trot should look when viewed from the side, front, and rear. The trot must cover a great deal of ground with long strides, powerfully, effortlessly, and smoothly.

Dogs with ears that do not stand upright or have been cropped to stand up are disqualified from competition. Dogs with noses that are not predominantly black, who do not have a correct scissors bite, or have a docked tail are also disqualified. White dogs and dogs who attempt to bite the judge are also disqualified.

Looking at Colors

The breed standard states that German Shepherds vary in color, and most colors are permissible. However, strong, rich colors are preferable, and pale, washed-out colors, blues, and livers are considered serious faults. As previously mentioned, white dogs are disqualified from competition.

Let's take a look at these colors and see what they actually are:

Black and tan: This color pattern consists of a black saddle on the back, with black on the muzzle and ears, and usually black on the tail. The tan can range from a yellowish tan to a deep, dark reddish brown.

Black and red: This color pattern consists of a larger black saddle than is typically seen on the black and tan. The red is a dark orange-brown-red.

Black and silver: This is a variation of the black and tan except the tan is silver instead. The silver is almost an off-white.

Black: These dogs are all black with no other color.

Bi-color: Dogs with this color pattern are all black with just a few markings of tan or red, usually on the lower legs and perhaps a spot of color under the tail. A spot of color might also appear on the eyebrows.

Sable: This coat color is most often described as coyote or wolf coloring. The coat is lighter underneath, and the hairs have a darker tip. The shades of sable coloring can vary from very light silver to a darker red or a dark silver-black.

White: Although white German Shepherds have always existed within the breed from its origins, this color is not acceptable in conformation competition. White dogs can participate in performance sports.

> **TIPS AND TAILS**
>
> Many enthusiasts of white German Shepherds have been actively forming new organizations in the United States and Europe to recognize and promote dogs of this color. The United Kennel Club recognizes these dogs as White Shepherds.

The color of a German Shepherd does not affect the dog's temperament, character, or working ability. Dogs of all colors can be wonderful companions.

Other Variations

German Shepherds from different parts of the world tend to have some differences, as do dogs bred specifically for working or for conformation shows.

American German Shepherds from show breeders tend to have more angulation (bend) in the rear legs. The slope from the withers to the hips is more extreme, and the dogs are not as heavy as European or German dogs. However, American dogs have a gorgeous flowing trot.

German Shepherds from West German conformation show breeders tend to be heavier bodied with thicker bones than American dogs. These dogs also have a ground-covering trot. Dark, rich colors are preferred, and many are black and red.

Many breeders in Germany have bred these dogs specifically for schutzhund competition or for working as police dogs, search-and-rescue dogs, or for other occupations where a serious working dog is needed. These dogs are generally well built but may not be as refined as many conformation show dogs are. These dogs are intelligent, have a strong work ethic, and are physically powerful.

After World War II, breeders in East Germany were determined to revive the breed from the dogs remaining there. Today's East German dogs don't have the extreme rear angulation seen elsewhere, and the back slopes from the withers to the hips with a less-extreme slope. These dogs are heavy boned and solid. They are prized working dogs.

Other variations of German Shepherds exist, too. Some are advertised as new breeds, such as Shiloh Shepherds, Giant German Shepherds, Giant Shepherds, King Shepherds, and a few others. These can suit people looking for something different from the AKC standard of the breed. However, you should understand that these breeds are different and cannot compete as German Shepherds, should that be your goal.

Health

One day your German Shepherd will get sick. It's unfortunate, but it happens. She may be coughing and sneezing, or have diarrhea, or be vomiting.

We discussed health problems in Month 7, along with instructions for when to call the veterinarian. This month, let's take a look at how to care for your adolescent at home. Although caring for your German Shepherd at home is easier and less stressful for your puppy, don't hesitate to call your veterinarian if you are at all worried about your puppy or if she doesn't show signs of improvement.

Giving your adolescent puppy medicines and treatments can be tough sometimes, especially if she's hurting or doesn't feel well. In this section, we share some tips to make that chore as easy as possible for both you and your puppy.

Dealing with Common Upsets

A few bodily functions can become upset easily, but you can help your puppy through them at home. Each of these could signal a more dangerous condition or disease, so it's important to keep in touch with your veterinarian.

Diarrhea: German Shepherds can have a sensitive digestive tract. Anxiety, nervousness, excitement, or a new experience can cause diarrhea. Even a change in water can cause it.

You can treat the diarrhea at home as long your pup has no other signs of disease. To begin treating it, don't feed your adolescent for the next 24 hours. Offer her ice cubes instead of water for a few hours and then let her drink as much as she wants to avoid dehydration.

If your veterinarian has preapproved it, give your adolescent antidiarrhea medication as you would for a person of the same weight. Pepto-Bismol and plain Kaopectate (without salicylates) are generally considered safe for dogs.

After 24 hours, feed your German Shepherd a bland diet. This could include boiled chicken, puréed cooked pumpkin, cottage cheese, boiled rice, cooked oatmeal, or soft-boiled eggs. Feed her several small meals through the day.

> ### TIPS AND TAILS
>
> Call your veterinarian if you see blood in your puppy's stools, if the diarrhea persists for more than 24 hours, if foreign objects or parasites are in the stool, or if the diarrhea is accompanied by vomiting.

Vomiting: Vomiting can occur for many reasons, including overeating, eating too fast, eating nonfood items, eating spoiled food, or disease. Your German Shepherd may also vomit if she eats some grass. This doesn't mean she has worms, by the way, as is commonly believed.

If your puppy is vomiting, withhold food and water for the next 12 hours. If the vomiting and dry heaves stop after her stomach is empty and she's rested, begin offering her ice cubes every few hours. If there's no more vomiting, and the water from the ice cubes stays down, offer her a ½ cup mixture of ¼ cup water and ¼ cup pediatric electrolyte solution.

After 12 hours with no vomiting, offer your puppy a bland diet, as was recommended for diarrhea. Offer several small meals throughout the day rather than larger meals. Feed the bland diet for 2 or 3 days and then reintroduce her normal food.

> **TIPS AND TAILS**
>
> Call your veterinarian if you see blood in your puppy's vomit, if the vomiting doesn't stop after her stomach is empty, if the vomiting begins again when food is introduced, or if you see any other signs of illness.

Coughing: Many different things can cause this, from allergies to heart disease. However, in puppies and adolescents, the most common cause is a respiratory infection often called *kennel cough*. Even well-vaccinated puppies can develop this because many different strains exist.

Home treatment consists, first, of keeping her quiet. Limit her activities, because if she's active she'll start coughing more. Your veterinarian may recommend an over-the-counter cough syrup to calm her throat.

> **TIPS AND TAILS**
>
> Call your veterinarian if your puppy begins to show any symptoms other than coughing, if she develops a fever, or if the coughing doesn't lessen with the cough suppressant.

Treating Your Puppy

Your veterinarian can diagnose an illness, treat an injury, and prescribe medications. However, you'll need to be able to continue the treatment at home. And if you know how to do it, it can save you and your dog additional trips to the vet clinic.

Pills and capsules: To give your puppy a pill or capsule, sit on a chair and have her sit between your knees with her back to you. Reach over her head with one hand, and from above her head, take hold of her top jaw by pressing her lips against her top teeth. As her mouth opens, use your other hand to place the pill or capsule as far back in her mouth as you can. If the pill is too far forward, your puppy will spit it out, so try to get it on the back of her tongue. Then close her mouth and gently rub her throat to encourage her to swallow. Give her a treat now so she swallows for sure.

Pills in food: If the pill can be given with food, it's much easier to hide the pill in a bit of cheese or meat. But the key is to have two pieces. Hide the pill in one, show your puppy the second piece so she swallows quickly, and give her the second piece. Not all medication can be given with food, however, so always ask your veterinarian first.

Don't try to hide the pill in a bowl of food, such as your puppy's meal. Most German Shepherds will eat around the pill or spit the pill out. It could end up on the floor somewhere, and you may not realize she didn't get her medication.

Liquid medications: Liquid medications are usually given by eyedropper, syringe, or medicine bottle. Again, have a seat and bring your puppy between your knees, facing away from you. Close her mouth and slightly tilt up her chin. Place the tip of the eyedropper or syringe between her lips at her cheek. Be sure the tip is in her mouth, facing toward her throat, but not in her throat. Slowly administer the medication, stopping frequently so your puppy can swallow. Don't try to rush it, giving her too much, or she will choke and cough, spraying the medication all over.

Suppositories: Sometimes medication is administered via suppositories that must be inserted into the rectum. This is more common when a dog is vomiting and will throw up any oral medication, or if the dog is having bowel problems. To insert the suppository, lubricate the suppository with petroleum jelly. Hold your German Shepherd's tail with one hand, and lift it so the anus is visible. With the other hand, insert the suppository so it's completely inside the rectum. Then let go of the tail.

Eye drops: Have your dog sit between your knees, again with her back to you. Tilt up her chin. Steady the hand with the medication against her head. Then, with the hand not holding the medication, gently pull down the lower lid. Without touching her eye with the bottle, squeeze the prescribed number of drops in her eye.

You can use the same technique if your veterinarian recommends flushing the eye with saline solution or artificial tears. A towel over your knees can help keep this from turning into a mess.

Eye ointment: Again, have your dog sitting between your knees with her back toward you. Hold the medication in one hand while steadying her head with the other. Using the hand steadying her head, gently pull down on her lower eyelid. Rest the hand with the medication against her head so you don't poke her with the ointment tip. Place the prescribed amount of medication inside the lower lid, between the lid and the eyeball. Close her eye and very gently massage the lower lid to spread the medication.

Ear medications: Depending on the problem requiring medication for the ear, the application may vary. Your veterinarian will show you how to apply it. However, the most common treatments require the medication to be inserted into the ear canal.

Your veterinarian may ask you to clean your puppy's ear before applying medication. Again, she will provide instructions as to how this should be done and what can be used.

When the ear is clean and dry, and you're ready to treat your puppy, have her sit between your knees with her back toward you. Fold the flap of the ear being treated back over her head so it's out of the way. Place the tip of the ointment or bottle into the ear canal slightly—only as far as you can see, and no farther. Do not push the applicator into the ear, or you could damage sensitive tissues. Apply the amount of medication, and remove the applicator. Put the ear flap back up, and gently massage the base of the ear.

Nutrition

As your German Shepherd adolescent gets bigger and the two of you become more active, perhaps with training, exercise, and play, she's going to need more calories to keep up with all that activity. However, just feeding more food isn't always the answer because German Shepherds are rarely gluttons. Your puppy may stop eating when she's full, even if she hasn't eaten enough to satisfy her energy needs.

In addition, more food than normal can cause soft stools or even diarrhea. Your dog will then lose the benefit of that food because it will move through her system too quickly.

Satisfying your adolescent's nutritional needs can be tough. Without those calories, she won't have the energy to work and play, plus she'll lose weight.

Feeding More Fats

If your dog hasn't lost any weight but just doesn't have all the energy she needs for her increased activities, sometimes just adding some extra fat to her diet solves the problem. Calories from fats are the most easily metabolized, and the blood sugar remains more stable with fats than with other sources of energy.

The downside to fats is that if your German Shepherd isn't using that energy every day, the fats will be stored in her body. This is okay if she's thin, but it's not so good if she tends to gain weight.

Increase the fat in your German Shepherd's diet very gradually. If you add too much all at once, she'll have diarrhea—bad, stinky diarrhea.

To increase the fat in the diet, you can add one of the following per day per meal to her normal diet:

🐾 ¼ cup ground beef or bison with higher fat content, cooked

🐾 ¼ cup goat's milk cheese

🐾 1 tablespoon full-fat yogurt

🐾 2 tablespoons full-fat cottage cheese

If your German Shepherd's digestive system is used to one or more of these foods in these lesser amounts, you can increase the amount prior to a hard training session or competition without the risk of diarrhea.

Adding Home-Cooked Foods

You can also add some home-cooked food to your German Shepherd's diet to boost her nutrition. These can be added to her normal diet as a supplement, giving her a small amount on a normal basis, but increasing the amount given when she's more active than normal.

On a daily basis, the amount added to her diet should never total more than 10 percent of her daily diet. That way, the nutritional balance of her food will be maintained. However, if you and your dog will be having a busy weekend training or exercising, for example, beginning on Thursday, you can increase the additional food to 15 to 20 percent of her diet. Then on Sunday, go back to the normal amount.

Knowing When to Make Changes

Your German Shepherd's diet is one of the keys to her good health. Making frequent changes is not good for her and is apt to upset her digestive tract.

It's important to feed a good-quality food or a well-balanced homemade diet, and stick to that food or diet as long as your adolescent is thriving on it. Make changes if she's not doing well, has itchy skin and coat or a dull coat, and doesn't seem to be doing well.

That good food will probably be perfectly adequate for most of your teenager's activities. However, if you feel that she's losing energy, is losing weight, or in some other way could use some nutritional help, gradually add some healthy calories to her diet.

If she continues to look or act less than perfect, even with those extra calories, it's time to call your veterinarian. You need to be sure something else isn't going on with your puppy.

Grooming

Adolescent puppies love to play and have no problem getting dirty. In fact, during adolescence, she will get the dirtiest she's ever been or ever will be. She's bolder and more adventurous now than she was as a puppy, and when she's grown up, she'll be more dignified.

Bathing a German Shepherd is quite an undertaking, and it's not always convenient. Especially considering that you usually get as wet as she does. Thankfully, there is an alternative.

When you do have the time and inclination to give your adolescent a bath, you'll need dog-appropriate shampoo. But have you read the labels on some dog shampoos? They contain some scary ingredients. Let's take a look at these chemicals along with some alternatives.

Giving Her Waterless Baths

We discussed how to bathe your dog in Month 8, even though your German Shepherd shouldn't need frequent baths. This breed's coat is wonderful because a good brushing removes most of the dirt it picks up. Many owners avoid bathing their German Shepherd because it can be a pretty big project, especially trying to get the dog dry and brushed out afterward.

If your German Shepherd is just a little dirty, perhaps dirtier than brushing will clean up but not so dirty you're willing to give her a bath, you can try one of a number of different waterless bath products for dogs. These can be a good bath alternative for dogs who aren't too dirty.

These products generally come in either spray-on liquid or foam formulas. Some are sold as wipes, but those are more effective on short-haired dogs and don't work well on the German Shepherd coat. Many German Shepherd owners who have used these products recommend the foaming products. With the liquids, it's hard to see how much of the coat has been covered. With the foam, it's obvious.

Some of the products have a very heavy scent and some dogs react to the scent, rolling around on the floor or grass as if to try to rub it off as soon as they're released from bath time. So choose one with a lighter scent if you go this route. Products that contain tea tree oil have a pleasant or natural scent.

To use a waterless bath product, you can wet a portion of the dog—just what's dirty—or you can bathe all of her. Follow the instructions for the product you choose.

Tea tree oil is derived from the Australian melaleuca tree. This natural antiseptic has penetrating qualities that make it effective against many bacteria and fungi.

A Look at Shampoos

Hundreds of dog shampoos are available, and that's no exaggeration. You'll find shampoos for black coats and white coats, short coats and long coats. There are shampoos with conditioners added and ones with no conditioners. You can find medicated shampoos for dogs with itchy skin and anything else that can affect a coat.

Many German Shepherd owners are concerned about all the artificial ingredients in many shampoos and would prefer to avoid those. Paraben is a preservative used in many cosmetics and shampoos that's been linked to the development of cancer. Sodium laurel sulfate is another ingredient commonly found in shampoos that's been linked to several side effects, including skin ulcers.

More natural shampoos are available. Don't completely trust the name of the shampoo, however, because "natural" in a shampoo name doesn't have any legal definition, and the ingredients can vary. Read the ingredient list on the label and be sure you know what the ingredients are. Or you can ask your groomer for a recommendation.

Making Your Own Shampoo

If you want to forego all the chemicals, you can make your own shampoo.

One very simple recipe calls for equal parts of a clear, antibacterial soap such as Dial and white vinegar. Mix these together, rub them into your German Shepherd's wet coat, rinse, scrub again, and rinse again.

A similar recipe calls for 1 cup of an all-natural dish soap such as Ivory or Dial, 1 cup water, and 1 cup apple cider vinegar. Again, mix, rub, rinse, scrub, and rinse.

If your German Shepherd has itchy skin, a soothing oatmeal shampoo is a great idea. Run 1 cup dry oatmeal (not instant) through a blender or food processor until it's a fine powder. Add 1 cup baking soda, and mix well. Add 1 quart warm water and 1 tablespoon clear liquid antibacterial soap, and mix well. Wet your dog's coat and then work the shampoo into his fur, massaging him with the shampoo for 3 to 5 minutes. Rinse thoroughly.

> **TIPS AND TAILS**

Pay attention to your German Shepherd adolescent after using any shampoo—commercial or homemade. If her skin gets red or itchy, or if you see another reaction, rinse her again immediately to be sure all the soap is off her skin and coat. If the problem remains, call your veterinarian.

Social Skills

Not everyone is going to like your German Shepherd, and your German Shepherd isn't going to like everyone she meets. That's just a part of life.

When People Don't Like Your Dog

German Shepherds have a recognizable appearance, and people all over the world know what this breed is. Unfortunately, not everyone likes the breed based on its reputation as a law-enforcement and military dog. The public perception is of a dog with bared teeth, snarling and growling in the backseat of a police car. Or a dog at the end of a leash, leaping and growling, while a police officer anchors the leash's other end.

People often don't even take into account the times the breed is used for guiding the blind, assisting the disabled, searching for lost people, and the other beneficial occupations German Shepherds take part in every day.

Your German Shepherd may be from a reputable breeder, you may have spent hours socializing and training your dog, and she may be a well-loved member of your family. But there will still be people who won't like your dog, simply because she's a German Shepherd.

You aren't going to be able to change the opinions of everyone who dislikes your dog or is afraid of her. Whether they were hurt—perhaps even bitten—by a dog, didn't grow up with dogs and may be unsure about them, or just plain don't trust any dog, you're not going to talk people into liking your dog if they genuinely are fearful of German Shepherds.

What you can do is be sure your German Shepherd is well socialized and well trained. When your dog is a model canine citizen, she makes a good impression for all who meet her, even if they're still leery about her.

When Your Dog Doesn't Like Someone

There will be times when your dog doesn't like someone, too. The most common reason is that when someone doesn't like her, she's apt to feel that. She may react by ignoring the person or, especially when she's still young, she may be uneasy and growl.

Your adolescent may also react to someone if that person looks or acts different. Someone who dresses differently from how your puppy is used to seeing people dressed may trigger her protective instincts. People of an ethnic culture she's not used to can also attract your puppy's attention.

Sometimes your German Shepherd should be wary of people. If someone approaches you in a threatening manner, your German Shepherd will react, as she should in that situation. Someone approaching your house will cause the same reaction. As an adolescent, your puppy isn't always going to make good decisions as to who she should be worried about and who is fine. She's mentally immature and will also lack confidence at times, especially in strange or, in her mind, potentially threatening situations.

Redirect her attention from the person who concerns her back to you. You can then praise her for paying attention to you rather than the strange person.

> ### TIPS AND TAILS
>
> When your German Shepherd is all grown up and mentally mature, pay more attention to her reactions. When she's an adult, she'll be more perceptive, and when she chooses to dislike someone, there's probably a reason why.

Behavior

Your adolescent puppy's behavior is going to be the same this month as it was last month. She's still going to be unsettled and have mood swings from affectionate puppy to silly teenager. And you'll still need patience to work through this age.

It's not uncommon to see a regression this month. You may ask your puppy to sit and she'll look at you as if she's never heard that word before. Don't get angry; just understand it's a part of this stage of life.

Working Through Teenage Regression

One of the most common complaints from owners of German Shepherd adolescents is concerning their puppy's regression. They question why their puppy is ignoring them, why she's not listening to even basic commands, and why she's doing things she hasn't done since she was a very young puppy.

This regression is so normal in adolescents it's more normal for the teenager to hit this stage than not. One day this month, you'll ask your German Shepherd to do something she knows well, like "Stay," and she'll walk away from you. She won't even act like it's a problem.

She's not defying you; it's even more basic than that. She has selective hearing right now, and what you're saying isn't even registering with her. However, that doesn't mean she's allowed to ignore you.

Set her up to succeed. That means using her leash a lot during this time. The leash isn't just to take her for walks but also to teach her to listen again. she can drag the leash around the house as long as she's supervised so she doesn't get it tangled.

> ### TIPS AND TAILS
> Refresh her lessons often when she's ignoring you or not listening. Repetition can help her focus.

Some of your German Shepherd adolescent's behaviors aren't even a regression— they are a reversion to puppyhood. Your teenager may have been quite well behaved, showing you what she's going to be like as an adult. And then suddenly, one day when you're out on a walk, she's barking at people, jumping on them, and even grabbing at hands with her mouth. She acts like a dog who has never left the backyard or met other people. Obviously, this is horrifying because it makes you look like you haven't taught your German Shepherd a thing.

Take a deep breath. Again, this is adolescence, and this, too, shall pass.

The Need to Be Needed

Your German Shepherd is in the throes of adolescence, but at the same time, she's growing up. Unfortunately, her misbehaviors do tend to overshadow the advancements she's making.

During this month, your adolescent is showing the signs of a true working dog— she has the need to be needed. She isn't a pet or a luxury; she's a working dog who needs a job to do. She needs for you to depend on her.

This may show up in strange ways. She may come up to you and make eye contact with you, staring and whining while dancing on her front feet. She's trying to communicate with you, trying to ask you a question. Dogs are quite amazing in their efforts to communicate with us.

Some smart dogs, in their desire to be needed, will bring the leash when it's time to go for a walk. She may bring you your shoes, slippers, or a dirty sock she found on the floor in the laundry room. She may herd the cat to the middle of the family room, not letting the poor feline leave. She may decide lizards are no longer allowed on the wall in the backyard.

All these behaviors may be cute at first but very annoying when repeated over and over (especially for the cat). Just understand that your teenager is trying to find her place in the world. Her instincts tell her she should have a job to do, and she's trying to create that job.

In the next section, you learn how to teach her a few tricks that can serve as a job for her.

You and Your Puppy

More dogs are given up by their owners during adolescence than at any other single age. Most of this is driven by not understanding what's going on, not realizing that adolescence in dogs is much like the same tumultuous stage in humans.

It's important to remember that your puppy is not a monster. She's not a bad dog who's trying to disrupt your life. This is a normal part of growing up. (You probably went through something similar. Just ask your parents!)

When times get tough, just keep in mind all those things you love about your dog. Remember her connection to you, her affection, and her desire to be close to you. Think of all the fun you've had walking, hiking, playing ball, and just hanging out together. What about those big dark eyes that seem like they can see into your soul? There's so much you love about your dog. Adolescence is a bump in the road. You both will get past it together.

Speed Walking

Exercise is an important part of the process of working through adolescence. You can speed walk your puppy and in the process use up a lot of her excess energy. Speed walking is walking faster than normal without breaking into a run. How fast you walk depends on your physical condition.

If you're not quite ready for a long walk at a fast pace, you can work up to it gradually. Begin the walk at a quick pace that's comfortable for you. When you begin to feel uncomfortable, slow down to your normal walking pace. When you've rested, pick up the pace again. Alternate normal and fast as much as you can. Over time, as your fitness level improves, you can extend the time you're walking fast.

While you're walking, have your German Shepherd heel. This is especially important while walking fast because you don't want her to step in front of you and potentially trip you.

> **HAPPY PUPPY**

If your German Shepherd isn't used to sustained fast walking, build up to it gradually. You want her muscles as well as her pads to toughen gradually. Her pads can get scuffed or torn if you do too much before they get a chance to toughen.

Getting the Newspaper

Bringing you the newspaper in the morning can be a good job for your German Shepherd. If the delivery person drops it at the end of the driveway, send your dog after it. You can stand in the doorway in your robe and slippers without offending your neighbors.

To get this started, have a rolled-up section of an old newspaper. Use some tape to make the roll fairly snug.

In the living room, when you and your dog are both relaxed, show her the paper. Shake it in her face a little to get her excited. If she touches it, praise her, "Good girl!" Do this several times and then take a break.

Play with her with it again, but this time, wait for her to touch it with her mouth. Praise her. Again, do it several times and then take a break.

Now you'll introduce the command, "Sweetie, get the paper!" Tease her with the paper, and when she touches it with her mouth or even closes her mouth on it, say, "Get the paper! Good!" Repeat this several times and then take a break.

When you have the paper in your hand and she reaches up to touch it with her mouth, you're ready to move on to the next steps. Now start tossing it for her. Start with just a few feet in front of you. Tell her, "Sweetie, get the paper!" and praise her when she goes to get it and brings it to you.

Over several weeks, gradually increase the distance you throw it until you can toss it across the room and down the hall and she willingly chases after it. Then move the game outside.

Put your German Shepherd on a long leash. Toss the paper a few feet away, and encourage her to go get it. Praise her when she does. Over several training sessions, gradually increase the distance until you can toss it the length of your driveway.

At this point, she needs to learn to go get it without your throwing it. After all, chasing something that's been thrown—like her ball—is much more fun. So with your dog on her long leash, ask her to sit and stay, then walk about 6 feet away and place the paper on the ground. Then ask her to go get it. When she does go get it, praise her enthusiastically. If she hesitates, take a step forward and encourage her.

Once she'll go get it when it's 6 feet away, increase the distance, again gradually. Eventually you'll be able to place it at the end of the driveway and send your dog after it.

The Military Crawl

Recently Liz saw a handsome black-and-red German Shepherd doing a neat trick at a public function honoring military veterans. This striking dog had on a camouflage jacket, a cammie cap, and a holster with a plastic gun. A red, white, and blue ribbon around one front leg topped off his costume.

As his owner talked to the crowd about honoring veterans, the dog did some tricks. The applause was great, and the dog was enjoying both his work and the applause from the audience. But one trick really stood out.

As the owner was talking, he mentioned the hardships veterans face, including crawling on their bellies through the mud. Those words were the dog's cue, and he dropped to the ground, and in his camouflage uniform, began doing a belly crawl. The audience loved it.

Teaching your dog to crawl isn't difficult. To begin, you'll need some good treats and a bench or low table that's short enough your dog has to crawl to get under it yet high enough so she can fit. A picnic table bench would work.

Here's how to teach her:

🐾 Have your dog lie down on one side of the bench, facing it.

🐾 Step to the other side of the bench, hold the treat under the bench, and tell your dog, "Sweetie, crawl."

❧ When her head comes down to sniff the treat, slowly pull the treat under the bench toward you so she follows it.

❧ When she comes out from under the bench, praise her and give her the treat.

Continue practicing with the bench until your adolescent knows and understands what the trick is and is doing it well. Then ask her to crawl without the bench. Continue to use the treat in front of her nose for a while. If she's hesitant to crawl and instead wants to get up, put one hand on her shoulder to remind her to stay down.

The Leg Weave

The leg weave is another trick that looks awesome when done well. This trick consists of your German Shepherd weaving through your legs in a figure-eight pattern. If you think it's impossible for a large dog to do this, think again. This trick is actually more impressive when a big dog does it, even if she has to duck a little.

To begin, you'll need a pocketful of high-value treats. Have one treat in each hand. Don't put her on leash for this one.

❧ Have your German Shepherd in front of you, facing you. Stand with your legs shoulder-width apart. Let your adolescent smell the treats.

❧ Don't give her any commands yet, but with your right hand, reach behind your right leg and lure your dog from front to back between your legs.

❧ Continue leading her by the nose, and bring her back in front of you by making a circle around your right leg with the treat. Praise her when she walks around, and give her a treat.

❧ Do this several times until she's comfortable with it. Take a break and play with your dog.

❧ At your next training session, do the same thing except with your left hand, your left leg, and circle her to the left.

❧ Again repeat several times and take a break.

Practice this exercise several times over several training sessions until your dog is comfortable circling both legs. To put it all together, again have a treat in each hand:

❧ Tell her, "Sweetie, weave," and have her circle your right leg.

❧ When she comes back in front of you, immediately draw her back between your legs to circle your left leg.

🐾 When she comes to the front again, praise her, pop the treat in her mouth, and tell her how wonderful she is!

Over time, you can decrease the hand motions and emphasize the verbal command. Eventually, you'll be able to simply stand with your legs shoulder-width apart and ask her to weave.

The Step Weave

If you really want to show off, once she knows the leg-weave trick, teach her to weave as you walk. Well, you really aren't going to be able to walk per se, but you can take slow-motion steps.

When you have her weave a figure eight around your legs, take one exaggerated step forward and have her weave around that leg. Then take another exaggerated step and ask her to keep weaving.

The end result is you walking with slow, exaggerated, big steps while your German Shepherd weaves through your legs. It really is as great as it sounds. Your dog is going to look awesome, and you're going to look like a great dog trainer. Best of all, you'll both have fun, together.

Your German Shepherd is so smart at times, it might be scary. It's fun to watch him learn and think—and even more fun to watch him solve puzzles. Don't be surprised if he learns how to open doors—many German Shepherds do. They can also open the kitchen cupboard where you store the dog treats.

You know those commercials where the dog opens the refrigerator to get his owner a beer? Your German Shepherd can do that. But do you really want him to? After all, your roast beef is in the refrigerator, too. Never teach him anything—seriously or as a trick—you don't want him to do again in the future.

Although he's still going through adolescence, hopefully he's learned how much fun training is and is cooperating with you. When he's working with you—rather than against you—learning new things together is a blast.

Physical Development

Your puppy's coordination is going to get better this month. The lessons you began last month, helping him to step and jump over obstacles at low heights, should continue this month. There are also some new exercises you can add that will help him get better.

As his coordination continues to improve, so will his speed. Long-legged adolescent puppies aren't very fast when they're tripping over their own paws, so coordination needs to come before speed. It's not important that he's fast—after all, he's a German Shepherd not a Greyhound. But watching him run fast is a joy.

One of the best ways to help your puppy continue to increase his coordination as well as his confidence is to build him a confidence course at home. A confidence course is similar to an agility course that has a variety of obstacles but with easier, scaled-down obstacles.

The obstacles can be as simple as a picnic table bench turned over on its side for your German Shepherd puppy to hop over. The bench creates a small jump that isn't too high so it won't damage the growth plates of his bones.

With the bench right side up, you can ask him to hop up and then walk the length of the bench. The narrowness of the bench requires him to place his paws carefully and to balance himself.

You can also build some obstacles. They don't have to be elaborate or expensive. In fact, you can build all of the following obstacles for less than $200.

Tire jump: To build this obstacle, you need two 4-foot lengths of 2-inch-diameter PVC pipe, four 3-foot sections, and two 12-inch sections. You also need two right-angle joints and four T joints. A saw to cut the pipe and some PVC glue to fasten them together round out your supplies list.

The frame is rectangular. Start at the base of one side. You need one of the 3-foot sections and one of the T joints. Cut the 3-foot section in half, and glue each half section to each side of the joints with the top of the T facing the ground.

In the opening of this T joint, glue a 12-inch section of pipe. Glue another T joint to that section, with the crosswise opening of the T joint facing to the side. To the top of the T joint, glue a 4-foot section. Top that with a right angle. If you consider the 3-foot sections extend front to back, the T joint opening above the 12-inch section faces to one side. The top right-angle joint faces the same direction.

Repeat for the other side, building a twin to this first side. With both sides glued and looking identical, you can fasten them together. Place one 3-foot section between the Ts above the 12-inch section and the other 3-foot section at the top. When both are in place, glue them.

When the PVC frame is all together and the glue has set, you can hang a tire. A motorcycle tire works well, but so can a bicycle tire. Use a length of rope to suspend the tire from the top and two pieces of rope to anchor the tire at each side at the bottom.

Teach your puppy to jump through the tire jump by luring him with a good treat. Put the treat in front of his nose and lead him through the jump, saying, "Sweetie, jump! Good!"

> **HAPPY PUPPY**

If your puppy appears worried about an individual obstacle or any of this training, stop, play with your puppy, and begin training again. Keep it slow and positive, with lots of praise and treats, and keep his tail wagging.

Weave poles: This is the easiest obstacle to build, and when you have the pieces, you can put them together in minutes. You need 10 pieces of 3-foot-long PVC that's 1½ to 2 inches in diameter. You also need 10 pieces of rebar or a similar type of stake that can be pounded into the ground. It needs to be a smaller diameter than the pipe.

Decide where you want the line of weave poles to be, and pound in one piece of rebar. Pace off three steps, or about 2½ feet, and pound in a second piece. Repeat for three more pieces, placing them in a straight line.

Then go back to the first piece of rebar. You're going to create a second line of rebar about 12 inches to the side of the first line with the poles staggered midway between the poles in the first line. Finally, place the PVC pipes over the rebar.

The first step in introducing the weave poles isn't going to include any weaving at all. Instead, just walk your puppy down the aisle created by the two lines of poles and then praise him. Have him trot down the aisle and then run down the aisle. Finally, have him sit at one end of the poles. Go to the other end, and call him to come to you.

When your German Shepherd can go down the aisle of poles with no difficulty, you can begin teaching him to weave. Relocate the second line of poles so it's about 6 inches from the first line, with the poles still staggered midway between the first line. When viewed from one end, the poles should form a zigzag.

Walk your dog between the poles. Because the gap is smaller now, he's going to have to make a small weave as he walks among the poles. As he does, tell him, "Sweetie, zig!" (Use "zig" as a command because "weave" is used as a command for the trick where he weaves around your legs.) Praise him as he weaves his way down the line.

Practice this way for several weeks so he can build the muscle memory and flexibility to go through the poles easily. Don't ask him to run through the poles; he'd just crash through them. You're trying to build skill and flexibility right now.

> ### HAPPY PUPPY

Alternate these training sessions with obedience and trick training. If you concentrate on any one thing to the exclusion of others, your puppy will get burnt out on it—and so will you! Keep the training fresh and exciting so you both want to do it.

After several weeks, or when your puppy can move through the poles easily, move the second line closer to the first—about 3 inches away. Continue practicing as you have been, not forcing speed but letting your puppy slowly build flexibility. Be enthusiastic, praise and reward him, and make this a big game.

Wait several weeks again before making the last change. When your dog is ready, incorporate the second line into the first so you have a line of 10 poles, each standing about 2 feet from each other.

Reintroduce this by first using a treat to lure him through the line of poles several times. However, if you introduced this slowly enough and with repetition, after being allured a few times he should be ready to do it on his own.

Closed tunnel: This is a fun obstacle that's easy to make. You need four sections of heavy plywood that are 2 feet by 2 feet square. You also need some angle iron braces to reinforce the corners, screws to put it all together, 6 feet of hook-and-loop tape with adhesive backing, and a large California king–size sheet. (The color and design of the sheet are your choice.)

Build a box out of the four sections of wood and the angle irons with four sides and no top or bottom; those are open. Reinforce the box well with the angle irons because your dog is going to be running through the box.

To introduce your German Shepherd to the box, turn it on its side so the top and bottom become the front and back and are open. Leave your puppy at the front of the box, walk to the back, and reach through with a treat, saying "Sweetie, come through!" When he follows the treat, praise him and give him the treat.

After a few days of him first walking and then dashing through the open-ended box, you can add the sheet. Choose one side of the box to be the bottom. Fasten the hook-and-loop tape to the two sides and the top (but not the bottom edge) at one end of the box. Let's call that end of the box the front. The hook-and-loop tape is at the front edge of the box, going up both sides and across the top. Peel the adhesive off the top piece of hook-and-loop tape, and stick one edge of the sheet to it. If it doesn't adhere well, you might want to sew the hook-and-loop tape to the sheet.

Pull the loose end of the sheet away from the box so it extends all the way out. Now gather it up in your hands and drape it over the front of the box so it's somewhat blocking the front of the box but there's still an opening.

Send your dog through the box, encouraging him as he goes under the draped sheet. You want him to get used to the idea of the sheet gradually. Over several practice sessions, let the sheet block more and more of the front opening.

> ### TIPS AND TAILS
>
> If he's been going through the tunnel well but hesitates with the exit partially blocked, gather up more of the sheet so it can be seen but the exit is fully open. Let him do this a few times and then gradually allow the sheet to drape more.

When he's going through easily, pull the sheet out and away from the box. Let it fall to the ground. The hook-and-loop tape holds one end of the sheet to the box but the rest is spread out on the ground.

Now send your dog into the open end of the box, "Sweetie, go through!" and run to meet him at the far end of the sheet. Praise him, "Sweetie, awesome! Good job!" when he pops out from under the sheet.

Ladder: The ladder is not for your German Shepherd to climb. At this age, he's too uncoordinated and would hurt himself. Instead, you can use the ladder to help teach more paw and leg coordination. To do this, you simply lay a ladder flat on the ground.

With your puppy on leash and some good treats in your pocket, walk him up to one end of the ladder. Encourage him to step into the gap between the rungs, saying, "Sweetie, step! Good!" Move slowly because this is very different and he's going to have to figure out where his feet need to go. Encourage and praise him as you move the length of the ladder.

If your puppy jumps off to one side to avoid the ladder, take him back to the beginning and work a little slower the next time. Point to the gap between rungs to show him where you want him to go. Use lots of encouragement.

> **HAPPY PUPPY**
>
> If you and your puppy have fun with these obstacles, there are many more you can build or put together. In the next chapter, we talk more about agility, what it is, and how you can get involved.

Health

This month should find your German Shepherd healthy, fit, and full of energy. That doesn't mean there's nothing to discuss considering his health, though.

Have you thought about health-care costs for your adolescent? Unfortunately, the price of veterinary medicine isn't cheap. Accidents and illnesses never announce themselves ahead of time so you can save money to cover those costs. However, you may want to look into veterinary health insurance, as many other pet owners have done.

Something else to plan ahead for: disasters. Granted, we often get warnings about hurricanes and blizzards, but tornados, earthquakes, and wildfires can arrive unannounced. Making some preparations ahead of time can help keep you and your German Shepherd safe, or as safe as possible, in the face of a disaster of any kind.

Considering Pet Health Insurance

Health insurance for pets might be a new idea for many people, but the first insurance company for pets actually originated about 30 years ago. Veterinary Pet Insurance (VPI) was the first company to offer pet health insurance, and it remains the largest pet health insurance company today, with more than half a million policyholders.

There are many benefits to pet health insurance. Your dog can be taken care of even if your budget is tight. Most policies have a co-pay, but other costs are covered. Insurance companies also cover tests you might not otherwise pay for. Pet health insurance is much like your own health insurance; it's there so you can have the care you need when you need it.

Many companies also offer wellness care coverage, or preventative medicine. With this coverage, more people can focus on keeping their dog healthy rather than simply on responding when the dog is ill or injured.

Veterinary Pet Insurance listed the following as the most common reasons for dogs visiting the veterinarian:

❧ Ear infections

❧ Skin allergies

❧ Skin infections

❧ Noncancerous growths

❧ Upset stomach and/or vomiting

❧ Intestinal upset and/or diarrhea

❧ Arthritis

❧ Bladder infection or urinary tract infection

❧ Bruise or contusion

❧ Underactive thyroid

Other health issues that are normally covered include the following, in order of frequency of coverage:

❧ Allergic reactions

❧ Skin cancer

❧ Sprains and strains

❧ Torn toenails

❧ Fungal skin disease

☙ Eye injuries and/or infections

☙ Abrasions

☙ Seizure disorders

☙ Kidney disease

☙ Liver disease

☙ Heart failure

☙ Tooth removal

☙ Addison's disease

☙ Foreign object in the stomach

☙ Lyme disease

Many more health problems are covered, including diabetes, bronchitis, urinary incontinence, and torn knee ligaments. The list of covered problems is long, and most health-care companies post a list of what's covered and what's not on their website.

Most companies do not cover health problems related to genetics, and that list varies by breed and by health-care company. For example, with German Shepherds, several companies do not cover hip dysplasia, elbow dysplasia, and degenerative myelopathy. However, many companies are now offering extended coverage policies that do cover these health threats.

Before you invest your money in a pet health insurance policy, take a look at several different companies and review the policies they offer. A good website to do that is Pet Insurance Review, at petinsurancereview.com/dog.asp.

Planning for Disasters

Liz and her dogs have been evacuated due to natural disasters several times. In Southern California, where they live, the disaster in question is often wildfires. Thankfully, their home has been spared, but unfortunately, many others have not. In the wildfires of 2003, more than 2,000 homes were destroyed in San Diego County.

Disasters happen anywhere and anytime. With some disasters, you may have to hunker down at home and see them through, while other times, you may need to evacuate. In any case, you need to be prepared.

A disaster-preparedness kit can be a life saver as well as make life immediately after a disaster more livable. When evacuated because of one wildfire, Liz and her two German Shepherds, Watachie and Michi, lived at the local beach for 3 days while her husband helped fight the fire. So she and the dogs, as well as a cat, rabbit, and ferret, lived out of their pickup truck camper because it was impossible to get a motel room with all the animals. Without a disaster kit, they would have been miserable.

Liz uses a plastic trash can with wheels to store and carry her disaster kit. She keeps it just inside the side garage door so that even if the garage is damaged, she can reach it and wheel it out. Be sure the trash can fits in the trunk of your car.

The San Diego County Office of Emergency Services recommends that every person should have immediate access to several important documents, including their Social Security card (or number) as well as a driver's license for identification. You also need to have your medical information and medical coverage contacts. Have your personal banking information, but also have some cash on hand.

Following are other items that should be in your combined disaster kit for dogs and people:

Dog medical information: The first items to get for your disaster kit should be your pet's medical information, including vaccination information and dates, and copies of any prescriptions. Update this information regularly. Have your veterinarian's name, address, and phone number, too, as well as the local emergency veterinary hospital.

Family medical information: You should also have the same medical information for yourself and everyone in your family. That includes doctors' names and contact information, health coverage, prescription information, eyeglass or contact prescriptions, and vaccination information.

First-aid kit: In Month 7, we list the items you should have in your first-aid kit. Be sure everything is updated regularly in the kit, and replace items that have been used. You should have a first-aid kit in your home, in your car, and one with your disaster supplies.

Nonperishable dog food: Pack enough canned dog food or dehydrated dog food for at least 7 days. Before Hurricane Katrina, the recommended time was 2 days, but in the aftermath of Katrina, Hurricane Rita, and several other disasters, 7 days is now recommended. Every 6 months, when you check your first-aid kit, pull out the stored food, use it, and restock your disaster kit with fresh food.

Nonperishable food for people: You need 7 days' worth of food, too. Just as with your dog's food, rotate yours.

Food preparation supplies: Include dog bowls, paper plates, glasses or paper cups, spoons, plastic wear, aluminum foil, storage containers, plastic bags, and garbage bags. If you have any camping gear, store that near your disaster kit.

Water: Store more water than you think you'll need. A case of bottled water is a good start. You may want to keep a couple 5-gallon jugs stored near your disaster kit, too. The bare minimum of water per day for an adult human and an adult German Shepherd is 2 quarts. However, when active or in times of stress or hot weather, more is needed.

Your German Shepherd: Be sure you have a collar with identification tags, an extra leash, a crate, and photos of your puppy in the unfortunate event that she get separated from you. Also have some basic grooming tools, including nail clippers.

> ### TIPS AND TAILS
>
> Emergency shelters must make room for pets. However, pets are generally required to be crated. So be sure a crate is easily accessible and your German Shepherd fits comfortably in it.

Sanitary supplies: For people, have toilet paper, paper towels, feminine products, sanitary wipes, tooth brush and toothpaste, and liquid soap. For your German Shepherd, have plastic bags for picking up after him as well as a couple towels and a bottle of waterless shampoo.

Tools and supplies: To hear information from the emergency broadcast system, you need a battery-operated radio and extra batteries. A couple flashlights and extra batteries for those are always needed, too. A manual can opener, a pocketknife, a pair of heavy-duty scissors, and matches are good to have as well. A small tool box with a Phillips screwdriver, a straight-edge screwdriver, pliers, and a hammer is also a good idea.

Electronics: If you have an extra battery for your cell phone and laptop, pack those near your disaster kit. Have an extra charger, too, including a car charger.

Clothes and shoes: Plan on appropriate clothing for at least 7 days. Include a couple blankets and sleeping bags if you have any.

It's also important to know what you'll do in a disaster. Having a plan of action can help prevent panic. This plan should take into account the type of disaster that occurs in your region. Where Liz lives, wildfires and earthquakes are the biggest threat. Wildfires require evacuation, sometimes a distance away from home, and that must be planned for.

Earthquakes don't give any warning so they're weathered at home. However, afterward there may be disruption in travel so stores may not have their supplies replenished. Having supplies at home is important. Plus, earthquakes may disrupt electricity.

Plan for disasters that happen in your locale, for both staying at home and leaving. If you're stuck at home, you have all your supplies with you, but you may be without power. Can you still cook, or would you need to eat cold foods? What if you don't have any water? What if the water system is contaminated? Water decontamination tablets are good, as is a large pot in which to boil water. Bottled water can keep you supplied for a few days.

If you need to evacuate, where can you go with your German Shepherd? Would relatives be willing to take you in, or would you need to go to a shelter or a motel? Make plans ahead of time; call those relatives today, or check on pet-friendly motels near you.

Have a point of contact that would be far enough away it wouldn't be affected by a local disaster. Be sure everyone in your family can check in with this person so everyone can be accounted for.

Planning and preparing for an emergency ahead of time is so important. You'll still be worried and scared, but with this advance preparation, you'll have less to worry about.

Nutrition

Hopefully, your German Shepherd adolescent is doing well on his food. If he is, don't make any changes.

This month, let's continue your education concerning the pet-food industry so that should you need to make any changes, you have the knowledge to choose wisely.

A Closer Look at "Natural" Dog Food

Many consumers opt for foods advertised as "natural" as a way to eat more healthily. To most people, *natural* means the food is straight from the source, unadulterated, as Mother Nature intended it. The same is true for dog food: many dog owners choose dog foods labeled "natural" in hopes of providing better-quality food for their dog.

Many dog foods are labeled as natural in some manner, whether in the manufacturer's name; in relation to the ingredients, implying that the ingredients are naturally grown or produced; or pertaining to the food as a whole, implying the entire mass-produced, processed food is a natural food. The word *natural* is used so much because manufacturers know that in the consumer's mind, *natural* means "healthy." However, in the pet-food industry, *natural* doesn't necessarily mean that at all.

In fact, the Association of American Feed Control Officials (AAFCO) defines *natural* as, "A feed or ingredient derived solely from plant, animal, or mined sources, either in its unprocessed state or having been subjected to physical processing, heat processing, rendering, purification, extraction, hydrolysis, enzymolysis, or fermentation, but not having been produced by or subject to a chemically synthetic process and not containing additives or processing aids that are chemically synthetic except in amounts as might occur unavoidably in good manufacturing practices." Plus, many foods include synthetic vitamins, minerals, and other trace elements. This definition means manufacturers can render poor-quality meat animals, bake the food to a crisp, add synthetic vitamins and minerals, and still call it a "natural" food.

> **DOG TALK**
>
> **Natural** doesn't pertain to the quality of the ingredient or food or mean the food is raw. Instead it pertains to how the food is grown, processed, and handled.

Unfortunately, *natural* has no legal definition, and manufacturers have known for a long time that consumers like the word. Consumers like the assumed definition rather than the real definition, or lack of a legal definition, so companies use the word frequently and liberally.

A Look at Organic Pet Foods

Unlike *natural,* the term *organic* does have a legal definition, and if it's not used correctly, violators can get in trouble.

> **DOG TALK**
>
> **Organic** means a food or product grown or produced using environmentally sound techniques, with no synthetic pesticides, chemicals, or fertilizers. Organically processed foods cannot contain genetically modified organisms or chemical food additives.

In 1990, Congress adopted the Organic Foods Production Act (OFPA), which established organic food standards. These standards apply to growing, producing, and handling crops and livestock. Products labeled "100% Organic" and displaying the "USDA Organic" seal are grown, produced, or contain only organically produced ingredients. Products that contain at least 95 percent organic ingredients—with the other 5 percent approved by the USDA for use in organic products—may also display the organic seal.

This applies to dog foods as well as foods for people. A dog food labeled "100% Organic Beef Dog Food" must be entirely organic beef with no other ingredients except water or salt. It may contain flavors and additives only if they are on the USDA list as approved for organic foods.

A dog food labeled "Organic Beef Dog Food" must contain at least 95 percent organic beef. The other 5 percent may include water, salt, and other ingredients on the USDA-approved list for organic foods.

A dog food labeled "Organic Beef Dinner" must be 95 percent organic beef, but the other 5 percent may be nonorganic ingredients. That word *dinner* creates the exclusion for nonorganic ingredients.

The National Organic Standards Board (NOSB) is a committee of farmers, environmentalists, consumer advocates, retailers, scientists, and a USDA certifying agent. This committee, and subcommittees, review materials for the lists of approved or disapproved foods or substances. They also make recommendations for organic pet-food standards.

A Look at Human-Grade Foods

As of this writing, only one dog food can legally use the phrase *human grade* on its foods: The Honest Kitchen. In fact, the AAFCO doesn't have a definition for human-grade pet foods, and without an established definition, it isn't supposed to appear on dog-food labels.

> **DOG TALK**
>
> **Human grade** means all ingredients in the food, as well as the processing plant and procedures, are suitable for consumption by people.

The Honest Kitchen went to court and defended its right to use the term. The court agreed the company has the constitutional right to truthful advertising and free speech, and because of its business practices, the company can use *human grade* on its foods.

However, because there is no legal definition in the pet-food industry for this term, beware. The manufacturer should be able to prove—as The Honest Kitchen did—that the ingredients, physical processing plant, actual processing standards, packaging, distribution, and transportation all meet the requirements for human foods.

Buyer Beware

As with so many things, you need to be aware that although many companies don't intentionally try to deceive potential pet-food purchasers, they do tend to tell you what they think you want to hear. If the advertisements say the food provides what you want for your dog, you'll be more apt to buy that product.

Always read advertisements and labels with a good dose of skepticism. If it sounds too good to be true, it likely is, so do some research. Some excellent dog foods are available commercially; some others aren't as good but do have excellent marketing departments.

Grooming

At this age, your German Shepherd is bolder and more inquisitive, and the two of you may be doing more activities away from the house. That might mean your puppy is getting dirtier.

Cleaning him up after a hike in the woods or an adventure at the local beach might seem a little more difficult, but it doesn't have to be.

Getting Out Oil and Grease

Various kinds of oils and greases can be tough to get out of your puppy's coat because many dog shampoos won't break up the oil and grease so it can wash out. The oil and grease can also cause the coat to clump and matt.

A bigger problem is that your German Shepherd may try to groom himself to remove the foreign substance, and ingesting those oils and greases can cause health problems. Cooking oils and meat greases are not toxic but can certainly lead to vomiting and a horrible case of diarrhea.

Motor oils and greases made from petroleum products can be toxic, so you need to remove those from your puppy's coat right away. If you believe your puppy has tried to groom himself and has ingested any oil or grease, forget about bathing him and instead get him to the veterinary clinic right away. Treatment for the ingestion can begin first and he can be bathed at the clinic later while being treated.

Symptoms of petroleum-product poisoning include difficulty breathing, vomiting, tremors, and convulsions. It can be fatal, so get veterinary care immediately.

Many professional groomers use the dishwashing soap Joy to remove oil and grease from fur. In fact, it works so well, wildlife rehabilitation specialists who try to save birds covered in oil after disasters also use Joy.

Start by getting your German Shepherd wet down to the skin. Then beginning at his head, start massaging the Joy into his coat, working down his neck to his shoulders and then the rest of his body. If he has any oil or grease on his face, suds up that area last, avoiding his eyes.

Be sure to work soap into each paw, rubbing the soap in between each pad and around each toenail. He'll lick at any oil or grease left between his pads. Massage his skin and coat for a full 5 minutes, giving the soap time to work. Then rinse thoroughly and repeat.

After the second soaping and rinse, work a mixture of 2 cups white vinegar to 1 gallon warm water into his coat, and rinse again. The vinegar water helps remove anything left in the coat, including any soap residue.

Removing Gum and Other Sticky Stuff

How many times have you gone for a walk and stepped in gum someone spit out on the sidewalk? It's tough to get gum off the bottom of your shoes. And it can be just as hard to get it out of your German Shepherd's coat.

Many groomers recommend applying ice to the gum or sticky stuff before attempting to remove it. Place your hand or something else between the ice and your dog's skin while trying to freeze the gum. When the gum is very cold or frozen, try to break it out of the coat. You may have to reapply the ice several times as you're working at it.

You may also be able to use a small amount of vegetable oil to remove the gum. Massage the oil into the coat around the gum with your fingers. Then see if the gum will slide out. Of course, now your German Shepherd will need a bath to get the oil out of his coat.

Sometimes the only thing you can do is trim the sticky stuff out of the coat. If you need to do this, trim carefully so you don't cut your puppy's skin. Slide a comb between the sticky stuff and his skin, without pulling up the skin. Then trim on the outside of the comb, away from the skin. Snip very slowly and in tiny cuts so you don't make a mistake.

Parting with Paint

Just recently Liz was painting her agility equipment, and two of her dogs felt they needed to help. The agility equipment is painted red, white, and blue and both dogs had bits of all three colors on them.

If the paint your dog gets into is nontoxic, you don't have to worry too much about it. Many times it will fall off the hair when it dries. Or when you brush your dog, the brushing action will remove the paint. And as your dog sheds, the hairs—and paint—will be lost. But if you don't want to wait, you can remove it.

If the paint is a latex or acrylic, it may wash out just fine. Try using some Joy to work out the paint. Then rinse well and follow up with a vinegar rinse.

If the paint is not one made for water cleanup, do not use paint solvents on your puppy: they are toxic. Instead, try to get the paint out with mineral oil, wash well with Joy, rinse, and follow up with a vinegar rinse. If the paint doesn't come out, you'll have to trim it out using the same technique as described for gum earlier in this section.

Getting Out Glue

If your dog gets glue, hot glue, or other adhesives into his coat, they are not going to come out easily. The glue will clump with his hair.

Wearing rubber gloves so you don't end up stuck to your dog, try to wash out as much as you can. Use Joy to wash, rinse well, and rinse with vinegar, as for gum and other sticky stuff. Then trim out any remaining glue. After you've trimmed his coat, you may want to wash that spot in his coat again just in case any glue remains.

Removing Burrs, Foxtails, and Seeds

In the spring and summer, grass and weed seeds are the bane of dog owners. Although your German Shepherd's coat doesn't pick up the seeds as much as dogs with fluffier coats do, the seeds are designed to stick. Most have barbs or hooks that latch on the coat. As the dog moves, the hooks and barbs grab more hairs, and soon a tangle forms. If the seed gets into your German Shepherd's paw between the pads, those barbs and hooks hurt.

You can pull out many grass and weed seeds from your puppy's coat. Just be careful you don't get a barb in your fingertips!

If the seeds won't pull out, you may be able to brush or comb them out. If the seeds don't brush out, use a little hair conditioner—a good, thick, slippery kind—to work out the tangle and seed. Then rinse out the conditioner.

If you still have a tangle with the seed in it, you'll have to trim it out. Use the scissors technique explained earlier in this section.

Dealing with Porcupine Quills and Cactus Spines

Porcupine quills come in different sizes and forms, depending on the species of porcupine. When touched by another animal, the quill releases from the porcupine's skin and embeds itself in the other animal's skin.

Cactus spines don't always detach from the plant, again depending on the species, but many are barbed. When they make contact with skin, they don't pull out but rather work deeper into the skin.

Don't try to pull out cactus spines or porcupine quills on your own—they're very painful. Take your dog to the vet instead. Most veterinarians recommend sedating the dog for removal. This is especially true if the dog got them in his face or paws or has a lot of them.

When He Smells Like a Wet Dog

The wet-dog smell your German Shepherd adolescent occasionally has is caused by oils from his skin as well as bacteria that can build up on his skin. Some dogs are more prone to it than others. Humidity can also cause this smell. If it's been rainy or more humid than normal recently, you may smell the odor more.

Although giving your dog a thorough bath can get rid of the bacteria as well as the skin oils on his skin, it doesn't always get rid of the odor, and no one really knows why. Perhaps the hairs absorb some of the odor.

Many of the waterless shampoos can help, though. These clean your puppy and his coat without using any water. Some of the heavily scented waterless shampoos definitely mask the odor, but they might also bother your German Shepherd's sensitive nose. Don't use those. You can use an unscented or lightly scented waterless shampoo to clean him.

Social Skills

Although as an adolescent your German Shepherd's behavior is still a little uncertain, now is still a great time to broaden his horizons. His brain is open to learning anything right now, so use it. Taking him with you, even on short overnight trips, helps him learn what traveling is all about. New places, sights, sounds, and social skills are great for him at this age.

He'll go to new places, spend the night someplace different, walk along the beach or harbor, hike in the mountains, or smell all the new smells in a big city. He can go camping or spend the night in a motel or visit with your relatives. His biggest lesson, though, is that when the trip is over, he'll go back home. German Shepherds love to have things orderly and controlled, so learning that traveling ends up back home is important to them.

Begin Traveling Young

It's important to begin traveling now, while your German Shepherd is still young, so this, too, becomes a normal part of his life. Even though his adolescent behavior can be a little unpredictable at times, you shouldn't wait until he's older to take him places. He's still flexible now and able to absorb new experiences easily. After all, during his socialization outings, he's facing new experiences all the time.

His first travel experience can be a long day trip. Perhaps there's a quaint town nearby you've wanted to visit. If this is a 2-hour trip, that's fine. Drive up, stopping as needed to let your puppy take a potty break. Walk around town, perhaps have lunch at an outdoor café where your German Shepherd can do a down stay while you eat, and drive home.

If he did well on this outing, maybe your next one can be an overnight trip. Then later, try a several-day camping trip. Just combine the things you like to do with your dog as much as possible.

TIPS AND TAILS

Try not to make the first trip a long one. That can be unsettling for your teenager. One night away and a return home can be a confidence-booster.

Before You Travel

Ensuring your German Shepherd has proper identification is important all the time, but it's even more vital when you travel. Be sure he has a collar ID tag that has your cell phone number printed on it in case he gets lost.

Before your trip, schedule a well-puppy checkup. Be sure your puppy's vaccinations and flea and tick treatments are up to date. Let your veterinarian know where you're going, and ask if there's anything your dog needs before visiting there. If you don't live in an area where heartworm is a problem, for example, ask if the parasite is an issue at your destination location. If you're traveling across state lines, a health certificate may be required. Again, ask your veterinarian. She'll know the requirements.

When you decide where to travel, be sure your destination allows large dogs. Many hotels and motels state they allow dogs but then have a 20- or 30-pound limit. You don't want to be caught unaware when you check in. When you call to make reservations, be up front that you have a large dog.

> **HAPPY PUPPY**

FIDOFriendly.com is a great resource for those traveling with dogs. It can help you find places where dogs are welcome.

You'll want to pack a bag for your German Shepherd. Include the following in it:

- 😼 Enough food for the entire trip as well as a couple of extra days' worth, just in case
- 😼 Food and water bowls
- 😼 Medications, including heartworm, flea, and tick preventatives, if needed
- 😼 Crate and bedding
- 😼 Extra leash and collar
- 😼 Plastic bags to pick up after him
- 😼 Toys and chew treats to amuse him
- 😼 Grooming tools, including nail trimmers

Update your first-aid kit, too, with supplies for you and your dog. It's also a good idea to have a current photo of your dog just in case you get separated.

On the Road

Your German Shepherd needs to be restrained in the car. Just as people need seat belts, your dog needs that safety, too. If you have a big-enough vehicle, you can use his crate. Just secure it with tie-downs so the crate won't move around.

If your car isn't big enough for a full-size German Shepherd crate, use a seat-belt harness. These harnesses, available at pet-supply stores, secure your puppy to your car's seat belt.

Carry more water than you think you might need. If you get delayed in hot weather or the car breaks down, you and your puppy both will need the water. A cooler with both ice and cold water is a great idea.

If you're traveling in warm climates, consider a battery-powered crate fan. It can move the air around even if the car is off.

Never, ever leave your dog unattended in the car. It only takes a few moments for your dog to overheat and die of heatstroke.

Stop for a break every couple hours, especially on the first trip you take with your puppy. You can top off the gas tank, grab a drink or snack for yourself, and take your German Shepherd for a walk. Let him stretch his legs and relieve himself.

> **TIPS AND TAILS**
>
> While traveling, keep your German Shepherd on his leash. It only takes a moment for him to be startled and frightened and dash away. As much as you might trust him, keep him on leash and safe.

Making Travel Fun

Although your teenage German Shepherd's safety is important while you're traveling, don't spend the whole trip worrying about him. He's going to be fine as long as he's with you.

Instead, spend time doing things you'll both enjoy. Go for lots of walks, investigate a new park, and sit on a bench and watch the people go by. Have your meals at outdoor cafés—the nearby air will be full of so many things for him to smell.

Do some research before you leave home and find some dog-friendly places where you and your puppy can have some fun. Then go visit these places. Enjoy the trip, and most importantly, enjoy the time spent with your German Shepherd.

Behavior

At times, your German Shepherd adolescent might totally confuse you. He may react in a way you don't understand or do something you don't expect. In this section, we look at some of the things that have flummoxed other German Shepherd puppy owners.

Dealing with Jealousy

German Shepherds love their owners, and when they choose one special person, they will love that person their whole life. They can also be protective of that person and jealous when someone else gets close, no matter if that someone is human or canine.

When hugging their significant other, many German Shepherd owners will find a long nose trying to weasel between the two people. Other German Shepherds wiggle in between an owner and another dog or cat.

Jealousy isn't a problem as long as your dog backs off when you ask him. However, if he barks, gets protective, or becomes nasty, have him do a down stay at a distance or give him a time-out in his crate.

Putting a Stop to Crotch Sniffing

As you're well aware, dogs sniff the anal and genital region of other dogs. The scent glands located there give off personal information about that other dog—a personal cologne, if you will. If your dog gets a chance, he'll sniff humans in the same region.

People don't appreciate that long nose poking in their crotch, so your dog needs to learn that this is rude behavior. When you see him aiming for an inappropriate area, give him a quick "Hey!" to distract him and turn his head away.

When your dog is on leash out in public, don't let him get anywhere near that close if you know he'll be sniffing that direction.

Understanding Panting

A dog owner asked, "Why does my dog pant when he isn't hot?" Dogs pant to lose heat; the only place they sweat is on the pads of their feet. By panting—blowing air over that big tongue—your puppy can lose a lot of heat.

Dogs also often feel heat differently from how humans do. Keep in mind your German Shepherd is wearing a fur coat. In addition, the darker your dog, the more he feels the heat, especially out in the sun. Individual dogs also have different heat tolerances; some are more sensitive to the heat than others.

Dogs also pant for behavioral reasons. When he's stressed or worried, your puppy might pant. So even if your dog is cool, he may pant in the veterinarian's office or in a strange situation. Build your puppy's confidence in other situations, and this confidence will carry over to times when he's stressed or worried.

Understanding Yawning

Dogs yawn when they're tired, just as we do. But they also yawn to try to calm a situation.

For example, if your puppy is having trouble in a training situation—perhaps he doesn't understand what you want—he may yawn while facing you. Or if he's in class and another dog is making a fuss, your puppy may yawn toward that puppy.

> **TIPS AND TAILS**
>
> Other calming signals include blinking his eyes and looking away from the person or dog who is causing the stress.

The Wagging Tail

Most dog owners assume that if a dog is wagging his tail, he's happy. Most of the time that's true, especially if you have a dog with a happy disposition.

However, a wagging tail really means the dog is feeling emotion:

🐾 A happy German Shepherd's tail will be higher than his normal relaxed position and wagging faster than normal. The happier he is, the faster it will wag.

🐾 An excited German Shepherd's tail will wag back and forth but will be lower than the happy dog's tail.

🐾 The friendly German Shepherd will swish the end of his tail back and forth, but it won't wag as much as the excited or happy dog's tail.

🐾 A puppy who's feeling worried or anxious will wag his tail very low, even between his back legs.

🐾 The German Shepherd who is feeling too big for his britches—who's ready to take on the world—will lift his tail high and wag it slowly back and forth.

The tail's motions are a means of communication, just like all his other postures. The tail alone doesn't convey the message—it's his entire body language.

Rolling in Bad Stuff

A German Shepherd owner asked, "My German Shepherd rolled on top of a dead squirrel, back and forth. Why did he do that?" Experts really don't know why dogs do this, but rest assured, your German Shepherd isn't the only one who has.

Some behaviorists feel that predators—which includes the canine species—roll in stinky stuff to camouflage their natural smell. Other experts disagree. No one really knows why dogs do it.

We might not know why dogs roll in smelly stuff, but we do know many dogs have preferred smells, like a personal cologne. Some like dead animals, some like cat odors, and some like garbage. It seems to be a personal preference.

Dealing with Mounting

The owner of a spayed German Shepherd asked why her female adolescent would mount (hump) other dogs—males and females—while playing. She assumed only male dogs did that and was also confused why her dog was mounting both males and females.

Intact males and female adolescents often mount other dogs because hormones are raging through their system. They feel this action is what they should do, so they do it. Plus, in reality, the intact dog may find that this behavior feels good. By mounting other dogs, the intact dog is also performing what comes naturally when hormones are raging. This is a behavioral rehearsal for reproduction.

Although spayed and neutered dogs won't reproduce, spaying a female dog (and neutering a male) doesn't remove all of the dog's hormones. Some behaviors will continue, although at a lower rate.

Many dogs mount during play sessions with other dogs because they get excited. Not necessarily sexually excited, but just plain overstimulated. All the dogs were running and playing and your dog was so happy and, well, he couldn't help it because the dog in front of him was just standing still.

Mounting can also be an attention-getting behavior. If the group of dogs is playing and your dog wants to be the center of attention, mounting another dog will certainly get him attention. Your dog doesn't care if the attention was a spin in place, a growl, or snapping jaws. It was still attention.

When your dog is playing with other dogs and begins to mount one, interrupt him immediately. Most adult dogs dislike this behavior, and it's a sure way to start a dog fight.

A dog who mounts another dog of the same sex isn't necessarily gay. Your dog is simply taking advantage of the fact that the dog near him was available.

Adolescent dogs hump people for the same reasons they mount other dogs. Your puppy might have also discovered that when he humped someone's leg, it got a reaction. Sometimes any reaction is a good one, according to puppies anyway.

Stop the behavior immediately. When he tries to grab a leg with his front legs, yell at him, "Hey!" and knock him off your leg. Then have him lie down and stay until he calms down. If he won't hold a down stay, put him in his crate.

Eating Cat Food and Feces

Many dogs, especially puppies, are attracted to cat food. The reason is simple: puppies are always hungry, and cat food is higher in fat than puppy food. It smells good and tastes even better, so once the puppy gets a mouthful of cat food, he's always going to want some more.

Cats have a short intestinal tract and don't digest commercial cat foods well, especially those containing cereal grains. In addition, fat is sprayed on the cat food so the cat will eat it. When the cat doesn't fully digest the food, the dog is attracted to the feces. Lacking the social mores people have, your German Shepherd puppy isn't disgusted by it at all. To him, this is just another snack.

To ensure this doesn't happen in your home, keep the cat food and the litter box in inaccessible places for your puppy. Never trust your adolescent to ignore either the food or the litter box.

Burying Bones

Many dogs like to bury bones and special toys. Some dogs bury them and then stand in front of the buried bone as if to say, "Go away. There is no bone here!"

Burying bones and leftover food probably has its roots in hunting behaviors. For most of the canine race's history, food was survival. Canines would eat as much as they could and then try to hide what was left over so scavengers wouldn't steal it.

Although hopefully your German Shepherd will never go hungry, that instinct is still there. If he's picking the wrong places to bury stuff, teach him where he can bury them. Turn over some dirt so it's soft, and give him a head-start by half-burying a few chew toys. Use praise to encourage him to dig there.

Drinking from the Toilet

This habit really disgusts most dog owners. Most dogs who can reach the water in the toilet, such as your big German Shepherd, like to drink from it. The water in the toilet is cleaner, fresher, and colder than the water in his dish. It makes sense that he prefers it.

If you don't like this behavior or if you use drop-in toilet-bowl cleaners, keep the toilet lid down. That's an easy fix.

Making a Bed

Many German Shepherds really appreciate their comfort and will circle and circle before lying down. Some even like to scratch at their blankets and arrange everything just so before getting comfortable.

Although throughout history wild canines didn't have blankets and dog beds for comfort, many wild canines did and still do scratch up a nest of grasses or other vegetation for a bed. Domesticated dogs' habit of circling comes from that old instinct to create a comfortable sleeping place.

Training

Environmental enrichment is a technique zoos use to keep captive animals happy. By hiding treats and things to play with in the animal's enclosure, the animal is more active mentally and physically. You can use this science to keep your German Shepherd happy, too.

Environmental enrichment stimulates your puppy's brain, but so should your training. His brain is ready and willing to learn, so polish those training skills.

Environmental Enrichment

At the San Diego Zoological Society's Safari Park in northern San Diego County, the African lions get some interesting items for environmental enrichment. Zookeepers there freeze 5-gallon buckets full of meat chunks, blood, and water. When they're frozen solid, they give these to the lions in various areas of their enclosure. The lions have to find the frozen treats and then get to lick, paw, claw, and chew on the treats to get the good stuff frozen inside.

At the elephant enclosure, food is given in the serving areas but also stashed away in other places, including in food-dispensing toys. One looked like a 50-gallon plastic drum with two holes at the top. It was suspended high in a tree, and the elephant had to reach up to the drum, tilt it, and get her trunk inside to get the food. This is a challenge for an intelligent animal who needs mental stimulation.

Your German Shepherd is also an intelligent animal who needs mental challenges. We've encouraged you to use food-dispensing toys several times in this book, and these continue to be good for your adolescent, both now and on into adulthood. But there are other ways to amuse him.

Have him do a down stay, hide some treats in another room, and release him to search for the treats. Initially, until he understands the game, you may have to point to the hiding spots. But once he understands, he'll do it on his own. Then, hide treats all over the house. Again, in the beginning, help him search for them. Play the same game in the backyard.

Purchase several inexpensive buckets at your local discount store. In different places around the backyard, invert the buckets and place a treat under each one. Each time you do this, change the location of the buckets so your dog has to search for them.

In the heat of the summer, get a child's plastic wading pool. Fill it with water and drop in some carrot slices, apple slices, ice cubes, a couple tennis balls, and some treats. Encourage him to get in and get the treats.

Once you start playing with environmental enrichment, you'll find out what gets your teenager excited and what doesn't. Then you can design some new activities for him.

Polishing His Training Skills

Your brilliant adolescent's brain is capable of learning anything you can teach him right now. He still doesn't have the concentration he'll have as an adult, but he does have the learning ability.

Keep your training sessions short and active. You can tell when he's getting distracted because he won't focus on you or will pay attention for half a second. Then his eyes will wander and he'll look at the birds, the butterfly flittering by, or the jogger passing on the sidewalk.

Use this month to polish your German Shepherd's training skills. Take a look at the exercises he already knows, and make them better. When he works with you during training sessions or when you're asking him to do something for you in the house, how does he respond? Is he slow, waiting to do things on his own time? Does he ignore you, waiting for a second or third request? Or is he just sloppy? Work on having him cooperate a little better.

To do this, have a vision of what you want. If you watch your dog trainer's dog and are envious of how he works with her, what is it you like so much? Does a neighbor's dog work with his owner as if the two were a real team? Decide what you'd like from your teenager and later, from your dog as an adult. Having this vision of what'd like from your German Shepherd can give your training focus. When you have that goal in your sight, you can then work toward it.

Practicing His Leash Skills

The most important leash skill for your German Shepherd is not pulling on it. He's already a big dog, and when he decides to pull, he can unbalance you, hurt your arm or shoulder, and potentially hurt himself.

In Month 4, we introduced leash training. Refreshing those skills is never a bad idea:

😸 Put the leash on your adolescent and go outside. Don't ask him to do anything; don't give him any direction. Just start walking.

😸 If he walks with you, keeping the leash loose, praise him.

😸 If he starts sniffing, run and walk away from him. Let the leash tighten quickly. If he immediately moves toward you, praise him.

😸 If he moves ahead of you and tightens the leash, pulling, turn around and walk the other direction.

If, after a few about-turns, he decides to keep an eye on you, praise him enthusiastically, "Sweetie, good! Awesome job!"

> ### HAPPY PUPPY
>
> When he's doing this fairly well, make a game of it. Walk in zigzags, turning quickly, going different directions. Challenge him to keep up with you, and keep the praise coming when he does.

The heel is also a leash skill. You taught him this last month, so he might still need some work on it. You can still make it better:

😸 During some of your training sessions, hold a high-value treat in your right hand.

😸 If he gets distracted, dip that hand down to his nose as you tell him, "Sweetie, watch me!"

Bring your hand up toward your face. When his eyes follow your face, praise him!

Keep the heel sessions short and sweet, because they require a lot of concentration.

Heel for 20 feet, stop, and sit your puppy. Heel 20 more feet, turn around, and sit your puppy. Heel 10 feet one direction, turn around, heel 10 feet the other direction, stop, and sit your puppy. Quick and snappy training is important right now to help keep your puppy focused.

Practicing Quick, Straight Sits

Lanky adolescents often take their time when sitting. They have to coordinate that long back and those long legs so they don't rush anything. Plus, when they take their time, they can end up sitting every which way that isn't right next to you.

For the most part, it really doesn't matter when or where or how your German Shepherd sits, but if you want to polish his training skills, teaching him to sit quickly right next to you is a good exercise.

 With your dog on leash by your left side in the heel position, hold the leash in your left hand and have some good treats in your right hand.

 Ask him to heel, and walk so you have a wall or fence by your left side, leaving just enough room for your teenager to walk between you and the wall or fence.

 As you come to a stop, immediately have the treat at his nose and bring it up and back quickly, using the same motion when you taught the sit in Month 4, but quicker. The faster hand motion tells him to move more quickly into the sit, and the wall helps keep him right next to you as he sits.

 Praise him and give him the treat.

> **HAPPY PUPPY**
>
> Don't ask him to do sit after sit after sit. That's boring even with the treats. So practice several different things, and scatter some sits near the wall throughout your training session.

When his sits have become quicker and he's sitting straight next to you, it's time to decrease the size of the wall. Walk next to a picnic table bench turned on its side.

Or place a 2×4 board on the ground, and walk next to it. He knows how to sit next to you; he just needs a cue to help him. Gradually phase out the wall or board, and really reward him when he sits nicely by your side without any extra help.

Practicing Faster Comes

There isn't much better than watching a German Shepherd in full run, covering ground as fast as if he's flying. Most adolescents tend to use that extra power and speed when they're doing something they want to do, like chasing a rabbit. Coming when called, however, isn't always that exciting. There are a few ways to increase the speed of the come, and both of them are exciting enough your teenager ought to be very happy to cooperate.

If your German Shepherd is fairly reliable when called and will come to you rather than dash away, he can be on his leash. If your puppy is apt to head the opposite direction when you call him, however, fasten a 20- to 30-foot leash to his collar.

🐾 Let your puppy sniff the grass and get distracted. If he's on a regular leash, just drape it over his back. If he's on a long leash, hold the end of it.

🐾 When he's not paying any attention to you, turn and run away from him. You don't need to run fast; you just want him to chase after you.

🐾 As you turn and move away, call him, "Sweetie, come!"

🐾 When he catches up to you, praise him enthusiastically, "Sweetie, good! Awesome dog!"

🐾 If he doesn't immediately come to you, let the leash get taut as you run. As soon as it tightens, he'll come to you. In this case, praise but not nearly as much as you would when he came with no help or with no reminder from the leash.

Another technique is particularly effective for German Shepherds who are ball-crazy. If your teenager loves tennis balls or other balls, he'll love this one:

🐾 Ask your dog to sit but not stay.

🐾 Step away from him. If you can go 10 feet without him moving, that's great. If you can go 20 feet away, that's even better.

🐾 If he moves from the sit when you're a distance away, that's fine. You're not practicing the stay right now.

🐾 Call him to come, and as he begins moving toward you, hold out the ball, let him see it, and throw it behind you, away from him.

🐾 As he picks up speed, praise him.

🐾 When he brings the ball back to you, praise him again.

With this technique he really isn't coming to you, but instead he's running after the ball. However, he began moving toward you when you called him and only then did you add a technique to speed up his motion. That's good, too.

You can mix up all the come techniques you've learned and do them in one training session. That keeps your puppy thinking, and keeps the training exciting for him.

You and Your Puppy

It can be hard to keep your cool when you have a 70-pound adolescent puppy in the house. When he comes trotting out from a back room with a half-chewed leather shoe, you may want to scream.

Remember, none of this is personal. Just as with human teenagers, adolescents react to whomever is closest to them. With your puppy, that's you.

Keeping Your Calm

Child-rearing experts suggest parents practice calming techniques so they don't lose their temper with their acting-up children. Thomas W. Phelan, PhD, author of the popular book *1-2-3 Magic: Effective Discipline for Children 2–12,* says one of the biggest mistakes parents make when dealing with children is too much emotion. He continues by saying that when children make mistakes, the parent needs to be consistent and calm.

This applies equally well to raising a puppy. When you get angry or lose your temper, you're more apt to do something you'll regret later. You may yell and scream, shake your chewed shoe in your puppy's face, or even physically intimidate him. None of these things are good dog training or even particularly effective.

If you have to stop and count to 10 to calm yourself, do it. Your puppy isn't going anywhere, and the situation will be the same as it was before you counted. But you'll be calmer and clearer-headed and better equipped to handle the situation.

Using Time-Outs

There's nothing wrong with giving your puppy a time-out when he needs one. You may have heard not to use the crate as a punishment, and that's absolutely true. However, giving your puppy a time-out isn't punishment; it's a chance for him to stop reacting, calm down if he's overstimulated, and begin thinking again.

The time-out is most effective if you can interrupt your puppy in the act of mis-behaving, gently take him by the collar, and walk him back to his crate. Don't talk to him. Just walk him to his crate, put him inside, close the door, and walk away.

Then go make yourself an iced tea or pour a glass of wine. Sit down and remind yourself why you added a puppy to your household and how much you love him. Yes, even when he acts up.

Out and About

If your teenager decides to misbehave when you're out in public, don't make a scene, and don't allow your puppy to make a scene, either. Not only does this reflect badly on all German Shepherds, but you also don't want your puppy to learn he can get away with bad behavior out in public or when other people are around.

If he begins to misbehave, nip it in the bud quickly. If he needs to get his brain back in gear, do some quick heel and sits. Or have him do puppy push-ups: down, sit, down, sit, down, sit, followed by praise and treats.

If he's behaving badly on the leash, have him down and stay. Hold the leash close or even put a hand on his shoulder to help him do it.

In the worst-case scenario, take him back to the car and make him do a down stay there. No bouncing around in the car—you mean it. A down stay.

> **TIPS AND TAILS**
>
> If your puppy is *really* acting out, take him away from the distraction—behind a building or down an alley or on the other side of the parking lot—and let him calm down.

Keep Him Moving

Your teenager can only concentrate on one thing at a time. So if he's acting badly, is antsy, and can't hold still, don't ask him to do a down stay. If he can't hold still, don't let him be still.

Keep him moving, and make him think. Practice his obedience exercises, and even review his tricks. Just keep him moving, and don't let him stop.

Soon, he'll be more than happy to stop and do a down stay for you, but be sure you wear him out first. He needs to learn in the best way for him at the time that you won't allow bad behavior.

Don't Forget to Play!

When all the bad behavior is over and your teenager is once again that puppy you fell in love with, don't forget to play with him. Play will help solidify the bond the two of you share and will give you a chance to smile again.

> **HAPPY PUPPY**
>
> Konrad Lorenz, Nobel Prize–winning expert on animal behavior, said that play develops a dog's mind. By stimulating your dog's mind during play, you can actually create a more intelligent dog.

What you do for play really doesn't matter. What does matter is that the two of you have fun.

Approaching Adulthood

Month 11 | Month 12

Socialization in public

Ready for more advanced training
Slow growth—reaches adult size
Annual vaccinations and checkup

What a journey you and your German Shepherd puppy have been on the past few months! She joined your family as a baby puppy and is now an adolescent who's rapidly approaching adulthood. The two of you have had some great times, learned a lot, and weathered some challenges together. As you've probably learned by now, there's no companion quite like a German Shepherd. She's an intelligent and devoted dog who is happiest when involved in every aspect of your life.

But even now, during this twelfth month, she's not yet grown up. Most German Shepherds this age are still in the turmoil of adolescence, and that can continue for a few more months. Rest assured, though, that the signs of adulthood will gradually increase.

Physical Development

It's hard not to think of your German Shepherd as an adult because she looks more adult than puppy these days. She's in proportion now and has lost most of the awkwardness of puppyhood. She's not a grown-up yet, though, and she won't be for a while.

Although your adolescent's body is continuing to develop, grow, and change, the differences aren't as obvious as when she was younger. At 4 and 5 months of age, for example, she changed daily. When she woke up from a nap, she looked like she'd grown as she slept! Those changes have slowed now. But if you take some photos of her on her first birthday and take new photos on her second birthday, you'll see some definite differences.

Adult male German Shepherds are between 24 and 26 inches tall at the shoulder at 12 months, and females are between 22 and 24 inches tall. Your puppy has most of her height now but she'll continue to grow slightly over the next year.

Most puppies this age weigh between 65 and 75 pounds. This is an average, though, and some will be heavier and others lighter.

German Shepherds are not considered adults, physically, until they're 3 years old. Although most of the growth and development has occurred by 2 years, your puppy will still change until she reaches 3 years old. By then, her chest will be larger, her hips will be slightly broader, and she'll have more muscle.

Males will continue to look more masculine, with a broader head and a bigger chest. Because males are larger than females, they take longer to mature. If you compare your male 1-year-old to a female of the same age, your male might be a little clumsier.

Females look obviously feminine without looking weak or fragile. They're also more coordinated.

Health

The more you know about your German Shepherd's health, both as an individual and as a member of her breed, the better choices you can make for her. That includes deciding, with your veterinarian's input, what vaccination schedule you want to use for her throughout her adult life.

Knowing what health problems can potentially affect German Shepherds is also important. Recognizing the signs and symptoms of disease can help you decide when to call the veterinarian.

Establishing an Adult Vaccination Schedule

At this age, your German Shepherd isn't yet ready for her next vaccinations; that won't be for a few more months. However, your veterinarian may have already sent you a reminder so you can schedule an appointment and mark your calendar.

Most veterinarians recommend an annual booster for a distemper combination a year after the last puppy vaccination. He may also recommend other vaccines depending on your location and any local disease outbreaks.

After these, however, vaccination schedules change. In years past, annual boosters were given each year of your dog's life, but that's changed.

The American Veterinary Medical Association (AVMA) now says, "Dogs and cats at a low risk of disease exposure may not need to be boostered yearly for most diseases. Consult with your veterinarian to determine the appropriate vaccination schedule for your dog or cat. Remember, recommendations vary depending upon the age, breed, and health status of your pet, the potential of your pet being exposed to disease, the type of vaccine, whether the pet is used for breeding, and the geographical area where the pet lives or may visit."

Talk to your veterinarian about vaccines. Some discussion points might include the following:

🐾 What is your German Shepherd's risk of exposure? Does she go to dog parks, dog shows, training classes, or other places where she meets a variety of other dogs? If she does, she's more apt to be exposed to disease.

🐾 Which vaccines are you concerned about? What would be the risks to your German Shepherd should she get sick? Is the disease treatable with a high probability of success?

🐾 What is the risk to people should your puppy get sick?

🐾 What is the risk to other pets in the home should your puppy get sick?

🐾 What's your German Shepherd's overall state of health? Would a vaccination cause more harm than good?

🐾 What's the potential for a reaction from a specific vaccination? Has your puppy had reactions from vaccines in the past?

Once you and your veterinarian have discussed these issues, you both can make a decision that will satisfy both of you.

> **TIPS AND TAILS**

The rabies vaccination is legally required a year after the puppy rabies vaccination was given. After this booster, rabies is given every 3 years.

Testing Titers

Some pet owners and even veterinarians are questioning the wisdom of giving booster vaccines every year, and more pet owners have been asking how long vaccination protection lasts. Unfortunately, that's hard to say because every dog's immune system is different.

Checking the animal's antibodies for a particular disease, a process called testing the *titers,* can help determine if the vaccine's antibodies are still present in your dog's system.

DOG TALK

A **titer** is a test that measures the amount of antibodies to a particular disease your dog is carrying in her body.

Although this test can be a wonderful alternative to vaccinating your German Shepherd every year—especially when it's not necessary—as with everything else, the system isn't perfect. Antibody tests aren't available for all canine diseases, and standardized levels of antibodies have yet to be set. Plus, more research is needed to determine exactly what minimum titer levels indicate when a dog is safe from disease.

Knowing the dog's history and lifestyle, along with the titer levels, is important in deciding whether a booster vaccination should be given.

Discussing Vaccinosis

No discussion of vaccinations can be complete unless the elephant in the room—*vaccinosis*—is introduced. Many veterinarians as well as dog owners are concerned about the number of animals with serious long-term health problems.

DOG TALK

Vaccinosis is a chronic illness that results from vaccinations. It may include immune system diseases, lupus, or cancer.

Vaccinations have been implicated in these health problems for several reasons. Vaccinations affect the animal's immune system—that's how they work, after all. Many of the diseases are autoimmune diseases, including lupus, immune system suppression, and bone marrow suppression.

In addition, many dogs who develop vaccinosis later in life suffered reactions after getting vaccinations many years earlier. The reactions might have been mild, such as lethargy and a lack of appetite for a day or two, but even mild reactions should be recognized and reported to the veterinarian.

In addition, it's vitally important that only healthy dogs be vaccinated. If your German Shepherd is sick or has a compromised immune system, she should not be vaccinated at that time. Although she may not get sick from the vaccine itself, her immune system could react and cause any number of autoimmune diseases like arthritis, colitis, pancreatitis, cancer, or leukemia.

Adult Health Problems

Breeders have been working hard to improve the health of German Shepherds, and some health challenges that were once common in the breed are now significantly less so. However, these dogs in general still have some problems you should be aware of in case it occurs in your German Shepherd.

As you read about these issues, take another look at those health threats listed in Month 6, too. When it comes to your German Shepherd's health, the more knowledge you have, the better. Then, should something in your dog's health change, you can get her veterinary help.

Here are some other health problems known to affect the breed:

Allergies: You may notice your German Shepherd is biting and scratching at herself, often incessantly. Many owners say their dog wakes them up during the night scratching or chewing. If she's scratching, she might be allergic to pollens, grasses, dust, dust mites, molds and mildews, or any number of other things, including food ingredients. If you think your German Shepherd might be having an allergy attack, talk to your veterinarian. Tests can sometimes determine exactly what allergies your German Shepherd has. Treatment options differ depending on the allergies.

Cancer: Cancers of various types have been found in this breed, but hemangio-sarcoma is found in German Shepherds far too often. This cancer grows from cells that make up the lining of small blood vessels. It's malignant, and although it can occasionally be found as a lump on the dog's body, it often grows internally with no visible sign. Surgery and chemotherapy can sometimes give your dog some more time, but this cancer eventually causes death.

Osteosarcoma is a form of bone cancer most often found in large-breed dogs, including German Shepherds. It usually first appears in the long bones of the front legs, although it also develops in the hind legs, ribs, or jaw. This is an aggressive cancer that spreads quickly and often to the lungs. Amputation of the affected leg as well as chemotherapy can improve quality of life and may buy the dog some time, but it won't cure the cancer.

Just because German Shepherds are prone to certain diseases doesn't mean your dog will develop them. Getting your puppy from a breeder who chooses her breeding dogs wisely—without these diseases—and then providing the best care for your dog is all you can do. So don't worry, but be aware so you can get your dog veterinary care if symptoms appear.

Cauda equina syndrome (CES): The first signs of CES are usually pain in the lower back and problems getting up after lying down. There may be lameness in one or both back legs, too. In German Shepherds, a narrowing of the lumbosacral vertebral canal, which puts pressure on spinal nerve roots, is usually what causes CES. Your veterinarian will need to diagnose this condition because it's often mistaken for hip dysplasia. Treatment options vary and may include surgery and/or medications.

Degenerative myelopathy: This degenerative disease of the spinal cord causes weakness of the rear legs. It, too, is often mistaken for hip dysplasia. Sometimes the toenails of the rear legs will drag on the ground or the dog will stand with a foot flipped over so the top of the foot is on the ground. It also can progress to paralysis of the rear legs.

Degenerative myelopathy is suspected of being an autoimmune disease wherein the immune system attacks the myelin sheath that covers the nerves. It's similar to multiple sclerosis in people. Your veterinarian will be needed for a diagnosis.

There is no cure for this condition, but exercise, physical therapy, diet, supplements, medications, and veterinary management may slow its progression. A screening test recently has been developed so breeders can eliminate dogs carrying this disorder from their breeding program.

Inflammatory bowel disease: Many forms of this disorder exist, but the one that most commonly affects German Shepherds is lymphocytic-plasmacytic enterocolitis. The first signs of this are recurring diarrhea and vomiting. Other signs are weight loss and malnutrition. The disease has been associated with giardia, food allergies, and an overgrowth of bacteria in the intestinal tract. There is no cure, but veterinary care, medications, and a controlled and limited diet can often manage it.

Pannus: This is an autoimmune disease of the eye. A chronic inflammation of the cornea, this first appears as redness around the edge of the cornea. The third eyelid may also be red and swollen. If left untreated, this disease can cause blindness. Treatment usually consists of eye drops that contain steroids and avoiding ultraviolet light.

Perianal fistulas: Fistulas are draining openings in the skin that appear around the anus. At first, they may appear as small openings in the skin, but if untreated, they may increase to open wounds. Constipation, painful defecation, a foul odor, and an increased licking of the anal region are all potential symptoms. It's thought there's an inherited tendency toward this disorder; it may also be an autoimmune problem. Treatment may consist of surgery to remove the fistulas as well as antibiotics for secondary infections.

Von Willebrand's disease: This is a bleeding disorder caused by a deficiency in a plasma protein that enables clotting. Dogs with a cut or a tooth coming in during teething bleed more than normal and for a longer period of time. This also becomes obvious when a puppy undergoes surgery, such as spaying or neutering. Thankfully, this inherited disorder is seen less in German Shepherds today than in the past.

If you suspect anything is wrong with your adolescent now or as she grows up, call your veterinarian. Don't hesitate because with many of the more serious diseases, early treatment can make a difference. Ideally, your German Shepherd will live a long, healthy life without any of these health threats.

Nutrition

Although you may need to make some changes to your German Shepherd's diet as she grows up, don't be in a hurry to do so. She may be a year old by the end of this month, but there really isn't anything magical about that age. She's still growing and still needs a good-quality diet.

As Your Puppy Grows Up

If your adolescent German Shepherd is eating a food labeled for all life stages, there's no need to change foods. If she's doing well, has a bright and shiny coat, is healthy, and has energy for training and play, keep her on the food she's on.

If your dog is primarily a pet and most of her exercise comes from a daily walk and games of retrieving in the backyard, an adult maintenance dog food will be fine.

If you and your dog are training in a couple of canine sports and you plan on competing at some point, your dog should probably eat a premium-brand dog food for all life stages rather than an adult maintenance.

If your adolescent tends to be thin and doesn't put on weight well, a higher-calorie premium food might be the answer. Or feed her an all-life-stages food and supplement it with some additional calories (cottage cheese or yogurt) and protein (meat or eggs).

If your German Shepherd is gaining too much weight, kick up her exercise. If that doesn't burn off her extra weight, cut back on her food and add some fiber so she doesn't feel like she's still hungry after she eats.

> **TIPS AND TAILS**
>
> Continue to feed your German Shepherd twice a day. Although for many years dog owners were told once a day was fine, that opinion has changed. Meals twice a day are healthier for your dog.

Make changes slowly. Take several weeks to change from one food to another, adding small amounts of the new food as you decrease the old food. If your adolescent develops soft stools, slow down the change even more.

Dealing with Food and Health Issues

The food you feed your German Shepherd has an impact on her overall health. Not only does it affect her weight—too thin or too heavy—the food must also provide energy for training, exercise, and play.

Dry kibble foods, especially those that contain sugar and simple carbohydrates, can cause dental problems. Bits of the kibble can lodge in the gums, causing inflammation and leading to tartar and plaque.

Ingredients in a food that contains several proteins and carbohydrates can trigger food allergies. Dogs with allergies usually do better on a food with one unique protein (often a different or unusual one such as bison or venison) and one unique carbohydrate (such as sweet potato).

Foods that contain a great deal of carbohydrates, especially cereal grains, can cause ear infections. Sugar, such as from sugar beets and other sources, can also trigger ear infections.

> **TIPS AND TAILS**
>
> Yogurt that contains live active cultures of probiotics can ease many digestive upsets by helping keep the digestive system working at its best. Yogurt can also tempt a picky eater because it smells good to the dog. Full-fat yogurt can also keep weight on a thin German Shepherd. A heaping tablespoon at each meal is great.

A variety of foods can cause gastrointestinal upsets, most commonly cereal grains and glutens. German Shepherds with a sensitive digestive tract should not eat wheat, corn, soy, or beet pulp. Sensitive dogs should eat as few artificial colorings, flavors, and preservatives as possible.

Food can also trigger vomiting. It can be a reaction to an ingredient, a sign the food might be spoiled, or simply your dog eating too fast.

What your German Shepherd eats is more than simply something to fill her belly. It's the single-most important thing for her continued good health and, hopefully, longevity.

Grooming

Over the past few months, you've learned a lot about grooming your German Shepherd. Hopefully, you're comfortable cleaning her teeth and ears, can wipe her eyes, and have toenail trimming down pat. You've also worked to make her comfortable with her daily massage while you check her over for any problems. Ideally, you've also come to terms with her shedding. You know how to brush her and how often you need to do it to keep her coat in good condition. You've got a good vacuum cleaner, too, and know how to use it. You can get sticky stuff and matts out of her coat and can bathe her with little difficulty. You know how to care for your adolescent.

So what else do you need to know? What about a skunk? Skunks aren't afraid of dogs, especially skunks that live around residential neighborhoods. Unfortunately, very few German Shepherds will back away from skunks.

Then, what about clothes for dogs? Before you protest, "My German Shepherd will never wear doggy clothes!" think about protective boots and life-preservers. There actually are some doggy clothes you may want to try out for your German Shepherd.

Getting the Skunk Out

Skunks, perhaps because they aren't afraid of dogs, seem to attract dogs' attention, and very few German Shepherds will voluntarily leave one alone. Once a dog has been sprayed, she doesn't seem to be deterred, either. It's almost as though she's even more fascinated with this funny-smelling creature.

Skunks spray by forcibly expressing the material in their anal glands, located on either side of the anus. Dogs have these glands, too, but cannot express them as skunks do—and most importantly, cannot aim them. Skunks can be very accurate when spraying.

A dog who's been sprayed by a skunk is a miserable canine, and her owners will be even more disturbed. Although nothing will get the smell out, we do know of a formula that helps tremendously:

- 🐾 If at all possible, bathe your German Shepherd outside. Don't bring her in the house until she's clean.

- 🐾 Mix together 1 quart of 3 percent hydrogen peroxide (get this at the drug store), ½ cup of baking soda, and 2 teaspoons of liquid dish soap with grease-cutting properties (such as Dawn or Joy).

- 🐾 Wet your adolescent thoroughly, getting her wet to the skin.

- 🐾 Work the peroxide formula into her coat, beginning where she took the hit from the skunk and following through over the rest of her body.

- 🐾 Really work in the mixture with your hands and fingers, getting it down to the skin. Continue to massage the mixture into her coat for at least 5 minutes to let the ingredients work on the oil from the spray.

- 🐾 Rinse well and then repeat.

Don't save any of the peroxide mixture, if any is left over. The chemical reaction can cause an explosion in an airtight container.

> **TIPS AND TAILS**

Forget the tomato juice bath that's long been recommended. It doesn't work and just makes a huge red mess.

Outfitting Your German Shepherd

Many, if not most, dog owners seem to think only tiny dogs—the toy breed dogs who are often carried about in their owners' arms—wear dog clothes. But dog clothing consists of much more than frilly pink outfits for those toy breed dogs, and many have practical applications for German Shepherds.

Boots: Shoes or boots for dogs have become popular recently, especially for dogs walking on difficult surfaces such as hot asphalt, hot sand, abrasive sand, or gravel that could injure the dog's paws. Many German Shepherd owners who have to walk their dog in cold weather regions put boots on their dogs. This protects the dog's feet from the melting agents used to treat snow and ice that are potentially dangerous for the dog. Working dogs, and search-and-rescue dogs in particular, wear dog boots when searching areas that could injure their paws. Urban searches in collapsed buildings can be particularly dangerous.

If your German Shepherd ever walks with you in places or during situations where her paws could be harmed, introducing her to some boots would be a good idea. Check out dogbooties.com for some boots for your buddy. Follow their instructions for sizing the boots.

Introducing your German Shepherd to the boots isn't difficult. Have some good treats at hand, and put your dog on leash so she can't dash away from you. It's best to introduce two boots at a time rather than all four. Put one boot on a front paw, checking to be sure it's on correctly and it fits. Praise your puppy and give her a treat. Then put on the other front boot, fit it, and praise and reward her.

Then, using the leash to keep her with you and some treats to help keep her attention, go for a short walk. Praise her for her attention, and distract her if she focuses on the boots. After just a few minutes, take the boots off and make a huge fuss over your puppy.

Gradually, over a week or two, use the same technique to get her used to all four boots at the same time. Pay attention to her paws to be sure the boots fit correctly and aren't causing a problem when she walks.

Vests for visibility: Vests that increase your German Shepherd's visibility using reflective strips or glow-in-the-dark material are great when you walk your German Shepherd in the early morning, evening, or at night. This is especially true when you have a dark dog who might not be easily seen. Bright-orange vests are great if you live in a rural area, especially if you're in an area where hunting is common. Plus, a German Shepherd wearing a bright-orange vest is less likely to be mistaken for a predator.

Several companies make safety vests for dogs. Search online for "safety vests for dogs," and compare the various types, colors, sizes, and prices.

Introducing your German Shepherd to a vest is easy, and most dogs accept the vest with little concern. Just use your training skills, including some good treats, and put the vest on your puppy before going for a walk. Distract her when the vest bothers her, and praise her when she leaves it alone.

Life jackets: As a general rule, German Shepherds are excellent swimmers. However, just as people who are good swimmers also wear life jackets at times, so should dogs. If you take your German Shepherd with you aboard a boat; when you go swimming; or if you'll be in potentially swift, rough, or cold water, a life jacket for your dog is a great idea. Plus, most dog life jackets have a handle on the top of the back. This makes a great grab handle should you need to get hold of your dog.

Several companies make life jackets for dogs. Take a look at petstreetmall.com/ Dog-Life-Jackets/615.html for more information.

Other clothes: Although your German Shepherd won't need much in the way of other clothing, there are some other things you might want to keep in mind.

For example, many people are worried about large and potentially aggressive dogs—German Shepherds included. It's amazing how much fear can be alleviated by having your dog wear something bright and colorful. A brightly colored bandanna around her neck is attractive and makes her look more like a well-loved member of the family.

At Halloween, costumes are always fun. Just be sure the costume fits your dog and doesn't restrict her movements. Be sure to teach your German Shepherd to wear it a few weeks ahead of time so she's comfortable on the big day.

Social Skills

As your German Shepherd puppy moves from adolescence to adulthood, in a few months you'll need to help her through a few more social changes. There shouldn't be anything drastic, and nothing the two of you can't handle.

One of the most important things you can do now, and as your German Shepherd grows up, is to be sure she gets out of the house and yard on a regular basis. A daily walk is the perfect way to do this. Vary your walks, and go to different places so you both can see new people, dogs, and sights. Varying the routine also keeps the two of you from becoming bored.

Mixing Teenagers and Adults

Adult dogs are incredibly patient with puppies. They allow puppies to chew on them, jump all over them, and steal their toys. Many adult dogs will even let a puppy get away with stealing a treat. Dogs are a wonderful lesson in patience with babies.

Now that isn't to say adult dogs don't teach puppies; they do. They correct biting with body language, as well as with a growl and snarl. They let a puppy steal a toy or treat, but don't let the puppy barge in on dinner. Adult dogs are patient but do set limits.

As your German Shepherd adolescent grows up, you'll find that adult dogs are less patient with her if she misbehaves. If she charges an adult dog, even in play, the adult will block the charge with a growl and snarl, and maybe even a flurry of harsh barks.

If this happens, don't yell at the other dog and tell the owner his dog isn't friendly. Instead, back up the adult dog by praising him, leash yours if she's continuing to be rude, and walk your dog away. She gets to play and interact when she behaves nicely. If she's rude, she doesn't get to play.

Adult dogs who have been raised with other polite adult dogs have social rules they are expected to follow. We can't always determine what each adult dog's rules will be because much of it is determined by how that dog was raised. Plus, some dogs are more patient than others. You just have to introduce your adolescent to them and see how things go.

A Social Conundrum

Out in public, dogs are on leash and should be on leash unless in a fenced area. Being on leash is also the safest for dogs because no matter how well trained your German Shepherd adolescent is, she is still a puppy and can get distracted, decide to chase a squirrel, or run off after something else that catches her attention. However, being on leash can hamper natural canine communications.

Basically, three things can happen when dogs greet each other on leash:

They ignore each other: If you walk past another dog and owner and the two dogs ignore each other, that's fine. By ignoring each other, both dogs were controlled—both self-control and owner control. After all, you go for walks without interacting with every person you see. Your German Shepherd doesn't have to interact with every dog she sees, either.

They play: Should your German Shepherd puppy go up to the dog you meet and greet him nicely, the two dogs may want to play. This is fine and shows your puppy is well socialized.

However, there is a down side to this. Once she plays with the dog she meets, she may anticipate a play session with every dog she sees on a walk and may try to pull you toward each dog. If the next dog plays, that pulling behavior has been rewarded and your puppy will try to pull even harder to the third dog. So even though the play is good, it's also a problem.

She can meet a few dogs while on the walk, but if she pulls, you need to turn around and walk away. Pulling should never become a self-rewarding behavior. If she pulls, she never gets to play.

They get ugly: If your German Shepherd puppy goes up to greet a dog who isn't social, or if she rushes up to greet an adult dog who thinks your puppy is being rude, a fight may ensue. Obviously, that isn't an outcome you want. Not only could this cause one or both dogs injuries, but now your puppy may think all other dogs are a threat. She may avoid other dogs in the future, or she may try to charge other dogs to begin a fight herself.

> ### TIPS AND TAILS
>
> Avoid all dogs who charge toward you dragging their owners behind them. This is especially true if the owner is shouting, "It's okay! My dog is friendly!" Although the dog might be friendly, she also might not be. Plus, she's rude if she's charging toward your dog.

In all these situations, you need to teach your German Shepherd adolescent to ignore all other dogs while on leash unless you give her permission to interact with the other dog. By paying attention to you, your German Shepherd will be safe and won't be causing a problem.

Practice the "Leave It" (ignore it) you worked on several months ago. Refresh it by practicing with a dog biscuit as you did initially and then when out on walks, tell your dog to ignore neighbors' dogs behind their fences. When you see a dog out on a walk, tell your puppy to ignore that dog walking past.

Follow "Leave It" with a "Watch Me" (pay attention to me) so you're telling your puppy what to do: ignore that dog and now look at me. Have a treat in your pocket to help her look at your face and then praise and reward her.

When you see another dog on your walk and your German Shepherd turns and looks at you on her own, throw her a party! Praise her, give her a handful of treats, jump around, and be silly. Acknowledge her self-control and her understanding of what you want from her. She'll love all the attention.

No Isolation, Please

During early puppyhood, you knew about the importance of socialization and made a point to take your German Shepherd to a variety of places. You made sure she walked on different surfaces, heard sounds, and met people. Socialization at that age was very important for your German Shepherd's mental health and development.

What many owners don't understand, though, is that German Shepherds should never be isolated from the world around them. A German Shepherd who spends too much time alone, at home, without social interactions, will become bored, depressed, and potentially fearful. As we've mentioned several times, although German Shepherds can be wonderful companions, they were not bred to be pets. This is an intelligent working breed that needs mental stimulation, social interactions, and physical exercise.

When isolated, the dog will lose her socialization skills and may become fearful or aggressive. Isolated German Shepherds also tend to develop obsessive behaviors; they may pace back and forth and back and forth for hours at a time. They often bark way too much. They may lick an ankle or paw so much a wound develops.

It's vitally important that you continue taking your German Shepherd out of the house and yard. Let her go out front with you when you visit with neighbors. Take her for walks in different places. Let her go camping with you or go for walks in the local forest. Continue training with her. Just make a point not to isolate her from the world.

The Joys of the Daily Walk

Several studies have shown that dog ownership is good for people in many ways. Petting and touching a dog is known to lower a person's blood pressure. The companionship of a dog alleviates loneliness. But also, walking a dog provides exercise and decreases social isolation for both the dog and the owner.

By walking your German Shepherd every day, the two of you get some mild exercise, and by doing so, also see other people and dogs. You get to spend time outside, in good weather and bad, and see the birds flying past, the butterflies in the summer, and the neighborhood kids' snowmen in the winter.

One day recently, as Liz was walking her dogs at the local boat harbor in her hometown, she listened to sea gulls squawking, sea lions barking, and the noises of the boats tied up to the docks. She enjoyed the blue sky, the smell of the Pacific Ocean, and the sounds of the waves. Liz smiled and greeted other people who were walking that morning, and her dogs visited with some kids playing in the grass. She enjoyed watching her dogs' reactions to the sights and smells around them.

Yes, making the time to walk your dog every day requires some scheduling efforts on your part. But the payoff is huge.

Behavior

A well-balanced adult German Shepherd has a wonderful mind. She's bright and intelligent, wants to learn, and has a desire to work. German Shepherds seldom zone out when they're awake. Instead, that mind is always thinking. This means you have to think faster than your adolescent. Learning to read her body language helps you understand what she's thinking.

Reading Her Body Language

Spending time with your puppy, learning everything you can about her and how she reacts to things, is the first step in learning how to think like she does. But watching her teaches you a lot, too. Look where she looks, and try to figure out what she's hearing. There's no way to understand what she smells—we can't even imagine it—but you can look for visual cues as to what she might be sniffing.

Learning to read her body language is a great way to help understand your German Shepherd's thoughts. Here's what to look for:

Relaxed: She's standing comfortably, with her head in its natural position. Her ears are up but not stiff and may swivel to catch sounds. Her mouth is open slightly with the tongue out. Her eyes are open but the whites aren't showing. Her tail is low in a normal position and may be wagging in a relaxed manner.

Friendly and excited: Her head is more forward than up, and her ears are at attention facing forward. Her eyes are wide open, and she's looking directly at what interests her. Her mouth may be closed so she can sniff with her nose. Her tail is down, and although the tip may move slightly, the tail is more still than moving. Her legs are poised under her so she can dash toward what interests her.

Worried: Her head may be low, depending on how worried she is. The more worried she is, the lower her head. Her mouth is closed, although her tongue might appear at the front of her mouth to quickly lick her nose. Her ears may focus on what scares her and then fall back to lie on her head. Her tail is low, and if she's very worried, it might clamp tightly to her back legs. Her body posture is held tightly together with her back arched and her hips tucked.

Ready to rumble: Everything is up and forward. Her head is up, her ears are erect and forward, and she's up on her toes and bouncing like a human boxer. Her eyes are open and staring, her mouth is open, and her tongue is out. She's holding her tail higher than normal.

Watching dogs communicate via body language is fascinating. Although most dogs share similar language, and each breed has certain tendencies, every dog also adds a few personal quirks to her own body language. It's fun to find those in your own puppy.

Enjoying Her Sense of Humor

German Shepherd puppies love to play, and they carry that attitude into adulthood. Retrieving games are a favorite, as are scenting games, hide-and-seek, and, of course, chasing critters. Trying to catch the water spraying out of the hose or the sprinkler is also great fun.

You may also find that your adolescent has a great sense of humor. You may walk out the back door one day to find your puppy has hidden around the corner of the house, and when you walk out, she suddenly barks behind you. If you startle and yell, she'll be so pleased her trick worked.

If you pick up the dog toys and put them away, she may act like someone is coming to the door. As soon as you walk away from the dog toys in the toy box, she'll double back and grab a toy out of the toy box. She distracted you so she could get a toy, and again she'll be so pleased with her cleverness.

> ### HAPPY PUPPY
>
> Laughter is not limited to humans. Primates laugh and enjoy humor while rats chirp when they're having fun. Dogs have a specific laughing-type pant with their mouth open and lips pulled back that appears to be the canine version of a laugh.

Many animals enjoy humor, but it takes an intelligent dog to come up with some of the tricks German Shepherds routinely use. Just be sure the practical jokes your adolescent comes up with are safe. If they're not, put a stop to them.

Everything in Its Place

A schedule is important to your German Shepherd. This breed has a definite need for things to happen when they should. Meals, play, training, people coming home from work, and bedtime all need to happen on time as far as your puppy is concerned.

However, that doesn't mean you can't vary from your schedule once in a while. A Friday night date isn't going to psychologically scar your dog. However, she may bark a few times when you do finally get home.

As your German Shepherd grows up, she's going to want everything in her world to be orderly, too. Obviously, you can't be sure your neighbor doesn't rearrange his lawn furniture or the kids across the street put away all their toys. But don't be surprised if your adolescent notices the differences.

She's also going to notice things that are different with people. An intoxicated person walking down the street will catch her attention, as will the police officer on horseback and the new sign in front of your favorite store. German Shepherds are observant, and because they like things to be orderly, she's going to notice things that are unlike the others or have changed.

Giving Her a Job

Several breeds of dogs, to be happy, need a job to do. Border Collies, Australian Shepherds, Corgis, Doberman Pinschers, and Rottweilers are all happiest when they have a sense of purpose. So are German Shepherds.

This breed was bred to work, to do a job, and they have a strong desire to be needed. When bonded with a person or family, that need to work, to do something, anything, for that person is strong. If not given any direction from you, you may find your adolescent brings you a shoe, a towel from the bathroom, a magazine dropped on the floor, or several of her toys. She's asking you for direction or praise for doing these simple things for you.

> ### TIPS AND TAILS
>
> If your adolescent or even adult German Shepherd is destructive in the house, several things can lead to this behavior, including a lack of exercise, a lack of training, boredom, and the desire to do something for you.

You can satisfy this need in a number of ways. Obedience training is certainly the easiest. Practice training skills often and in different places. Don't limit it to simple exercises like sit and down, but also practice leave it, watch me, stand, stay, heel, and come. Practice these on leash and, when she's ready for it, off leash.

Teach your dog some tricks. Start with simple ones and move up to more elaborate ones. These are training, just like obedience training, but they're a lot more fun. If you subscribe to the morning newspaper, send her down the driveway to get it each morning. She'll be so excited to do this for you! She can learn to pick up the damp towels off the bathroom floor and carry them to the hamper. Granted, it would be easier for you to do it by yourself, but it's a lot more fun when she does it.

Training

You can use your training skills to challenge your German Shepherd's brain in many ways. Teaching her more obedience skills (or perfecting the ones she has) is certainly one way. Trick training may be fun, but it's still training. It gives you a chance to make your training skills better as you teach your German Shepherd puppy new things. Plus it's always fun to show off your puppy's skills.

German Shepherds can also participate in many different performance sports. This breed excels in tracking, search-and-rescue work, and schutzhund, but you're not limited to just those sports. There are many others you and your adolescent may enjoy.

One great way to put your adolescent to work is to teach her to find an item you name. Lost your keys? Ask your dog to find them. She can also find your wallet, purse, the family cat, or even your spouse. All you need to do is teach her what "Find it" means and the names of a variety of different items.

To teach her the name of an item, you need that item, such as a toy she likes—for instance, a ball—and some really good treats.

 Have your adolescent on leash and ask her to sit in front of you. Have the ball in one hand and some treats in the other.

 Let her sniff the treats in your hand, and then hold out the ball, holding a treat behind the ball so she has to touch the ball to get the treat.

 Move both hands toward her nose as you tell her, "Sweetie, ball."

 She doesn't know what you're saying yet, but she wants the treats so she'll nose the ball. When she does, praise her, "Good! Ball!" and give her the treat.

🐾 Repeat this four or five times, take a break, and play with her with the ball. Then repeat the exercise again.

Over several days, when she's moving her head toward the ball, draw your hand back so she has to reach to touch the ball. Then keep the hand with the treats close to your body and have her reach only toward the ball. Continue to reward with praise and treats, however.

After a few more training sessions, move your hand with the ball toward the right, the left, and finally set the ball on the floor.

When you feel she understands that the ball's name is "ball" move on to teaching "*Find it.*" You'll start teaching this with treats, but as soon as she understands, you'll switch to the ball.

> ## DOG TALK

"**Find it**" means search for the named item.

🐾 Have some really high-value treats, like Swiss cheese or pieces of beef.

🐾 Ask your adolescent to sit. Praise her. Then let her sniff one of the treats in your hand.

🐾 Tell her stay, and walk away from her. Hide one of the treats about 6 feet in front of her. Just tuck it slightly behind something. In the house, this could mean placing it behind a chair, with the treat showing a tiny bit.

🐾 Go back to your puppy, praise her for staying, and release her as you tell her, "Sweetie, find it!"

🐾 Move forward with her, point to the treat, and tell her, "Sweetie, find it!"

🐾 When she finds the treat and eats it, praise her, "Good to find it!"

🐾 Do this a few times, hiding the treat in several easy-to-find places, and then take a break. Play with your puppy and then come back and repeat the exercise.

Over several training sessions, do this in different places—other rooms in the house, out in the backyard, and in the front yard. But keep the hiding spots nearby and easy for your adolescent to find.

After a week or two of training, when your puppy is eager to go find the treats, make the process a little more difficult. But do this very gradually so she doesn't get discouraged. Hide the treat completely rather than barely hiding it. Hide it 12 feet away rather than 6. Next, shoot for 20 feet away.

When she's doing this very well, turn her away as you hide the treat. Don't let her see where you hide it so she really has to use her scenting abilities to find it.

> **HAPPY PUPPY**

When she can't see you hide the treat, she's going to use her scenting abilities to find it. If she's smart, she's going to follow your tracks as well as the smell of the treat.

Once you've made the find it game more challenging and she's succeeding in finding it, bring back her ball and play find it with the ball rather than the treats. Start with the beginning training steps, hiding the ball close and barely hidden, but then make it more difficult as soon as you see she understands the new game.

Later, you can follow these same steps and teach her the names of a variety of different items and then have her find those items. You can also teach her to identify people in the household by name and then find them by name. That's a lot of fun.

Participating in Performance Sports

You and your German Shepherd can participate in many different performance sports, both competitively or just for fun. Most of these provide exercise for you and your dog, a chance to increase your training skills, and a mental challenge for your bright dog.

You can begin training in these sports now, or if you prefer, wait until your dog is a little more mentally mature. Just keep in mind, you can always begin training now and wait to compete until your puppy is more grown up. The choice is yours.

Agility

Agility is like a combination of an obstacle course and an equine jumping competition. You and your German Shepherd have to follow a set course, and you guide your dog from obstacle to obstacle while she climbs, jumps, or goes through the various obstacles.

The obstacles can vary somewhat depending on the organization holding the competition, but some of them can include the following.

Weave poles: When photos of agility are published in magazines or online, one of the most common is of a dog going through the weave poles. A dog weaving through the upright poles is quite amazing to watch. The poles are spaced from 20 to 24 inches apart, and the dog flexes her body as she weaves among the poles.

Tunnels: These are generally about 2 feet in diameter so your German Shepherd will have to duck to get through. Some of the tunnels have a flap of fabric she'll have to push through while others are just a long tube.

Jumps: There are many different types of jumps. Some are simple bar jumps, some are solid that the dog can't see through, and others may be flat and wide (called a broad jump). Or you might see a window-type jump that looks like your dog is actually jumping through a house window. The height of the jump depends on the dog's height.

Teeter or seesaw: Much like a child's teeter-totter, this is a plank balanced on a center support. Your German Shepherd must walk up the plank, balance at the center, and walk down the plank when the far end lowers.

Dog walk: This elevated obstacle requires the dog to maintain her balance, much like a balance bar in gymnastics. The difference is that the dog doesn't have to perform acrobatics but instead walks up the ramp on one end, walks across the level plank at the top, and walks down the ramp on the far side.

A-frame: This is a pyramid-type obstacle. Two solid wooden boards meet at the top, forming an A-frame. The dog must climb up one side and descend the other side without jumping off in mid-climb or descent.

These are just a few of the more common obstacles in agility. If you're interested in this sport or just want to look into it more, many dog trainers and dog-training clubs offer agility training. Call around to trainers in your area and ask about classes. Several organizations, including the American Kennel Club (AKC), offer competitions in which your German Shepherd can earn titles.

Conformation Competition

If your breeder sold you your German Shepherd puppy as a show puppy, your dog may be able to compete in conformation dog shows. The best known of these is the televised annual Westminster Dog Show held in Madison Square Garden in New York City every February.

We described the German Shepherd breed standard in Month 10, but unless you've had experience seeing what those standards mean, it's tough to evaluate your own dog. Talk to your breeder, and ask for an opinion as to whether your dog should compete.

To start, go watch a few dog shows in your area. Watch what happens on the sidelines before the dogs go into the ring—especially the grooming. Then watch the competition and talk to people outside the ring. Leave your dog at home when you go watch. Dogs not entered in the competition are not allowed on the dog-show grounds.

Before entering and competing in a conformation dog show, take a handling class. This teaches you how to show your dog, move her around the ring, and stack (or display) her. There's an art to doing this right, and it takes practice.

Herding

German Shepherds are synonymous with law-enforcement work, guide dog work, and protection, but don't forget that this breed was originally a herding dog. It's great fun to introduce your German Shepherd to sheep, watch her fascination with them, and see her instincts kick in.

If you just want to see if your adolescent has some herding instincts, herding-instinct tests are designed for that express purpose. A trainer introduces your dog to sheep and then encourages her to use her instincts. If your dog does well, she can move on to practical training or competitive training.

You don't have to have livestock of your own to do herding work, although that would make things easier. Many dog owners interested in herding who live in rural areas do add a few ducks, goats, or sheep to their menagerie just for that purpose.

Several organizations offer stock-dog titles of various kinds, from working with sheep, ducks, or cattle. Plus, there are opportunities to compete in formal sheep-dog trials or working ranch–type exercises. Contact local dog trainers for a referral to a stock-dog trainer in your area.

Obedience Competition

Several organizations offer obedience competition for titles, including the AKC. There are various levels, from the basic, called Novice, through the advanced, called Utility.

Novice: In Novice competition, your German Shepherd is required to heel with you both on leash and off leash following a pattern called out by the judge. That pattern contains left and right turns, an about-turn, and both slow and fast paces as well as the normal walking pace. You and your dog also have to heel in a figure-eight pattern around two people. Your dog also has to come when called and sit in front of you. On the judge's command, she must move back to the heel position on your left side. She also has to do a sit stay and a down stay as well as a stand stay while the judge touches her.

Open: In the middle level of competition, your dog has to heel off leash, come when called, and, during the come, drop in place on your signal. She has to retrieve a thrown dumbbell and retrieve the dumbbell over a jump. She has to jump a broad (flat jump) and do both sit and down stays while you leave the ring and go out of her sight.

Utility: This advanced category is even more difficult. Your dog must heel with you off leash and perform a number of commands via hand signals—no verbal commands. She must also find and retrieve a metal and a leather article you've touched from among several identical objects that do not have your scent. She has to run away from you on command, turn, and sit. Then you direct her to a jump on your right or on your left, and she has to turn and jump the correct one.

> **HAPPY PUPPY**
>
> Although advanced training can be tough, especially for the first dog you train to this level, it's immensely rewarding. You and your dog will have a lot of fun, and it's quite an accomplishment when you win your first ribbon or trophy for a job well done.

After Utility, there's still more you can do, including Utility Dog Excellent and Obedience Trail Champion, to name just two additional titles. If you think this might be something you'd like to try, find a dog-training club in your area that offers competition training.

Rally

In this obedience sport, your German Shepherd can compete and earn titles. The judges can arrange a number of difference exercises in any way they please. So each time you compete, the course will be different. That keeps it fun and interesting.

Exercises can include heeling, making a left turn, making a right turn, making an about-turn, weaving through traffic cones, stay, jumping, and more. Additional exercises can be walking in a 360-degree circle to the right or left, doing a stay while you walk around your dog, doing a side step while heeling, and backing up.

Many dog trainers teach rally classes, so talk to your trainer. Dog-training clubs also offer classes.

Schutzhund

This is the premier German Shepherd sport. Although other working-dog breeds can also compete with many schutzhund clubs, some are specifically for German Shepherds. This sport originated with this breed.

> **TIPS AND TAILS**
>
> Schutzhund doesn't promote attack-dog training or aggressive, out-of-control dogs who bite. Instead, this sport is all about utilizing the dog's instincts and teaching obedience and control.

Dogs can earn titles in several levels of difficulty, from the easiest, Schutzhund I, through most difficult, Schutzhund III. Several organization offer competitions and titles, but most of them share several exercises.

The obedience portion of schutzhund includes heeling on and off leash, heeling with distractions, and retrieving a thrown dumbbell, as well as several other exercises. The exercises get more difficult as the dog progresses from level one to level two to level three.

The tracking portion for Schutzhund I consists of a 20-minute-old track the dog's owner walked. For Schutzhund II, the track is older, longer, and walked by someone other than the owner. For Schutzhund III, the track is the most difficult, and the dog must find three dropped items as she follows the track.

The third part of schutzhund is protection. Note it's called *protection* rather than *attack-dog training*. The goal is for the dog to protect her owner from a threatening person and never use more force than is needed to do the job. Dogs who are too aggressive or not under the owner's control won't make it in schutzhund.

If you're interested in this sport, take a look at Appendix E for a list of schutzhund organizations. You can contact these groups for a trainer in your area.

Search-and-Rescue Volunteer Work

This is a very rewarding volunteer opportunity for dogs and their owners. There's nothing better than using your dog's natural abilities to find a person who is lost or injured.

However, search-and-rescue (SAR) work is also time-consuming. The training your dog needs is only one part of the process. You also need a considerable amount of training.

Here's a small sampling of SAR work:

- 🐾 The owner working a SAR dog cannot get himself lost, so map reading, orienteering, and GPS training is mandatory.

- 🐾 Some searches are in rural areas, and the owner must be able to traverse a variety of terrains, keeping himself and his dog safe. You will encounter hills, valleys, creeks, rivers, and rocks. Plus, there's the danger of poison ivy, poison sumac, and poison oak, as well as wildlife and insects.

- 🐾 Rubble searches are needed after earthquakes, tornadoes, and other disasters. These, too, need to be performed with safety in mind for both dog and owner.

- 🐾 Base-camp skills, learning to organize a search, handling the radios, dealing with people who show up wanting information, and so much more are all also part of SAR work.

This is just one piece of the training required and hasn't even touched on the skills the dog needs. The dog must be able to track, air scent, ignore distractions (which can include other people and wildlife), and communicate to her owner when the person has been found.

Depending on the organization that oversees the SAR unit, other volunteer requirements may be needed. Some are run by the local sheriff's department, which may require that the volunteers also complete the sheriff's department volunteer program. Some SAR units are members of a national organization with their own requirements.

SAR is a wonderful volunteer activity but requires a great deal of time and dedication. It also costs some money because most volunteers must purchase their own equipment.

Therapy-Dog Volunteer Work

This is one of the most rewarding volunteer activities you can be involved in, especially because you and your dog do this together. Therapy dogs visit people in nursing homes, retirement complexes, assisted-living facilities, hospitals, and more. Many libraries like to host reading programs with dogs because a child can read to the dog rather than a person. The dog is patient, doesn't critique, and lets the child read at his or her own pace.

Therapy dogs provide warmth, affection, something to touch, and something to talk about to other people. Of course, the owner is very much a part of this, too, by presenting the dog and initiating conversation.

Therapy dogs must be well socialized to people and have a good foundation of obedience training. Many dog trainers offer therapy-dog classes, so talk to your local trainer. (See Appendix E for a list of therapy-dog organizations.)

> **TIPS AND TAILS**
>
> The trainer can also help you decide what type of therapy-dog work to do. If you and your German Shepherd both like children and your dog is gentle with them, you might want to participate in reading programs or visit special-education classrooms. Or you may prefer to visit the elderly. Sometimes it's best to visit a couple of different kinds of facilities or situations before making up your mind. But talk to your trainer about this, too.

Tracking

Tracking has several applications. Tracking and scenting games, often called nose work, are a lot of fun. Plus, you and your dog can compete for tracking titles through several organizations, including the AKC.

Dogs can earn several titles through the AKC. Each has requirements for the types of tracks the dog must follow.

Tracking Dog: Your German Shepherd must follow a 440- to 500-yard track that's between 30 minutes and 2 hours old. The track has from three to five turns.

Tracking Dog Excellent: The track is 800 to 1,000 yards long, with five to seven turns, and is 3 to 5 hours old. The track crosses a variety of terrain, including plowed land, streams, bridges, lightly traveled roads, and brush and trees.

Variable Surface Tracker: This track is 600 to 800 yards long, 3 to 5 hours old, and covers a variety of surfaces. The goal is to provide a track laid over surfaces normally found when tracking in a real-life situation, such as when looking for a lost person. That means it can be on vegetation, bared soil, concrete, asphalt, or even through a building.

A dog who earns all three tracking titles is awarded the Champion Tracker title.

You can also do tracking training and earn titles through a schutzhund club. If you have any interest in doing search-and-rescue work, your dog needs to know how to both *track scent* and *air scent*.

Many dog trainers offer tracking and scenting classes. Call your local trainer and ask for a referral if he doesn't offer them.

Working Dog Association

The Working Dog Association (WDA) is the performance branch of the German Shepherd Dog Club of America. The WDA hosts schutzhund trials, conformation shows, and breed surveys. The goal of both organizations is for a German Shepherd to have titles at both ends of her name: a breed championship in front of her name and working titles at the end of her name.

For more information on this program, go to the German Shepherd Dog Club of America website, gsdca.org.

Breed-Specific Legislation

Participating in performance or working sports with your German Shepherd can serve several purposes, including challenging your dog's mind and body, as well as strengthening the relationship you and your dog share. However, there's another benefit to advanced training with your dog you might not have considered: boosting public perception of your dog and the German Shepherd breed.

Many breeds, including German Shepherds, have been the focus of *breed-specific legislation* for many years. Although Pit Bulls and related "bully"-type breeds are the primary focus right now, other breeds, including German Shepherds, Doberman Pinschers, Rottweilers, Shar Peis, Chow Chows, and Akitas are also in the spotlight.

Breed-specific legislation has been widely used, with some cities or counties banning the ownership or even presence of certain breeds. Airlines have banned some breeds, insurance companies refuse to cover certain breeds, and more.

This type of legislation is unfair because it punishes all dogs and their owners of certain breeds when perhaps only a few dogs of those breeds have caused problems. Those fighting breed-specific legislation encourage lawmakers and companies to focus on individual problem dogs and their owners rather than ban entire breeds.

When an entire breed is punished, dogs end up being destroyed or dogs and their owners go into hiding. German Shepherds are renamed and called Dutch Shepherds or Belgian Shepherds.

Breed-specific legislation doesn't have to be enacted to protect the populace or a company's assets from problem dogs. The owners of problem dogs are the ones who should be targeted rather than entire breeds. Most cities, counties, and states already have laws on the books regarding problem dogs; those laws should be enforced.

The owners of breeds that have been targeted can also help. Here's how:

- 🐾 Train your dog. Dogs who are well behaved in public also attract attention in a positive way.

- 🐾 Train your dog some more. A very well-trained dog, as well as a dog who participates in performance sports or activities, is also spotlighted in a positive way.

- 🐾 Be sure your German Shepherd's socialization is maintained so she's social when out in public.

- 🐾 Keep your dog healthy and well groomed.

- 🐾 If your German Shepherd is not going to be shown in conformation shows and/or is not going to be used for breeding, spay or neuter your dog. More than 70 percent of all dog bites are from unneutered male dogs.

If you want to help promote breed-neutral laws rather than breed-specific laws, go to the ASPCA's website at aspca.org and search for the page on breed-specific legislation.

You and Your Puppy

Your adolescent German Shepherd puppy is on the verge of growing up, and although she looks quite adult, she's still a puppy. It's important to remember that she's still maturing because she's going to continue to make decisions that might surprise you. Perhaps one day she'll grab something out of the kitchen trashcan even though she hasn't done anything like that in a long time. Things like this are just reminders that she's not yet grown up.

Even though she's still a puppy, she's in the process of growing up, and in the months that follow, she'll continue to mature mentally and physically. Some of the changes will be gradual—so gradual you won't even notice them until you look back one day on the way things used to be. The relationship you have with your dog is going to change, too, but again, that change will be gradual and happen over time.

Stand by Your Rules

At this time, don't slack off on the household and social rules you established for your puppy months ago. Because your puppy—your teenager—isn't yet grown up and isn't always making good decisions, it's important to remind her that those rules are still in effect.

In fact, because she's still an adolescent and continuing to challenge those rules, slacking off now in your enforcement of those rules could result in bad behaviors from your dog. She could challenge you even more than she already has.

If your adolescent's behavior does change—if she gets in the trash, chews up some shoes, or begins chasing the family cat again—consider that a wake-up call. Obviously, your teenager isn't taking you seriously at the moment. Take a look at the household and social rules you established several months ago. Now that you've had some experience raising this puppy, what's important to you? What do you want your German Shepherd to do or not to do in the coming years? Then talk to everyone in the household and reinforce the importance of presenting a united front. Everyone needs to enforce these rules just as they did when your teenager was a young puppy.

> **HAPPY PUPPY**
>
> Enforcing your rules doesn't mean your household has to become a military boot camp. Everyone in the household can still have a good time, including your dog. But that good time comes with a few rules. And remember, your German Shepherd likes having rules to follow.

A key to encouraging your teenage dog to cooperate with you is to continue to praise and reward her good behaviors. Be sure you acknowledge when she picks up her toy and not your shoe. Praise her when she walks past the overflowing kitchen trashcan. When you acknowledge and reward some behaviors, she'll continue to do those things that earned your praise.

When Can You Relax?

Remember, your dog will be about 3 years old when she's mentally mature. Females generally mature faster than males, and some big males will be closer to 4 before they're grown up.

Nothing will happen on one specific day to tell you your dog is grown up. This is such a gradual process, you might not even notice it. However, one day you may think back and realize she hasn't gotten into the trashcan, chased the cat, or ignored one of your requests in a long time. That may lead to discussions with other family members until you all agree—she's grown up.

By the time your German Shepherd puppy has grown up, all the household and social rules you taught her should be good habits. In fact, they should be well-established, automatic habits she does because it's what she's supposed to do.

At that point, you can relax. Your German Shepherd is now doing things you asked her to do because they're the right things for her to do. It won't be necessary for you to be so vigilant.

Your Changing Relationship

This is also the point you'll notice that the relationship you have with your dog is changing. An adult, well-behaved, cooperative and compliant dog is a wonderful friend. And she has become a friend rather than a puppy or a teenager. Instead of being her guardian or her teacher, you are now her friend as much as she is yours.

There's no human friendship quite like the friendship with a dog such as this. Your German Shepherd cares about herself and satisfying her needs, but she cares about yours even more than her own. She will make herself uncomfortable just to be with you. She will put her own safety aside to be sure you're safe.

Enjoy her and treasure her. She's your dog and your best friend.

Appendix A　Glossary

AAFCO　The Association of American Feed Control Officials, an association of local, state, and federal agencies charged by law to regulate the sale and distribution of animal feeds and animal drug remedies.

activated sleep　Sleep that consists of kicking, twitching, stretching, and other movements. This is normal for newborn pups and helps them develop muscle tone.

adolescent　A dog who is past puberty but not yet an adult; he's immature.

air scenting　A method of scenting wherein dogs follow a scent wafting in the air versus on the ground.

anorexia　A lack of appetite or inability to eat.

antibody　A substance made out of protein and produced by the immune system to protect the body against disease.

behavior rehearsal　Practicing a new behavior, with guidance, so it can be learned and then performed as a normal behavior.

behavioral consultant　A behavior specialist, usually also a dog trainer, who is not a veterinarian.

behaviorist　*See* veterinary behaviorist.

bite inhibition　A dog's ability to control how much force is used when he uses his jaws in play or in work.

breed standard　The written description of the perfect dog of a specific breed. The German Shepherd Dog Club of America created the German Shepherd standard.

breed-specific legislation　The practice of writing legislation that pertains to specific breeds and includes regulating the ownership and/or keeping of those breeds.

colostrum　The first milk a mother produces. It contains proteins, fats, vitamins, minerals, antibodies, and other substances to initiate the immune system.

"Come"　The command that means "Quit what you are doing and come here, to me, right now."

coming into season　Also called *coming into heat,* this is the common term for a female dog being receptive to breeding.

conformation dog show　A competition where dogs are judged according to their breed standard.

congenital health defect   A defect that exists at birth. It can be genetic or can be acquired before or during birth.

"Down"   The command that means "Lie down, roll on one hip, and don't move." The hand signal is to sweep your flat hand, palm down, toward the ground.

fear period   A time in a puppy's life when he becomes worried, anxious, or afraid for no apparent reason other than his age.

"Find It"   The command that means "Search for [the named item]."

free feeding   The practice of leaving food out all day long so the dog can nibble when he feels like it. This generally isn't recommended.

"Give"   The command that means "Put that item in my hand." The hand signal is to hold your hand open, palm upward, in front of his face.

glycemic index   A scale that measures the speed at which the body converts starches into sugars.

growth plates   Discs at the end of each long bone (of the leg, for example) that are composed of soft cartilage. The cartilage is eventually replaced by bone.

"Heel"   The command that means "Walk by my side with your shoulder next to my left leg." She needs to maintain that position no matter what the distractions.

human-grade food   Food in which every ingredient, as well as the processing plant and procedures, is suitable for consumption by people (and dogs).

Hz   The abbreviation for "hertz," a unit of measurement for sound and electronic waves.

intact   An unneutered male or unspayed female dog.

leader   One who guides or commands; a guiding force as part of a team. A leader is one who is looked up to. A leader can be another dog or a human.

"Leave It"   The command that means "Turn away from what you are looking at and look at me."

"Let's Go"   The command that means "Pay attention; we're going for a walk." The hand signal is to step off on your left foot (when he is at your left side).

lush coat   A longer outer coat that may be longer over the entire body, with thick hair behind the ears, around the ruff, and on the tail.

marking   When a mature dog deposits urine so other dogs can identify him and determine his age or sexual maturity. Marking also establishes territorial boundaries.

mastitis   An infection or abscess of one or more of the mother dog's mammary glands, often caused by bacteria from a scratch or wound in the skin of a nipple. Keeping the puppies' nails trimmed and smooth is one way to help prevent mastitis.

matt A tangle of hair that has turned into a knot. As the knot moves, the tangle gets tighter and pulls on the dog's skin.

melamine A compound used to make different items, including dinnerware, shelving, floor tiles, and fireproof fabrics. It has been added to food ingredients to boost the protein level during laboratory testing. If you see this listed on a dog food's ingredient list, do not feed your dog that food.

microflora Microorganisms that live in the digestive tract of an animal and perform various functions, such as training the immune system, producing vitamins, and preventing growth of harmful bacteria.

natural A term pertaining to how food is grown, processed, and handled, not the quality of the ingredient or food or raw or not raw state.

neonatal period The first 2 weeks of a puppy's life, when the puppy sleeps and eats and not much else.

OFA The Orthopedic Foundation for Animals, a nonprofit group that collects information about the incidence of orthopedic and genetic diseases in dogs. OFA evaluates and grades hip and elbow x-rays of dogs prior to breeding. A breeder provides the rating of your puppy's sire and dam.

"Okay" The command that releases your dog from whatever he's doing. "Okay" signifies "You are finished; relax," or "At ease." The hand signal is both hands palms up.

oppositional reflex A reflex that causes the dog to push against force. If you pull on the dog, she will pull back. If you push her, she will push against you.

organic A term describing a food or product grown or produced using environmentally sound techniques, with no synthetic pesticides, chemicals, or fertilizers.

pheromone A chemical secreted by an animal that another animal, usually of the same species, can interpret.

pica The practice of eating nonfood items.

prey drive The instinct that causes a dog to chase moving things, including animals as well as cars or bicycles.

puppy push-up An exercise designed to use your puppy's mind and body. He is to sit, down, sit, down, and sit again on your commands.

"Release" The command that means it's the end of the exercise for the moment.

resource guarding A behavior where the dog guards things that are important to him, including the owner, toys, treats, or food.

schutzhund The German word for "protection." It's also the name of a dog sport that combines obedience, tracking, and protection work.

scissors bite   A bite in which the inside of the top incisors meet the outside of the bottom incisors.

separation anxiety   A behavior problem that shows itself as extreme stress when the dog is left alone.

"Sit"   The command that means "Put your rear end on the floor and don't move." The hand signal is to scoop one hand upward, palm up.

socialization   The process of introducing a puppy to the world around him, including sights, sounds, smells, and surfaces, as well as other people and animals.

specialty show   A conformation dog show for a single breed of dog, held by a breed club.

"Stand and Stay"   The obedience exercise that means "stand upright with all four paws on the ground, and hold still until I release you."

"Stay"   The command that means "Do not move a muscle until I come back and touch you." The hand signal is your flat palm in front of Puppy's nose as you step off on your right foot.

styptic powder   A powder used to stop minor bleeding, especially when trimming nails. It contains several ingredients, including ferrous sulfate.

titer   A test that measures the amount of antibodies to a particular disease your dog is carrying in his body.

track scenting   Dogs tracking a trail of scent on the ground, from beginning to end.

tracking dog   A dog who follows scent on the ground or on vegetation that has been touched as the person or animal walked past.

transition period   The time between 2 and 3 weeks of age when your puppy starts to be more aware of his environment.

vaccinosis   A chronic illness that results from vaccinations and may include immune system diseases, lupus, or cancer.

veterinary behaviorist   A veterinarian who specializes in behavior.

"Watch Me"   The command that means "Ignore all distractions and look at my face," preferably making eye contact.

weaning   The process of gradually changing a puppy's diet from mother's milk to solid food.

whelping box   A large nest where the mother gives birth to her puppies. There's often a ledge around the sides, so the mother won't accidentally crush a puppy against the wall.

withers   The highest point of a dog's shoulders, behind the neck.

Body Condition Assessment

Obesity is becoming more prevalent in dogs today just as it is in human populations. Some sources believe 40 percent of dogs in the United States today are obese.

Although some health concerns, which include issues such as including hypothyroidism and hyperadrenocorticism, can cause weight gain, the primary cause of obesity in dogs is overeating and a lack of exercise. This affects older German Shepherds more often than puppies, but even puppies can overeat. It's important to monitor your puppy's weight because an overweight puppy is more likely to become an overweight adult dog with the health challenges that come with obesity.

To make things more complicated, many German Shepherds are not good eaters. They can be finicky and uninterested in food. So making sure your German Shepherd isn't too thin is also important.

There's an easy body condition assessment you can do to evaluate your German Shepherd's weight. This evaluation is good for puppies over 6 months of age; under 6 months the puppy's body shape is still too young. If your puppy is under 6 months old and you're concerned about his weight, talk to your veterinarian.

To evaluate your German Shepherd puppy's body condition, ask a family member to help you. Have her hold the front of your puppy's collar to help keep him still. She can then place her other hand under the puppy's belly to encourage the puppy to stand.

Stand at your puppy's tail and look down at his back. Does he have somewhat of an hourglass shape—wider at the shoulders and hips? This shouldn't be pronounced; if it's too extreme, your German Shepherd may be too thin. If you don't see an hourglass shape or your puppy is wider in the middle, he may be too heavy.

With your fingertips, feel your puppy's ribs. Can you feel the ribs? There should be a thin layer of fat between the ribs and skin, but you should be able to feel the ribs. If the ribs are prominent, your puppy may be too thin. If you can't feel the ribs, he's too fat.

Step away from your puppy, and look at him from the side a few feet away. He should have a waist; his belly should tuck up between the end of his ribs and his back legs. The tuckup shouldn't be extreme; if it's too much, he's too thin. But if there's no tuckup or if his belly is lower than his ribs, your German Shepherd is too heavy.

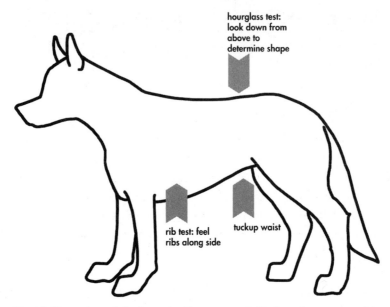

hourglass test:
look down from
above to
determine shape

rib test: feel
ribs along side

tuckup waist

Use this illustration to help determine if your puppy is ideal, too heavy, or too thin.

If your puppy is growing out his adult coat and you can't see his belly from the side, use your hands to feel for it. Place one hand under his rib cage as he's standing and run it along the underside of his ribs to his belly toward his back legs. You should be able to feel his waist.

If this assessment points toward a weight problem—either too heavy or too thin—call your veterinarian for an appointment. A young German Shepherd who is too heavy will need to consume fewer calories and increase his exercise; however, this needs to be done with care. Too few calories for a rapidly growing big dog can cause other health problems, including nutritional deficiencies. Plus, too much repetitive exercise can damage the bones and joints. Let your veterinarian guide you.

A German Shepherd who is too thin needs more than just more food. He may not be attracted to food and may need an appetite stimulant, or he may not be digesting his food well. Again, talk to your veterinarian and share your concerns.

Poisonous Plants

Many common landscaping, decorative, and houseplants are potentially hazardous to your dog. Some may cause a contact allergy, such as poison sumac or ivy; others can be potentially fatal. When ingested, castor bean, English ivy, and hemlock, for example, can kill a dog.

If you have any of these plants in your house or yard, either remove them or be sure your dog doesn't have access to them. If you aren't sure of the identity of a specific plant, take a close-up photo of it and ask at your local garden center or nursery.

Flowering Plants

These plants could be in a flower bed or used as potted plants. In some regions, some are also used as houseplants.

- Anemone
- Azalea
- Bird of paradise
- Buttercup
- Christmas cactus
- Crocus
- Cyclamen
- Foxglove
- Impatiens
- Jasmine
- Larkspur
- Lilies (including Asian, Day, Easter, Glory, Japanese Snow, and Tiger)
- Lily of the Valley
- Morning glory
- Snapdragon
- Sweet pea
- Verbena

Bulbs, Tubers, and Fungi

For many of these plants, the tuber or bulb contains the toxins, not the flower or green parts of the plant. Unfortunately, many times the bulb or tuber is what dogs are attracted to, especially when the bulb or tuber is planted with mulch or bone or blood meal to nourish the growing plant.

- Amaryllis
- Calla lily
- Daffodil
- Gladiola
- Hyacinth
- Iris
- Jonquil
- Lantana
- Mushrooms and toadstools (many varieties)
- Tulip

Trees, Decorative Plants, and Shrubs

Some of these plants are used frequently as landscape plants because they're attractive and easy to grow in many regions. Others are more commonly found as potted houseplants.

- Asparagus fern
- Bottlebrush
- Boxwood
- Caladium
- Creeping Charlie
- Croton
- Dieffenbachia (all varieties)
- Dogwood
- Dracena (most varieties)
- Elephant ear (all varieties)
- Emerald feather fern

😺 English Ivy

😺 Heavenly bamboo

😺 Hemlock

😺 Holly

😺 Horse chestnut

😺 Hydrangea

😺 Ivy (including Boston, Glacier, and others)

😺 Kalanchoe

😺 Mistletoe

😺 Nightshade

😺 Oleander

😺 Pennyroyal

😺 Philodendron (all varieties)

😺 Privet

😺 Rhododendron

😺 Sago palm

😺 Wisteria

😺 Yew

Vegetables, Fruits, and Nuts

This list contains a variety of plants that have different parts dangerous to dogs. If one specific part is dangerous, that's noted. If nothing is noted, the entire plant should be avoided.

😺 Avocado (leaves, stems, and pit)

😺 Eggplant

😺 Grapes (the fruit)

😺 Macadamia nut (the nut)

😺 Peach (and other stone fruit seeds/pits)

😺 Potato (foliage)

😺 Rhubarb

😺 Tomato (foliage)

Herbs, Weeds, and Miscellaneous Plants

This category is also a mixed one, with common herbs, noxious weeds, and a variety of other plants. Many, such as jimson weed and locoweed, are also toxic to many animals, including livestock.

- Belladonna
- Castor bean
- Jimson weed
- Locoweed
- Marijuana
- Milkweed
- Pokeweed
- Poison ivy
- Poison oak
- Poison sumac
- Pokeweed
- Sage

Household and Yard Hazards

Appendix D

Puppies, like young children, have no concept of what's good to eat (or play with) and what's dangerous. Never assume your puppy won't touch something. If it's different, out of the ordinary, has a smell, or is within reach, she probably will investigate it.

Problem Foods

A number of foods we normally consume can be a problem for our dogs. Some may cause mild gastrointestinal upset while others are poisonous and potentially toxic. If your puppy consumes any of these foods, call your veterinarian or emergency veterinary clinic right away.

- Alcoholic drinks (of any kind)
- Caffeine
- Chocolate (milk chocolate is the least toxic; dark and baker's chocolate the most toxic)
- Coffee
- Grapes and raisins
- Macadamia nuts
- Onions and onion powder
- Xylitol (including baked goods, gums, or candies that contain it)
- Yeast dough

As a general rule, don't allow your puppy to eat any spicy foods, fatty foods, leftover grease, or spoiled or moldy foods. They may not be toxic, but they're likely to cause gastrointestinal upset.

In the House

A wide variety of potentially hazardous materials are around your house—many of which you might not have realized could be a danger.

- Bug sprays and repellents (including insect traps)
- Cigarettes, cigars, pipes, and tobaccos

🐾 Cleaners and cleansers (including floor, kitchen, bathroom, shower, countertop, and toilet cleaners)

🐾 Craft supplies (including small parts that might be swallowed, like beads, and many paints and glues)

🐾 Holiday decorations (all holidays, including Christmas tree decorations, Halloween, electrical cords, ribbons, tinsel, batteries, and plants)

🐾 Laundry products (including detergents, bleach, and fabric softener sheets)

🐾 Makeup, hair-care products, and nail polish (as well as hair coloring and nail polish remover)

🐾 Mothballs

🐾 Plant-care products for houseplants (including fertilizers and insecticides)

🐾 Potpourri (especially those used over a candle or in a heated container)

Medicines

Almost all medications, if ingested in quantity, can have a detrimental effect on your puppy. If you believe your puppy has ingested a medication, call your veterinarian or emergency veterinary clinic immediately. Do not wait for a reaction to begin.

Keep all medications out of your pet's reach but especially these:

🐾 Cold remedies (including those with alcohol)

🐾 Pain medications

🐾 Prescription medications (of any kind but especially antidepressants and anticancer drugs)

🐾 Vitamins

In the Garage and Yard

To keep up our homes and yards, we use a number of potentially dangerous substances. We know what they are, and out of habit, we use them with care. But with a puppy in the household, we must be even more cautious.

🐾 Automobile care and maintenance products (gas, oil, antifreeze, cleaning products, waxes, and more)

🐾 Cocoa mulch

🐾 Home-maintenance supplies (including paints, paint removers, and supplies)

🐾 Rodent killers (including traps of all kinds as well as poisons)

🐾 Snail and slug poisons

🐾 Yard-care supplies (fertilizers, insecticides, herbicides, and fungicides)

Weather-Related Hazards

Some potential problems are only seen during certain seasons. This doesn't make them less of a hazard; in fact, because these products or hazards are only seen occasionally, they can be more attractive to a curious puppy.

🐾 Antifreeze

🐾 Blue-green algae in ponds (especially during hot weather)

🐾 Candles (lit or unlit)

🐾 Cocoa mulch (sold commercially as a garden mulch)

🐾 Compost piles (with decaying matter)

🐾 Frogs and toads

🐾 Ice-melting products

🐾 Insects (ants, spiders, scorpions, and others)

🐾 Snakes

🐾 Swimming-pool supplies

Resources

For more information on German Shepherd Dogs or anything else discussed in this book, here are a number of different resources you can check out.

Clubs

American German Shepherd Rescue Association
agsra.com

American Kennel Club (AKC)
akc.org

Canadian Kennel Club (CKC)
ckc.ca

German Shepherd Dog Club of America
gsdca.org

German Shepherd Dog Club of Canada Inc.
gsdcc.homestead.com

National Disaster Search Dog Foundation (SDF)
searchdogfoundation.org

United Kennel Club (UKC)
ukcdogs.com

White German Shepherd Dog Club of America
wgsdca.org

Performance Sports

German Shepherd Dog Club of America—Working Dog Association
gsdca-wda.org

German Shepherd Schutzhund Club of Canada (GSSCC)
gsscc.ca

North American Dog Agility Council (NADAC)
nadac.com

North American Flyball Association (NAFA)

flyball.org

United Schutzhund Clubs of America for the German Shepherd Dog

germanshepherddog.com

United States Dog Agility Association (USDAA)

usdaa.com

World Canine Freestyle Organization (WCFO)

worldcaninefreestyle.org

Health and Health Insurance

American German Shepherd Dog Charitable Foundation

agsdcf.org

ASPCA Pet Health Insurance

aspcapetinsurance.com

Pets Best Insurance

petsbest.com

VPI Insurance

petinsurance.com

Pet Sitters

National Association of Professional Pet Sitters (NAPPS)

petsitters.org

Pet Sitters International (PSI)

petsit.com

Therapy Dog Training and Certification

Love on a Leash

loveonaleash.org

Pet Partners (formerly Delta Society)

deltasociety.org

Therapy Dogs Inc.

therapydogs.com

Therapy Dogs International (TDI)

tdi-dog.org